Freud Stoopa in the Fifties

Michael Olesker

Front Stoops in the Fifties

Baltimore Legends Come of Age

The Johns Hopkins University Press · Baltimore

© 2013 The Johns Hopkins University Press
All rights reserved. Published 2013
Printed in the United States of America on acid-free paper
1 2 3 4 5 6 7 8 9

The Johns Hopkins University Press
2715 North Charles Street
Baltimore, Maryland 21218-4363
www.press.jhu.edu

Library of Congress Cataloging-in-Publication Data
Olesker, Michael.
Front stoops in the fifties :
Baltimore legends come of age / Michael Olesker.
pages cm
Includes bibliographical references and index.
ISBN-13: 978-1-4214-1160-6 (hardcover : alk. paper)
ISBN-13: 978-1-4214-1161-3 (electronic)
ISBN-10: 1-4214-1160-1 (hardcover : alk. paper)
ISBN-10: 1-4214-1161-X (electronic)
1. Baltimore (Md.)—Social life and customs—20th century.
2. Baltimore (Md.)—Biography. I. Title.
F189.B15O43 2013
975.2'6043—dc23   2013012850

A catalog record for this book is available from the British Library.

Frontispiece: "Wash Day," photograph by A. Aubrey Bodine,
copyright © Jennifer B. Bodine

Special discounts are available for bulk purchases of this book.
For more information, please contact
Special Sales at 410-516-6936 or specialsales@press.jhu.edu.

The Johns Hopkins University Press uses environmentally
friendly book materials, including recycled text paper
that is composed of at least 30 percent post-consumer
waste, whenever possible.

To Marni Olesker
and Brian Samet
and Adam Alter
so they will know where their new family came from

Contents

Acknowledgments

I am indebted to Bob Brugger for his help getting this book off the ground and to Greg Nicholl for his sensitive and smart editing and his good cheer along the way.

Also, special thanks to those whose memories helped me tap into the 1950s: Ken Ball, Jack Bowden, Tommy D'Alesandro III, Johnny Dark, Jules Dorner, Jack Edwards, Richard Holley, Leonard Kerpelman, Jerry Leiber, Barry Levinson, Clarinda Harriss Lott, Frank Luber, Morty Marcus, Clarence Mitchell III, Dr. Keiffer Mitchell, Michael Mitchell, Nancy Pelosi, Sharon Peyton, Joann Rodgers, and Ken Waissman.

I am also grateful to Jeff Korman, the manager of the Maryland Department of the Enoch Pratt Free Library, and to the ever-patient and helpful women at the Pratt's Periodicals Department—Reba Pile, Cheryle Moore, Lois Wright, Ruby Robinson, Delores Chambers, and Marian Massenberg—for their assistance as I plowed through microfilm covering every Baltimore daily newspaper from the dawn of 1950 through the awful nightfall of 1963.

Front Stoops in the Fifties

The Day the Fifties Ended

On November 22, 1963, the day the 1950s has a heart attack and dies, the fire at Saint Jerome's Parochial School is big news for about a minute and a half, and that's it. The sixties now arrives. Nobody knows the fifties are ending this day, since everyone assumes they vanished a few years ago, on their official date of expiration. As it turns out, decades never really begin or end on schedule.

This one dies with the gunshots in Dallas, Texas.

It dies with strangers huddled around transistor radios on street corners all over America, straining to hear each new bulletin updating the killing of John F. Kennedy, and dies with children listening to intercoms while school principals announce the worst news of their lives and then dispatch the kids home, where mothers are found weeping over kitchen sinks.

It dies with everyday disasters, such as this fire at Saint Jerome's, instantly erased from memory.

The school is located on Baltimore's West Hamburg Street, in a scruffy row-house area known as Pigtown. This is the usual working-class neighborhood of the era: bars on every block, the last of the coal men and the ice men still making home deliveries, and the local numbers runners slinking around in case the vice squad feels like getting serious today. Kids playing hooky scrounge around for discarded RC Cola bottles to make a killing at two cents a deposit. The hell with junior high, their education is poverty.

A young third-grade teacher named Mary Miller, hurrying to her lunch break just past noon, spots the fire and screams to the heavens for help. The blaze quickly goes to four alarms. The Rev. John A.

Mountain, pastor, watches helplessly from a playground hopscotch area with hundreds of children gathered around him, and nuns clutch rosary beads, and nearby housewives with their hair still up in curlers arrive just in time to mutter platitudes to each other about the good lord moving in mysterious ways.

This, while the fire demolishes an auditorium completed one week earlier to celebrate the Catholic school's seventy-fifth birthday.

When Frank Luber arrives, the flames are threatening the church and rectory next door. Luber's a newsman for WCAO, an AM radio station that'll dispatch a reporter to cover the usual municipal catastrophe du jour but mainly plays rock-and-roll phonograph records, as any Baltimore adolescent can tell you. On this sunny November midday, the airwaves carry the Chiffons' "One Fine Day," and Dion's "Donna the Prima Donna," and Elvis Presley embarrassing himself with "Bossa Nova, Baby." Within a couple of weeks this music will drift away, and all such performers will be declared outdated cultural artifacts, pushed aside by some brand new musical group from Great Britain calling themselves the Beatles.

But, in a matter of minutes, the air will be empty of all song.

At Saint Jerome's, much of Pigtown ceases normal activity and comes to gawk at the fire: grocery store delivery guys and municipal street sweepers and midday saloon regulars who came off the night shift at Bethlehem Steel and stopped in for a quick beer and a glance at the latest Baltimore Colts coverage in the morning paper and haven't quite navigated their way home yet.

Luber makes his way past them all to a huge pageantry of firefighting equipment. Looks like a pretty good story. Then he hears firemen utter a word: arson. Good, this makes the story even better. It's the school's second fire in as many days, and it means Luber's got a lead story at the top of the hour, which will scoop the city's two afternoon papers, the *Evening Sun* and the *News-Post*, and beat the hell out of tomorrow morning's *Sun*.

These newspaper guys don't even know it, but their day of dominating all news is passing in front of their eyes. The game starts to end right here. Scores of reporters and editors in every big newspaper city room in the country, and all will stand there helplessly chained to the past as the first sketchy reports arrive from Dallas. Radio stations are starting to deliver the earliest blurbs to everyone, followed quickly by television. For newspapers, the story will have to be taken from wire-service machines to editors to hunched-over linotype operators sitting in ancient composing rooms, while front pages already locked in will have to be laid out again and reprinted and then loaded frantically by the tens of thousands onto trucks finally huffing and puffing their way across metropolitan landscapes that have never been so crowded.

By the time the papers arrive, the news will already be everywhere and updated faster than any trucks can deliver it. For newspapers, it's the opening moment of long decades of coughing and wheezing their way out of existence. The changeover begins now, on this Friday afternoon, first with all radio stations replacing their music with news bulletins and then with television, which will break into the network soap opera *Search for Tomorrow*, and the quiz program *Truth or Consequences*, and the Mike Douglas talk show to announce the earliest assassination reports.

Now Luber spots a familiar face, a Southwestern District city cop named Jimmy McIntyre from Old Frederick Road, where they both grew up.

"You hear about the president?" McIntyre says.

The words barely penetrate Luber's brain. He's watching the new auditorium burn down and trying to pick up street sounds to play on the radio. McIntyre's voice arrives through the din of fire hoses.

"He's been shot."

"President Kennedy?" Luber says.

"Yeah. In Dallas, Texas."

"Good lord. Is he OK?"

"Don't know."

Luber heads straight for his car, where he's got a primitive two-way hookup to call the station. He is twenty-five years old, and he's news director at WCAO. It's an impressive title without much real-life muscle. The station's got huge numbers of listeners, but its entire news operation is three or four people. They rip off wire copy and read it over the air for a few ticks of the clock each hour, like practically every station across the country. And that's about it for news. We're not dealing any more with Edward R. Murrow hanging tough on a wartime rooftop in London during the blitz; this is the final hour of the 1950s, when the country prides itself on staying calm and orderly. If a major local story breaks, such as a school fire in a crowded row-house neighborhood,

Luber might escape the studio for half an hour and practice something resembling actual reporting. Otherwise, forget it, it's reciting wire copy or rewriting something from one of the local papers.

But now, as he calls the station, the burning Saint Jerome's and the firefighters scrambling madly about and the Rev. John A. Mountain and the nuns with their rosary beads staring at some vision of hell itself are all part of an instantly forgotten background blur.

"What's this about the president?"

"Doesn't look good," a voice back at the station says. "United Press says he's been shot."

"Oh, my God. How bad?"

"Don't know. You better come in right away."

The station's located at 1102 North Charles Street. Figuring the usual Friday afternoon traffic tie-ups, maybe it's a fifteen-minute ride from Saint Jerome's in southwest Baltimore to the heart of downtown. Luber navigates it in half that time, heads straight for the UPI wire-service machine, and finds everybody crowded around it: ad salesmen and secretaries and studio techs, people who have never in their lives bothered to glance at a news ticker. Nobody's thought about turning on a television—why would they? It's only 1963. There's no news on daytime television yet, just these game shows and soap operas aimed at housewives who haven't yet discovered there's life beyond Benjamin Spock and Betty Crocker.

Luber thinks the UPI machine's lost its mind. The noise alone is intimidating. Bells are going off, and typewriter keys beat out a frantic clackety-clack. He sees the word FLASH typed repeatedly across the top of the page like a movie scene. This is a guy who spends all his workdays checking the wire services every few minutes, hour after hour, and time goes by, and he's never seen the word on a real-life teletype machine until this moment. But now it's everywhere—FLASH! FLASH! FLASH!—and it's interspersed with terse updates out of Dallas.

No more Chiffons across WCAO's airwaves today, and no more Dion. Elvis will have to leave the building until further notice.

Luber heads for the studio and sits before a microphone with the latest bulletin in his shaky hands. What's he doing in this place at such a moment? This is a guy who left school a few years ago for a radio job at a small-time Annapolis station and then went to Decca Records to help promote Brenda Lee and Jackie Wilson. As if they needed *his* help. Twenty minutes ago, he was happy to beat the daily newspapers on an arson story out of some poor forgotten Pigtown parish. Now he's joining all those radio voices announcing the end of the world as we know it to millions of listeners.

Calm down, calm down. He's done this so many times, what's the big deal? In the last couple of years he's broadcast mayoral elections and domestic bludgeons and airplane crashes killing seventy-five. He's got a little seasoning on him. But all previous experience now belongs to some other world, made up entirely of small-town tales from Mayberry. That fire back at Saint Jerome's? It's in God's hands. The story's already lost to time and memory. This is history now, and Luber, leaning in to his microphone, joins its radio chorus of sorrowful, disbelieving voices.

"President John F. Kennedy . . . " he declares.

This is happening at stations all across America. In 1963 most of them play their phonograph records around the clock—maybe not rock and roll, maybe Sinatra doing "Love and Marriage" for the middle-aged hipsters—while an era drifts lazily past. Radio gives you a few paragraphs of perfunctory headlines each hour just to cover their asses with the FCC's public-service hall monitors, and then it's right back to the Four Lads records and Hampden Rug Cleaners commercials and more sounds of a nation in the midst of its sweet complacent mid-century ride.

It's beautiful back there in that America. The fifties is Marilyn Monroe standing over a breezy subway grate with her cotton candy dress billowing all around her. She's our national sex goddess. (But, this being the fifties, the sex is still hidden somewhere under gauzy layers, just out of reach.) The fifties is Willie Mays racing across center field to make a catch that resembles an optical illusion. (Just don't let the Say-Hey Kid try to move into your neighborhood.) The fifties is hula hoops and Davy Crockett coonskin caps and the neighborhood Good Humor ice cream truck with its bells tinkling so loudly that we don't quite notice the sound of boys just out of high school trudging off to wintry Korea.

In the fifties the old soldier Dwight Eisenhower oversees eight years of economic triumph and cultural sleepiness and then turns over the country to the young Kennedy, our first real video president. Ike holds press conferences, and the death of language follows. Kennedy faces a TV camera, and a nation falls in love. He's handsome and witty and knows how to turn a phrase. He makes us want to be better than we are. He inspires young people to rescue distant primitive people, one Peace Corps mission at a time. He makes it cool to be idealistic. He gets us through the Cuban missile crisis in one piece. He stands at the Berlin Wall, cheered by millions, and it's as if World War II never happened. When he tells Americans, "Ask not what your country can do for you; ask what you can do for your country," he makes our flesh tingle.

It's as if Kennedy's the role model for our longings: Maybe we could be just like him, if only we had a billionaire daddy, a Harvard education, and a Prince Valiant head of hair. He has the beautiful wife, Jackie. Nobody's heard yet about the various girlfriends. He has the two beautiful children. Nobody's even imagined him bedding a Mafia dame. He is the golden warrior who declares that America will "bear any burden, pay any price" to ensure freedom across the globe. Nobody yet imagines the full catastrophe of Vietnam. A moment ago we were all galloping across our New Frontier together, with our ideals clutched high against our chests. This isn't the way the story's supposed to end.

But now come words over all radio stations that sound like taps being played for an era.

On Dallas's KBOX radio, a reporter named Ron Jenkins, standing alongside the presidential motorcade, can be heard shouting frantically something that sounds like, "Put me on, Sal, put me on. Am I on?" Behind him, a wail of sirens like a mourner's anguish.

"It appears something has happened in the presidential motorcade route," Jenkins shouts into a telephone line. "I repeat, something has happened in the motorcade route." He describes people racing up a nearby street or falling face down onto the sidewalk. "I can see many, many police motorcycles," he says. "We understand there has been a shooting. Something is wrong here. Something is terribly wrong."

At stations around the country, network announcers break into regular programming with the earliest wire-service bulletins. You can hear each update in insurance offices and suburban kitchens and cars bumping along lonely back roads. We have commenced our first nationally broadcast shooting and dying, and it's about to kill something in each of us.

NBC's Robert MacNeil, scrambling from a motorcade press bus to a telephone, reports, "Several shots were fired as President Kennedy's motorcade passed through downtown Dallas. A crowd screamed as the motorcade went by. Police broke away and began chasing an unknown gunman across some railroad tracks. It is not known if the shots were aimed at the president. Repeat, it is not known if the shots were aimed at the president."

At WCAO, somebody hands Frank Luber another wire-service report: "The president was seriously wounded." The words go straight from the page to Luber's mouth. He can't believe what he's announcing. "This is not confirmed. It is a flash from Dallas that the president was seriously wounded by an assassin's bullets."

His words go everywhere. At Baltimore's federal courthouse, on Calvert Street, a clerk named Jackie Moloney listens to her radio and turns up the sound. It feels like some kind of bizarre bad-taste radio drama, like that old Orson Welles "War of the Worlds" broadcast back in the thirties that scared half the country. Have they started running those dramas again?

In a courtroom next to Moloney's office, 102 immigrants from a dozen different countries have gathered before Judge R. Dorsey Watkins for ceremonies to make them American citizens. Some carry small U.S. flags into the room, like children at a parade, and wave them in the air. This is the first day of their brand new American lives.

Nobody's heard a word about Kennedy and Dallas.

In her little clerk's office, a small crowd of courthouse workers and a *Baltimore Sun* reporter, Ted Hendricks, gather around Moloney's desk, and somebody brings in a second radio. It's as if the story's too unbelievable and they need a second source, they need to know if everybody's reporting the same impossibility.

They hear an NBC network announcer say, "We have just talked with two eyewitnesses, a man and his wife who were standing near the presidential motorcade. They said that a shot rang out behind them. One woman, who was in a hysterical condition, told us the president was hit in the side of the head and fell into his wife Jacqueline's arms."

"Oh, my God."

"Oh, good lord."

Everybody in the little clerk's office sucking in their breath as Robert MacNeil urgently updates his earlier report.

"People screamed and lay down on the grass as the motorcade went by," he says. "Police immediately fanned out over a wide area. A small Negro boy and a white man said they had seen a man with a gun in a window in a building overlooking the road."

On Grand Street in lower Manhattan, Kenny Waissman hears the news from a toothless elevator operator as he's leaving work. Later, Waissman will produce a Broadway musical called *Grease*, celebrating the innocent 1950s whose curtain is now descending across the landscape. Waissman's a Baltimore native, a graduate student at New York University working part-time at a place where they produce those runty little pencils for keeping score at bowling alleys. As he's leaving work, the elevator operator tells him, "They shot the president."

Waissman, dazed, starts walking uptown. It's a sunny day, and people have their car windows open and ten or fifteen people will gather around to listen to the radio together. Complete strangers, but right now it doesn't matter. As he walks toward Washington Square Park, Waissman can hear the assassination story playing itself out, one radio at a time.

He hears: "The president's head lay in his wife's lap."

He hears: "Governor Connolly of Texas also wounded."

And then: "Kennedy taken to Parkland Memorial Hospital."

He notices people all around him. It's the usual Greenwich Village Friday afternoon sidewalk crush, the boys in their desert boots and lumberjack shirts, the girls with the skirts starting to climb shamelessly above the knees like Jackie Kennedy's, and all the young folksinger wannabes with guitars who are starting to crowd out the old Village beatnik poetry types with their sandals and their goatees. But there's no street sound at all, just the damned news coming out of everybody's radios.

And there's something rattling about the very pace of things, something so unsettling you can't see straight: everybody wants more information, and they want it faster. Nobody's felt this way since Roosevelt's death or the end of the war eighteen years ago. People want the whole goddamn story right away. They're accustomed to the day's big news arriving on the front pages of newspapers, after it's had time to sort itself out a little and catch its breath. But those editions are hours away, and everybody wants to know now if it's true that their whole world has come undone.

Then it dawns on people: maybe television's carrying the story. Nobody takes TV news very seriously yet—how could they? Hell, it was only two months ago that they doubled the nightly network broadcasts—Huntley and Brinkley on NBC and Cronkite over at CBS—from fifteen minutes to half an hour. When the guys over at ABC heard this, they laughed out loud and said, "It'll never last. How are they gonna find enough news to fill thirty minutes every night?" And who could argue with them? It was only the end of the fifties, when the country could go months and nothing seemed to happen.

But now comes an endless weekend in which a nation will watch real-life drama on television, in real time, hour after hypnotic hour, and never for a heartbeat turn away. Heading uptown, Waissman listens to the latest bulletins and thinks, "This is the run in the stocking." That's how he phrases it. "Everything," he thinks, "begins to unravel now. It's the end of something, right in front of our faces."

In Pennsylvania, the writer Ken Kesey and his pal George Walker flip on their car radio. Kesey's great novel, *One Flew Over the Cuckoo's Nest*, has just been turned into a Broadway play, so he's in a celebratory mood. But, as they pull into a highway Howard Johnson's, he and Walker hear the radio bulletins about Kennedy. Inside the restaurant, word has already spread. As Kesey looks at the mourners around him, he thinks, "It's America with its shirt torn open in grief."

At the Lord Baltimore Hotel 250 members of the Maryland State Conference of Social Welfare listen to a speech entitled "Equal Opportunity"—it's about black people finally getting a fair shot—when M. Shakman Katz, presiding over the meeting, takes the microphone and says, "Someone has handed me a bulletin."

Sudden silence. Then Katz, his voice soft and breaking, says, "The president has been shot in Dallas." That's all he knows. He asks for prayers. People are already standing with their heads bowed. A moment later Katz asks, "Is there a doctor in the house?"

One woman has fainted and another, State Senator Verda Welcome, the only African American in Maryland's Senate, has broken down in uncontrollable sobs, her head buried in a handkerchief.

At the federal courthouse half a dozen people cluster around the two radios on Jackie Moloney's desk. Chief Judge Roszel Thompsen's there, and Judge Edward Northrop, and a clerk named Wilfred Butschky. Luber's bringing them the bad news on WCAO. The veteran Galen Fromme's the news voice over at WBAL, and both can be heard reading the latest wire service stuff aloud.

And then comes Edwin Newman of NBC. His voice sounds exhausted, almost disembodied. It's the beating of a national death knell. "Here is a flash from Dallas," he says slowly. "Two priests who were with President Kennedy say he is dead of bullet wounds suffered in the assassination attempt today. I will repeat, with the greatest regret, this flash from Dallas: two priests who were with President Kennedy say he has died of bullet wounds."

At the federal courthouse, Moloney screams, "Oh, no, no." She stumbles to a back room where her cries can be heard in Judge Watkins's court. Three more women join her, all sobbing convulsively. Judge Watkins, meanwhile, knows nothing. He's seated at the bench with a sweet, unsuspecting smile on his face. This is one of his good days, when he can offer all these brand-new citizens the official bighearted American embrace.

But now a deputy U.S. marshal, Fred Smith, standing near the courtroom door, hears the cries from Moloney's office and the newest bulletin on the radio, and he slips into Watkins's court. The roll of brand-new Americans is being called. Smith sees the little flags in their hands, the shy, expectant smiles on their faces. All are clothed in their innocence. Now Smith whispers the bad news to a deputy sheriff, William Harris, and Judge Watkins signals Harris to approach the bench. Then everybody in the courtroom watches Watkins slump disconsolately in his seat.

"I can't go on," he says. "President Kennedy . . . " barely getting the words out " . . . has just died."

All these joyful, smiling, brand-new Americans—here is their national welcome, exploding in their faces.

"We will all rise for one minute of silence," Watkins says.

As they stand there tearfully, disbelievingly, some are still holding up their American flags. A few show each other the official letters of welcome they just received in the mail. The letters are signed by John F. Kennedy. It's as if they're asking: How could he be dead when his name's right here?

"I don't understand," one man says in an eastern European accent. "You mean he was shot?"

At the Howard Johnson's in Pennsylvania, George Walker tells Ken Kesey, "The son of a bitch has killed him."

Not *some* son of a bitch; *the* son of a bitch.

"We thought we didn't have him," Kesey says. "The Europeans have him, the Muslims have him, but the United States? No, we're above that." Later, he'll recall, "This was the real loss: the opinion of ourselves as an innocent, wonderful, above-board nation. It was a loss of our feeling of invulnerability—that you could walk across the nation and be all right, nobody is going to hurt you."

At WCAO radio, Frank Luber finally exits the little news studio and hears the latest programming plan. Management has issued orders: no more rock and roll until further notice. In a time of national grief, there's no place for the likes of Elvis and "Bossa Nova, Baby." Play something classical, something funereal, something that's been filed away back in the dusty record library for the last twenty years. Rock and roll will pay its respects with silence.

In New York, Kenny Waissman's made his way to Columbus Circle on the upper west side. By the time he gets there evening has fallen and the worst of the news is everywhere. Waissman sees people walking the streets silently. Many hold lighted candles in their hands.

Better, they should curse the coming darkness.

So there we are when the curtain descends on the 1950s, 175 million of us gathered at graveside, one television set at a time.

We stare at these TV images in living rooms and club basements and neighborhood corner bars where people search for some kind of confirmation that this madness has really happened. Maybe if we watch long enough some authority figure like Walter Cronkite will appear on-screen to tell us there's been a huge mistake, that Kennedy's all right, he was only winged like Marshall Dillon in a TV shoot-'em-up, and he'll be better after a commercial break. Maybe they'll tell us he's gone with Jackie and the kids to Hyannis Port for healing but he'll be back at the White House in a couple of weeks. Anything, anything but this. We've been made vulnerable in a way we've never known: by the gunman Lee Harvey Oswald, by history, by TV itself. Murder has entered our homes, and it will linger. It's on every television set where there used to be innocent ball games and kids on late afternoon dance programs doing the cha-cha to Sam Cooke records and *I Love Lucy* reruns where all comic problems are solved inside thirty minutes. On television in 1963, until this moment, everything had its appointed time and place on three comforting mainstream networks, and all was geared to entertaining us and seducing us to buy merchandise that will make our lives ever more bountiful.

But now, at the tail end of a November weekend, comes this stunning panorama: the grieving Kennedys marching through the sunlit, haunted streets of Washington, D.C., and a little boy in short pants saluting his father's casket; a bugler playing taps at hallowed Arlington National Cemetery with its ghostly thousands; and a crummy Dallas police basement where the owner of a strip-tease joint emerges from the shadows to kill the reviled assassin Oswald.

So ends the slow, self-satisfied fifties, buried alongside John F. Kennedy. And now begins the country's long nervous breakdown, the years of pushing the limits of our maddest derangements. It's as if millions will suddenly decide to act out their anxieties and their rage, as if Kennedy's murder exposed some hypocrisy at the heart of the American dream, some bill of goods we'd all been sold, and TV has come of age just in time to grab everybody's attention whenever some malcontent with an issue feels like venting.

Somebody kills a president, it takes the limits off things. If a rodent like Oswald can change the world, then anything is possible. In the sixties we become a country choosing up sides against ourselves, fangs bared, doped up, on the make, out of breath, everyday life getting freakier all the time.

"A naked tribal wig-out," the critic James Wolcott will call the sixties, "that sucked us into a kaleidoscope and spat us out."

The army starts snatching kids off street corners—by the thousands, every day—for a war that's never officially declared in a place nobody can find on a map against a people in pajamas who have never in their lives threatened America. We blunder into Vietnam with our bombs and our missiles, and they crouch by their rice paddies and crawl through their tunnels. They will wait us out. The war goes on forever, killing fifty thousand of a generation of American kids who had no place to hide from the draft and no letter from a sympathetic doctor faking an infirmity for the skeptics down at Fort Holabird.

In the sixties, that's us on the six o'clock news, marching on Capitol Hill with reefer wafting through the air, feeling self-righteous and brave on the streets of Washington, where nobody's dropping napalm. And that's us in the sixties, too, Americans so enraged by the killing of Martin Luther King Jr. that we put the torch to scores of American cities.

Who says you can't fight city hall? You sure can, if you stage your fight with enough imagination. Take over a government building, that'll grab their attention. Burn down a neighborhood, that'll bring the TV cameras. Go build some more bombs, go kill some innocents in Asia, one more war to stop all future wars, right? All of this is the sixties.

They'll last from November 22, 1963, until—when? Decades don't go strictly by the calendar, they're made up of war and peace, money and politics, and whatever mood's in the air. Maybe the sixties ends when the last souls make it safely out of Vietnam, clinging desperately to the bottom of a helicopter. Maybe when they call off the military draft and all these earnest young people suddenly stop hollering about injustice and decide their future's in Wall Street profiteering. Maybe when Richard Nixon gets caught trying to slip one past Justice while she's got her blindfold on. After that, you could hear the world quiet down for a little while, as if we'd all simultaneously discovered how exhausted we were.

But what about the fifties? Decades later, many remember that time with affection and longing. We want our innocence back—as though it's something we inadvertently misplaced with our car keys. The fifties were innocent compared with so much that came later, but that naiveté sometimes seems willful, an enforced innocence. White people were innocent of the appalling limits imposed on black people. Men imposed restrictions on women to maintain a perception of female innocence and servility. Human sexuality was censored and confined. Sometimes it felt as if we were suffocating ourselves—until we finally began tearing our way out of our self-imposed straitjackets.

In retrospect it seems so much safer back there, before the general craziness started. But sometimes the fifties seemed so slow, too, and sometimes so boring that the decade took thirteen years—the dawn of 1950 to November of '63—to complete.

Or maybe not. You can't go strictly by the calendar. The giddy 1920s probably started in 1918, when World War I ended and set off a decade of boom markets and nighttime razzmatazz, and ended with the Wall Street crash of 1929 and the onset of the Great Depression. The dreary 1930s stuck around until December of '41 and Pearl Harbor. The forties was World War II.

Is that when the fifties started, August of '45, when the boys started coming home from the war? Or was it January of '53, when Eisenhower took the presidential oath? It's a little tough to say—and not nearly as easy as pinpointing the end.

Or maybe the fifties doesn't open with something big and powerful, like troop movements or a presidential inauguration. Maybe it crawls out of the 1940s in a thousand different places where the culture shifts glacially and nobody realizes until later. A little girl named Nancy D'Alesandro watches her mother organize an army of women for her husband Tommy, the mayor of Baltimore, and sees there's a place in the political world even if you're female. She'll become America's first woman Speaker of the House. A black youngster named Thurgood Marshall goes through Baltimore's segregated public school system and never knows a white classmate. He grows up and convinces the U.S. Supreme Court to let children of all colors sit in the same classrooms. And then there's this West Baltimore kid named Jerome Leiber, who will help change the way America listens to music and finally encourage boys and girls to dance a jitterbug, and share a laugh, across the color line.

So much that erupted in the sixties was there in the fifties, simmering just below the surface, as if biding its time. And so much began in Baltimore.

Like this kid Leiber, as we're just beginning to put the war behind us.

He's a white boy who slips into black neighborhoods and hears rhythm and blues. It sounds like some glorious secret being revealed. He goes to the movies and sees the adventures of Sam Spade and Charlie Chan and Boston Blackie. These stick in his brain and become the stuff of lyric. He listens to the language of noisy street corners and school locker rooms and cafeterias, which have never been translated into American music.

Leiber will put it all there, including the laughter.

Jerry Leiber found his first musical inspiration on the postwar street corners of West Baltimore and helped create such rock-'n'-roll legends as the Coasters and the Drifters. Leiber and song-writing partner Mike Stoller (*left*) also wrote songs for "some white kid" named Elvis Presley. (Corbis)

White Boy at Doo-Wop's Dawning
Jerry Leiber

Summer of 2010. All these years since he helped bring the untapped humor and hunger of the urban ghetto into mainstream American music, Jerry Leiber's on the telephone in Venice, California, where he hears a simple question about the songs he and Mike Stoller wrote: "Did you ever imagine they'd last half a century?"

"I don't know," he says in a soft, rheumy, slightly breathless voice. "When we sat down to write, we figured the stuff would last until maybe the following Tuesday."

He means "Hound Dog," for which Leiber wrote the words in about fifteen breakneck minutes pacing back and forth while Stoller sat at a piano banging out the tune, and then this raw pompadour named Elvis Presley turned it into one of the seminal romps of rock and roll.

He means those great comic operettas they wrote, such as "Yakety Yak" and "Charlie Brown" and "Poison Ivy," that the Coasters turned into the earliest musical laugh tracks echoing across the 1950s American racial divide. The songs don't quite introduce racial harmony across America, but they sure help put us in the mood.

And he means those lush, yearning heartache-and-pain ballads they produced, such as "There Goes My Baby" and "Stand by Me" and "On Broadway," songs the Drifters sang across that same racial chasm when white kids and black kids were first discovering, against all previous ignorance, the adolescent hormones they had in common, hormones that were completely unsatisfied by the sexless, antiseptic music of Perry Como or Patti Page or Percy Faith.

By 1958, when they were twenty-five, Leiber and Stoller had been dubbed the Gilbert and Sullivan of rock and roll. Big deal, Gilbert and

Sullivan. What did those guys know about seven-come-eleven crap games down in the boys' gym, like Leiber and Stoller's Charlie Brown? Gilbert and Sullivan, what did they know about needing an ocean of calamine lotion when "poison ivy" posed as metaphor for an outbreak of the clap? What did they know about finding a rose growing right up through the concrete in Spanish Harlem?

Leiber and Stoller—*they knew.*

"For me," says Leiber, "it all started on those streets back in Baltimore. The music, yeah. But that's also where I decided that black people were hipper, and smart, and nicer than white people. And, by the time I started writing music with Stoller, the only people writing what we were writing were black."

In the summer of 2010—a year before he died of heart failure at seventy-eight—Leiber was half a century and three thousand miles away from the corner of Riggs and McKean Avenues in shabbiest West Baltimore, where he grew up. But he remembered. This neighborhood was one of the birthplaces of rock-and-roll music, though nobody realized it then and almost nobody recognizes it even now. You'd need archaeologists poking through the recesses of Leiber's brain to locate such early traces. But it was Leiber in his youth who made the neighborhood one of those digs on the prehistoric map where white America began to notice vagrant underground sounds wafting out of black America and started clutching these sounds to its collective heart.

For this is where Leiber ran the mid-twentieth-century streets of the city. Baltimore was the nation's sixth-biggest metropolis back then, swollen by wartime industry, feeling pretty puffed-up about itself—as was much of the country.

The America we know in the '50s comes out of World War II like the heavyweight champ. In Europe and Asia, they're still sweeping the remnants of bombed-out buildings off their cratered streets, while here we're driving our brand-new Lincolns to the suburban country club. We're now the richest nation in the world. We've got 6 percent of the planet's population, but we produce 50 percent of its factory goods. In the old industrial cities like Baltimore, we've got working-class sixteen-year-olds routinely dropping out of high school, and who's to worry about it? The kids march straight from boring tenth-grade geometry into factories like the great Bethlehem Steel, where more than thirty thousand people are employed.

"The greatest metal-making capacity on earth," Mark Reutter will call it in *Making Steel: Sparrows Point and the Rise and Ruin of American Industrial Might*: "Out of its furnace fires came the steel for the tail fins of Chevy Bel Airs and Thunderbird convertibles, the tin plate for Campbell's Soup cans, the hulls of ocean tankers and Navy destroyers, the wire and girder plate of suspension bridges, and a thousand and one other products that made our culture of bigness and abundance possible."

In the 1950s Baltimore has more than sixteen hundred manufacturing establishments. One hundred thirty thousand people have jobs at these places, producing not only steel but parts for spacecraft, nuclear reactors, power tools, metal cans, car and truck bodies, missile warheads, hydraulic pumps.

Another forty thousand people have jobs connected to the city's port, which handles twenty-two million tons of cargo a year. Only New York handles more.

Out at Bethlehem Steel's Sparrows Point, there's an entire community built around the steel plant: homes and schools, churches and pool halls, a golf course and a yacht club. The mills' blast furnaces send columns of smoke and soot into the air, and it drizzles over everything in the area, and this is considered a blessing. Gold dust, the workers call it. Nobody calls it pollution. The soot means people are working.

And those jobs will be here forever, won't they?

Won't they?

In the '50s, we've never seen such prosperity. In Baltimore, Mayor Tommy D'Alesandro builds huge numbers of new schools, roads, recreation centers, parking garages, and thousands of public housing apartments to replace dilapidated housing left over from the previous century. Week after week he averages two or three groundbreakings of all kinds. Once, he does four of these in two hours. If there are recurring political photos capturing this era, they're the countless shots of all the mayors of America happily shoveling dirt.

After the long years of depression and war, the modern world's arriving in unanticipated ways. It's 1955 when the city sets up its first parking meters—more than six hundred of them—beginning with North Avenue between Howard Street and Greenmount Avenue. Ten cents gets you two hours of parking. Not so bad. Nobody imagines a day when ten cents at a downtown meter will get you three minutes.

It's 1954 when the city begins shutting down its public baths. Over the years a nickel gets you a shower, a dime gets you a bath, and extra towels are rented for two cents each. But brand-new Health Department regulations require a bath or shower in every new home built by 1956—and so, beginning with the public bathhouse at 131 South High Street, which dispenses roughly two hundred thousand baths a year, the era of public bathing is washed away.

At the end of the war, the city has 105 movie theaters. But they go dark one by one with the arrival of television. Who needs to spend money at the movies when Uncle Miltie's on the tube?

Television helps us buy into our own mythology. It feeds us endless images confirming what cheerful, upbeat, lovable people we are— Ozzie and Harriet, meet Jim and Margaret Anderson—and so do the magazines fat with advertising that overflow newsstands you find everywhere in stores and on street corners of all cities.

Life claims twenty-six million readers a week, and *Look* eighteen million, and the *Saturday Evening Post* fourteen million. When the country begins its 1960s convulsions, these magazines will wither and die one by one. They've lost their grip on the national zeitgeist. *McCall's* and the *Ladies Home Journal* claim a combined readership of thirty-six million, which will mean a lot when they run excerpts of that new book, *The Feminine Mystique*, by Betty Friedan. But Friedan's not finished writing until the summer of 1963, when the 1950s are finally about to expire. The most popular midcentury American magazine is the *Reader's Digest*, whose circulation is so huge they don't even bother running ads.

In the fifties we're still clinging to a feel-good identity drawn— literally—from the sunlit American imagination. This is reinforced every week on the cover of the *Saturday Evening Post*, where Norman Rockwell paints his valentines to an idealized America. They help sustain a common national self-image: the jug-eared soldier finally home from the war, with his folks out to greet him and their hearts all bursting; the beefy cop buying a soda for a runaway little kid before escorting him safely home; the pubescent girl gazing wistfully into the mirror while she waits for her maturity to show up any day now.

Nobody's imagining American grunts one day torching a Vietnamese village called My Lai, nobody's imagining police riots in Chicago, and nobody's imagining darling little girls growing up to drop acid at a place called Woodstock.

With Rockwell's sweet magazine covers, you know you're being manipulated, you can spot all the strings he's pulling. But you go along for the ride because it makes you feel you're part of something special. He's not issuing a call to greatness, he's holding up a mirror to great ordinariness: the nobility of everyday American folks.

Meanwhile, millions around the country are buying things previously unaffordable with brand-new credit cards. Half a century later, many will spend themselves into bankruptcy with it. But, for a generation that remembers wartime rationing, and the depression that preceded it, the credit card helps us make up for lost time. We're buying things we never dreamed we could have: washing machines and vacuum cleaners and power lawn mowers for new tract houses in the suburbs where kids can play football in grassy back yards instead of dodging Chevrolets on cramped city streets.

It takes a while for us to realize: those city streets are getting a little less cramped each year. In a place like 1950s Baltimore, you could hang out at a busy Gwynn Oak Junction, at Liberty Heights and Gwynn Oak Avenues, or on Eastern Avenue near Patterson Park, or on Pennsylvania Avenue before the heroin invasion, and a summer evening's pulsing with life. Teenage boys who've all pitched in for gas at twenty-five cents a gallon are packed into a jalopy, playing "Yakety Yak" up loud on the radio while girls from the neighborhood stroll up the block (some of 'em with pin curlers in their hair, even if it's Saturday night) slurping chocolate snowballs from the corner grocery. (But not too fast, or they'll get brain-freeze.) In East Baltimore noise filters down from Our Lady of Pompeii Church, where the neighborhood ladies gather to play bingo; in northwest Baltimore's Ambassador Theater, Elvis Presley just opened in *Love Me Tender*; in the tiny storefront West Baltimore Pentecostal church, a couple of kids and a cop on the beat watch the old men play checkers on a rickety card table just before the line starts to form outside the Royal Theater, where Sonny Til and the Orioles are singing.

So much of this will disappear with the exodus to suburbia. It begins in the immediate postwar years and picks up steam as millions of black people settle in cities and start to spread out and millions of whites decide to take a powder. Some mention race as they pack up the moving vans—"The colored are moving in," they say with a fatalistic shrug—but others mouth hypocrisy. They say they've always dreamed of a lawn. They would rather lie than admit simple aversion to people with dark skin, whom they've never actually met. In the fifties we're racing from the city to those blossoming suburbs in Buicks that seem to be forty feet long. They only get nine miles to the gallon, but so what? You can fill your tank at the local Esso station for a couple of bucks, and they'll throw in S&H trading stamps. The new cars have tail fins like rocket ships and roar across Eisenhower's gleaming new interstate highway system as if launching themselves into outer space like Russia's Sputnik.

In the fifties General Motors has six hundred thousand employees supplying cars to twenty-four thousand dealers. Everybody knows their unofficial company slogan: What's good for GM is good for the country. In Baltimore, when these sixteen-year-old kids drop out of high school, who's to worry about it? The kids troop down to the GM plant on Broening Highway. Why not? Those swell assembly line jobs will be here forever, won't they?

Won't they?

In the fifties, nobody's got home computers yet and almost nobody's got air conditioning, so what does this mean? It means we go outside. The parents plop themselves on front steps and beach chairs in their Bermuda shorts and wait for a cool summer breeze while they keep an eye on the kids, who are playing stickball and hopscotch and three-flies-in and S-P-U-D. They say hello to their neighbors, many of whom they know by actual name. "Hey, Louie!" "Hey, Gussie!" "What's new since yesterday?" "How 'bout those birds?" "And how 'bout that dress Uncle Miltie wore on the TV last night?"

Nobody thinks about pollution yet. Nobody frets over what level of sunblock to plaster over pale faces. Kids ride their Schwinn bikes in the street, with Topps baseball cards flapping in the spokes for cool sound effects, and not one of them wears a safety helmet. They're kids, let 'em play! In the fifties, we've got more than five thousand little leagues across the country, more than four million girls in Brownies and Girl Scout troops holding meetings every week in church basements.

That's the innocent America we wish to remember, no?

Then there's the other America, where people like Jerry Leiber live. It's getting a little edgy down there. Young Jerome's living along the encroaching edge of the black ghetto. The country fought the last world war to preserve some idealized American Way of Life, as everybody knows. But it finds itself, out of habit, still choosing up sides by race and religion and ethnic persuasion. You want evidence? Just watch some Italian kid try to dance with a Polish girl at a Saturday night CYO dance. Or listen to a Catholic schoolteacher warn her students not to play with public school kids—you never know which ones might be Protestants. Or just watch a black family try to slip quietly into a white neighborhood, the way it's happening exactly one block from the Leiber grocery store.

In cities such as Baltimore, the American melting pot looks more like a mosaic. The Italians have Little Italy, and two blocks north of this thousands of Jews huddle around their famous Lombard Street holy places: synagogues and delicatessens. Further east surrounding sprawling Patterson Park, the Germans and the Poles and the Greeks and the Slovaks separate themselves by narrow city intersections that sometimes seem as wide as the Atlantic and equally treacherous to cross. People tend to settle in with their own kind, though not always by preference.

In West Baltimore, there are specific streets around Druid Hill Avenue below North Avenue where the blacks are officially permitted to live. The city goes to great legal pains to keep them in their place. First, an early-century municipal ruling stops blacks from moving to white residential areas. Then, when the U.S. Supreme Court in a rare moment of racial enlightenment calls this unconstitutional, private gentlemen's agreements bar blacks (and Jews) from moving into certain neighborhoods.

And so, over on the west side of Baltimore you find black families jammed into their narrow stretch of turf and, on the fringes of this ghetto, working-class whites. All are scuffling for the dollar that just about disappeared during the depression years. They arrived across much of the city during World War II: about a quarter-million whites and about twenty-five thousand blacks, almost all from the South, and all looking for wartime industry jobs that finally rescued them from depression-era poverty. Baltimore built a hell of a lot of combat ships and planes. With the fighting over now, a lot of these folks stick around but still keep their distance across the racial divide.

Also on this crowded west side: those who run little corner groceries and mostly live right above the store. Manya Leiber's one of them. She had two daughters and the five-year-old son, Jerome, when her husband died. He left her a hundred bucks from an insurance policy. She used the money to open a candy store and then turned it into a grocery. Nobody down here knows from big supermarkets. You need a loaf of bread, you send one of the kids down to the corner. While Jerome grows up running the streets, Manya, short, stocky, and tough, runs the little store where she sells meat and potatoes and produce. Also cigarettes, which Jerome is smoking by the age of nine. This suits Manya fine. She thinks it's a sign that her boy is becoming a man.

She's already got him working like one. Jerome delivers five-gallon cans of kerosene and ten-pound bags of soft coal from the grocery store to nearby row houses, many lived in by poor blacks. They like Manya. She extends credit to them when other store owners see skin color and instinctively offer contempt. This is how the Leibers scrape by. All these decades later, you can still go down to Riggs and McKean and see the faded lettering painted on the old store's brick wall. "Groceries and Provisions," it says.

It's about the last indication that healthy life ever existed here or might ever exist here again.

The neighborhood's a mess. It was a mess in Leiber's time but only to a degree. Now it's the full urban disaster. All these boarded-up row houses, all these signs over the front doors of rotting buildings saying, "No Trespassing. Private Property. No Loitering." As if throngs of vacationers might otherwise wish to pause here and admire such a splendid panorama. The neighborhood's big legitimate business, at Riggs and Fulton a block east of McKean, is the T-Bird Bail Bond Company, whose motto is: "You Ring, We Spring." Around here, bail bonding is considered a growth industry. Police cruisers circle the block regularly. Here comes a fifteen-year-old girl with her ten-month-old baby by a father to be named later. She crosses paths with a beefy kid taking his pit bull for an afternoon stroll. It's a pit bull neighborhood, unfit for poodles of any sort.

Jerome on his postwar deliveries here had his own problem environment. For one thing, the neighborhood was lousy with competition. The coal man made deliveries, and so did the Koester's bread man and the ice man and the Cloverland milk man, whose truck bears the company advertising jingle: "If you don't own a cow, call Cloverland now. It's North 9-2222." Then there are the street A-rabs, black men riding their rickety old horse-drawn wagons and splitting the air with their shrill cries, only half-decipherable to the human ear, announcing fresh fruits and vegetables. Horse-drawn wagons, in the age of cars and trucks. Later, such wagons will be cited by those with short memories and misplaced nostalgia as a sign of Baltimore's enduring municipal charm.

But there's something else in the air, which will change the whole country. Fulton Avenue, one block from the Leiber grocery store, is the city's west-side racial dividing line. Blacks on the east side, whites on the west. But now, as the war's ending, blacks have begun moving across the street. For Sale signs, scores of them, are popping up all over the place. Whites start evacuating a block at a time. In March 1945, there are maybe fifty black families all along broad, lengthy Fulton Avenue. Four months later, hundreds of empty homes are available to them.

It's the dawning of a very nervous time, intensified by real estate people looking to cash in on everybody's anxieties. They're making phone calls, they're sending letters, they're sliding circulars under front doors. The message to white people around Fulton Avenue is always the same: The neighborhood's changing, so don't be the last to get out. The message to blacks is the opposite: Finally, here's your chance to step up.

Moving across this racial divide we find Jerry Leiber. He's a kid, what does he know? He knows he's making deliveries for his mother, that's all, and when he goes to these streets with black families he hears something he's never imagined before.

He hears teenagers standing under street corner lights who seem to be ad-libbing their way through melodies and making up words as they go along. "Bop-shoo-bop," what the hell kind of English is that? "Sh-boom-sh-boom." And the music comes out of radios and little record players in the homes where Jerome's making his coal and kerosene deliveries.

He hears a song called "Boogie Express," by Deryck Sampson, who lays down a jaunty piano rhythm. He hears a guy named Josh White singing "Outskirts of Town," where he wants to move so he can give up the ice man and buy himself a Frigidaire. Frigidaires? Who sings about Frigidaires? Not Joni James. Not Vaughn Monroe. In the postwar years, mainstream American pop songs stick to bland moon and June romantic lyrics. But the sound of ice men and street A-rabs and parents hollering at kids—these are the images that Leiber will absorb into his bloodstream and one day turn into song.

He surely hears the Orioles. They're a Baltimore group starting to hit it big on the rhythm and blues charts, which white disc jockeys call "race music." It's an oblique, polite way for white people to categorize "music for the colored." The Orioles are led by Sonny Til, born Earlington Tilghman, who brings with him Alexander Sharp, George Nelson, Johnny Reed, and Tommy Gunther. Baltimore guys, every one, scuffling for the buck with musical skills breathed into them since childhood inside some of these neighborhood storefront churches you see all over ghettoized West Baltimore.

They make the rounds of local black clubs, places like the Avenue Café, over on Pennsylvania Avenue, where the girls swoon over Sonny and his cool, elegant, soaring tenor as he sings "It's Too Soon to Know" and "Crying in the Chapel." Then Sonny goes home to Whatcoat Street, where he still lives with his mother so he can save a few bucks on rent. If they're lucky, maybe the *Afro-American* gives the group a line in an entertainment column. They haven't got a prayer of coverage in the daily *Sunpapers* or *News-Post*, which seem oblivious to all life in the black community except acts of felony.

But then Jubilee Records signs the Orioles to a contract. Arthur Godfrey gives them a shot on his national radio program. "It's Too Soon to Know" goes to number 1 on the race charts and 13 on the pop charts. Imagine this, white people listening to radio music that has an overtly black sensibility. It's 1948 now, when the top-selling song in America is Dinah Shore's "Buttons and Bows." Number 2 is "I'm Looking over a Four-Leaf Clover." There's no edge to American pop music. Hell, it's three years since the end of the war. Who's ready for edge? Most people who survived those years want the middle ground, where it feels safe, where we can all calm down after so much tumult.

In the midst of this comes the Orioles and "It's Too Soon to Know," which might be the first great rhythm and blues number to cross over. And it commences a style, barely noticed at the time, which will become known as doo-wop. It's the music that begins with kids who slip outside their narrow little row houses and apartment buildings and stifling housing projects, who have no money to buy instruments, but they harmonize on these street corners, in the hallways, and in school lavatories so they can exploit the great echo-chamber effect of porcelain toilets and sinks.

From the moment he hears it, this music entrances young Jerome Leiber. Who knows, maybe it's the ancient strains of cantorial singing he senses in it. "Listen to any cantor singing in a synagogue," he says years later, "and there's a little bit of Ray Charles going on." Or maybe it's a gender thing: Jerome's the only male in the household of the mother and two older sisters, and this stuff's got a distinctly masculine thrust to it. He starts walking and talking like some of the black kids he's meeting. He's a white boy who's seen the other side and can't get enough of it.

At the grocery store, he hears Manya yelling at him, "Take out the papers and the trash."

"Or what?" Jerome mutters under his breath to a pal.

"Or you don't get no spending cash," the pal says.

Does such a conversation actually take place? Of course it does. It happens every day in households across America where the exhausted parent nags the reluctant teenager to take care of chores, or else. In the Leiber household, though, this kind of language sinks into the crevices of Jerome's brain and remains there. When he meets Mike Stoller a few years later, they help re-invent pop music with a song called "Yakety Yak" that becomes a kind of comic anthem to the eternal parent-teen struggles.

In the apartment above the grocery store, such music is a mystery to the Polish immigrant Manya Leiber. She knows nothing about Sonny Til or Deryck Sampson or Josh White. She knows from European folk music. Or Chopin, or Mahler. This is what the Jews out of Eastern Europe still cling to in the postwar years.

Or, if they're further assimilated, they take pride in all those Jewish composers whose work makes up so much of the great American songbook: George Gershwin and Jerome Kern, Rodgers and Hammerstein, and Irving Berlin, who writes "White Christmas" and "Easter Parade," causing gentiles to say, "Look at this! A Jew writing songs celebrating our holidays! He's OK!"

All of which becomes America in its grand symphonic mix, no?

It's the stuff the veteran newspaper columnist Pete Hamill, writing years later in New York's *Daily News*, calls "the music that came out of the ghettos of the Lower East Side and Williamsburg and Harlem. It was made by piano players in whorehouses. It was played in clip joints run by gangsters. It was written by men born in other countries who came through Ellis Island and discovered America. It was given a rowdy grandeur by the children of immigrants." It was, Hamill wrote,

> the sound of America, the rhythms made by black slaves and their sharecropper children, the deep, mordant, triumphant challenge of the blues. They added the melodies of the world that was left behind, the Europe of memory, the Europe of Vienna and Milan, of Irish minstrels and vanished troubadours. They threw in the sound of traffic and subways and the mood of closing time in a gin mill. And from all that, they made something new. Their brilliant synthesis became American music.

In the postwar years the music of old Europe's beginning to be drowned out, and the new music's stirring to life in places such as West Baltimore, where it catches the imagination of the young Leiber. On one of his grocery deliveries, Jerome meets this black fellow named Dunbar. He's four years older than Leiber. Dunbar knows this rhythm and blues music and also knows how to fight. He teaches Leiber a pretty good left hook that will come in handy later.

"You remember Dunbar's full name?"

"Nah," Leiber says half a century later. "I just remember that he was a black kid who was a friend, and he looked after me." Affection lingers in his voice. "He took me up to his roof and let me pet his pigeons. And he smoked Old Golds, which was very cool. He liked me because I brought stuff to his mother. And I liked him because of the music."

"Was there also an empathy there? The Jews and the blacks, two outcasts?"

"Oh, absolutely. We were as vulnerable as them. All the time, there was anti-Semitism flaring up, and all the time the blacks had to duck their heads. We each knew what the other was going through. I identified with the blacks. My mother was extending credit to them, and I was doing those deliveries to their houses, and that's where I discovered this music coming out of their radios, stuff I never heard anywhere else. I was passing open windows and I'd hear it. Or there's a guy sitting on his front step, and he's making stuff up as he goes along.

My mother went to these immigrant social clubs where you heard Jewish music, Polish and Russian stuff. That stuff didn't move me. But the music in these black families' homes—I mean, the radios were like magic boxes to a young Jewish kid like me. The music just knocked me over. Some of that, I got from Dunbar. And, also, he taught me how to fight. The left hook, it made me feel like a tough guy."

Jerome's outnumbered, but he's scrappy. He's got a slightly mongrel quality about him, down to his eyes: one brown, one blue. (Years later, somebody asks him, "On your passport, what do you put down for color of eyes?" Leiber answers, "Assorted.")

He starts running with a bunch of neighborhood white boys. "Kid named Kelly," he remembers. "He was the leader. He's maybe fourteen. I was younger, but now I could fight. Kelly loved me. I brought him candy bars with nuts from the store. I'd bring it to him like a Mafia leader."

Much of the time, Jerome was on his own and getting a little wild. "There was them, and there was me," Leiber remembers. "The punks hanging outside my mother's store. Mostly Italian and Polish kids. I knew they were looking to knock my mother's place over."

Fights, all the time. The most memorable, a drizzly afternoon right outside the store. This little bunch of neighborhood kids hanging out, even in the crummy weather, for who's got some place better to go? They spot the Hebrew books Leiber's carrying. They start yelling, "Jewboy, get the Jewboy." Two cops are right there on the corner, but they find this Jew-baiting a fine amusement.

Leiber tries to get into the store, but the bullies are shoving him around. "*Jewboy, Jewboy.*" They knock the books out of his hands. Now it's not just a fight, it's religious transgression: Leiber thinks somebody's going to hell—maybe him—for letting the holy books hit the pavement. So he spots a kid he thinks he can take. He throws Dunbar's left hook at him. The kid staggers back. This impresses the others. Leiber throws another punch. He's doing pretty nicely, when somebody unfortunately breaks up the fight: Manya Leiber.

Here she comes, shoving all these punks aside, and she's marching Jerome into the store and smacking him a good one across the chops.

"Fighting again?" she cries in her thick Polish accent. "You gonna wind up in the 'lectric chair."

His teachers had the same worry. One of them sends a letter home, warning Manya there's trouble ahead for her son. More than sixty years later, Leiber laughs aloud at the memory.

"The teacher was angry," he recalls. "So she sends a note home to my mother, who didn't read. She knew Polish, she knew Yiddish. So I read her the note. It says, 'Your Jerome is incorrigible.' My mother leaps on this. 'Incorrigible!' She says, 'I knew it. A little bit of encouragement goes a long way.' She believed in me. She wanted to believe in me."

"What about the music?"

"This was another fight," Leiber remembers.

He starts making his way down to Howard Street, down to Fred Walker's Music Store, where he takes drum lessons. He makes friends with a teenage boy who's got a set of drums at home and lets Leiber practice every day on his way home from school. And he starts taking piano lessons.

Several blocks east of the grocery store, over by upper Druid Hill Avenue a few blocks above the black ghetto, lives Leiber's Uncle Dave, who has a piano on his top floor. Long after he has met Mike Stoller, with whom he will help invent rock and roll, long after they have both become famous, Leiber will recall this moment with Uncle Dave and a piano teacher named Yetta Schlossberg as a turning point in his life.

Yetta teaches classical piano. She is described as a homely woman with a kind heart. She has learned from Leiber about this strange new music he calls boogie-woogie. She wishes to encourage his musical enthusiasm and asks him to play a little bit. The music echoes through the house. After a few moments, the door whips open. There stands the formidable Uncle Dave like classical music's avenging angel. Uncle Dave's musical sensibilities have been offended. Piano lessons aren't for boogie-woogie, they're for Bach and Beethoven.

"Out of my house!" Uncle Dave cries, slamming down the keyboard cover so that Jerome barely snatches his hands to safety. "I give this woman room and board to teach you how to play the piano like a mensch, and you reward me with this garbage? These lessons are over. Take this music back to the gutter where you found it."

Uncle Dave will go to his grave without ever again exchanging words with his nephew Jerome. The battle lines in the generation gap are being drawn here in West Baltimore and will soon spread across the country.

Within a few years, the teenagers are deep into this thing that's now called rock and roll, and Jerry Leiber's writing songs with Mike Stoller while Uncle Dave is covering his ears from all the coast-to-coast racket.

A few blocks below Uncle Dave's home, on Druid Hill below North Avenue where black people are allowed to live, there's another family dealing with the changing times. In their home, the music on the radio is Beethoven, and it's also religious spirituals. As white Americans begin reaching for the sound of black rhythm and blues, this black family reaches for traditionally white music. But they want more than a simple song. The family is Clarence Mitchell Jr.'s.

(WX1)WASHINGTON,AUG.23--APPEAL COURT RULING--Students from Little Rock,Ark. sit on steps of the U.S.Supreme Court with their escort and Thurgood Marshall,attorney for the National Assn. for the Advancement of Colored People,after he filed an appeal in the court yesterday to vacate an Eighth Circuit Court of Appeals order which would delay integration in Little Rock's Central H.S. Left to right:Melba Pattillo,Jefferson Thomas,Gloria Ray,Daisy Bates,escort;Marshall,Carlotta Walls,Minnijean Brown and Eliz. Eckford.Students are attending negro Elks convention here.(AP WIREPHOTO) (1170700strWJS) 1958.

Thurgood Marshall took lessons first learned at Baltimore's Frederick Douglass High School all the way to the U.S. Supreme Court. He's surrounded on the high court's front steps in the midst of efforts to integrate America's public schools. (Hearst Newspapers LLC / Baltimore News-American)

Passport across the American Racial Divide

Clarence Mitchell Jr. and Thurgood Marshall

One spring afternoon in 2011, from his office on Druid Hill Avenue in broken West Baltimore, across the street from the Union Baptist Harvey Johnson Head Start Program, we find Dr. Keiffer Mitchell. He issues driving instructions over the telephone as though directing a rube from the cornfields of Nebraska to the back streets of lower Kazakhstan.

"That's Druid Hill Avenue," he says, carefully spelling it out. "D-R-U-I-D . . ."

"Yes, yes, I know where . . . "

" . . . Hill. H-I-L-L. Druid Hill Avenue."

Wonderful.

After all this time, and all this history, we have a man acutely sensitive to divisions that never exactly go away. Mitchell practices medicine on this busy thoroughfare, Druid Hill Avenue, that serves as a municipal dividing line. Blacks here, whites somewhere else. Head Start programs here, private nursery schools somewhere else. He spells out directions to a white man because sometimes even now you practically need a passport across the American racial divide.

Everybody in Baltimore knows Druid Hill Avenue, or should. Clarence Mitchell Jr. came from this neighborhood, and Thurgood Marshall, and Lillie Carroll Jackson and Juanita Jackson Mitchell. All were black, and all changed the course of history. Whites don't come from here. They drive through here, in haste, all car doors locked. It's a municipal reflex.

Keiffer Mitchell is a medical doctor despite the efforts of white people. They wanted him out of their public school. Hundreds of them stood outside Gwynns Falls Park Junior High in the autumn of 1954, ready to gang up on this dreamy, artistic twelve-year-old child. They told him to go back to Africa, even though he only came from West Baltimore. They said the hell with the Supreme Court and the hell with its brand new ruling integrating the public schools, we still don't want any blacks here. And then came Keiffer Mitchell's father, Clarence Jr., all by himself, and he marched up and down the pavement in front of all these screaming people and said he wasn't going anywhere until his son could live his life as fully as any white American child.

And that's the merest snapshot of Clarence Mitchell Jr.'s life.

Keiffer Mitchell's row-house quarters seem a combination medical office and museum of the American civil rights movement, all superimposed on the tattered surrounding neighborhood. Photographs cover the walls. There's Mitchell's dad, Clarence Jr., getting the Presidential Medal of Freedom from Jimmy Carter. There's his mom, Juanita Jackson Mitchell, befriended by Eleanor Roosevelt. There's his uncle, Parren Mitchell, the first black congressman from Maryland. There's Keiffer's brother, Clarence III, who was a state senator, and his brother Michael, who was also a state senator. There's John Kennedy; there's Lyndon Johnson. So many grand moments, and it all comes down to Keiffer Mitchell, seventy years old now, slender and soft-spoken, seeing patients all day long in the heart of this perennially impoverished West Baltimore neighborhood.

"Been here for thirty-eight years," he says, "and never been robbed once." There are locks on the doors and iron bars over windows. The bars cast shadows over a new campaign poster for Mitchell's son, State Senator Keiffer Mitchell Jr., displayed inside a first-floor window.

The office is located one block below the modest row house where the family lived for decades, back when the father, Clarence Jr., headed the NAACP's national office and the mother, Juanita, was the first African American woman to practice law in the state of Maryland, and visitors to the house included Paul Robeson and Duke Ellington and Marian Anderson and Eleanor Roosevelt, and the telephone would ring and young Michael Mitchell, picking up the receiver, would hear a man say, "This is John Kennedy. Is your father home?"

"He's at work."

"Is your mother there?"

"She's in the bathroom."

Young Michael never heard the end of *that* one.

Anyway, somebody should have declared the old house a historic monument. Instead, it's an empty ruin, like hundreds and hundreds of other row houses in this neighborhood: boarded up and falling down and plagued by so many gaping wounds that you can look from the sidewalk of Druid Hill Avenue and see all the way through to the grubby alley in back.

"What would your parents think of that?" Keiffer Mitchell is asked now. "All that work, all that history inside the old house, and now it's a forgotten wreck."

"My parents wouldn't have cared about that," he says, waving a hand dismissively. "They didn't care about bricks and mortar. My parents were revolutionaries."

≈

Well, it took a revolution, didn't it?

By the innocent fifties Clarence Mitchell Jr. in his middle age arose each morning in his row house on Druid Hill Avenue, with his wife and four sons, and he put on his suit and tie and looked in the mirror and never fooled himself. He knew that a second-class citizen stared back. When he traveled to Florence, South Carolina, one day, he was arrested at the train station for the crime of entering the White Waiting Room. In Baltimore his sons can't sit in a classroom with white children, and his wife can't walk into a downtown department store and try on a dress before buying it. The casual humiliations are ceaseless. This is why Mitchell never once fools himself. Instead he rushes to catch the morning train to Washington, D.C., where he spends his days trying to fool all the reluctant people who run the government of the United States.

He does this with his courteous patrician manner, designed to cover all inward seething. He's insistent but respectful. No threats, no talk of riots. He learns to smile at such bigots as Senator Strom Thurmond of South Carolina. He asks those such as Senator James Eastland of Mississippi why citizens whose grandparents arrived here in chains from Africa don't have the same rights as those who arrived in steerage from Hamburg and Cracow and Dublin. He does this with a mask over his face to cover the impatience and the anger of twenty million black American citizens.

But Mitchell knows something important. Black people aren't the only angry ones. He sees white people ready to resist. Blacks advance, whites dig in. Before the innocent fifties are over, the worst of the whites will put bombs inside churches to murder little black girls. But most whites just stand firm, or puzzled. They want to know why black people can't stay in their own neighborhoods, attend their own schools, work at their own jobs, and leave whites alone. The way it's always been in America.

Mitchell, a sophisticated man, knows that some of this resistance comes from bigotry, and some from ignorance, and some from fear. Law and custom have kept the races apart. Americans share the same cities at a distance. Stereotype and myth are handed down like family heirlooms, and relentless stories in the daily newspapers reinforce the worst of it: "Negro, 49, Held in Burglary." "Rape Charges against Negro." The headlines are always quite specific about felonies by blacks. No headline ever says: "White Man Held in Stick-Up." Or "White Bankers in Mortgage Scandal." Whites drive along streets where black people live in ghettoized homes that ought to be condemned, and they think: "What kind of people are these? Who could live like this? *They must not be like us.*"

In the innocent fifties we live in two different countries called America. As always. As the entire life of Clarence Mitchell Jr. gives testament.

Mitchell's born March 8, 1911. This is precisely three months after passage of a Baltimore City law that prohibits black people from moving into white residential neighborhoods. The new ruling's a disgrace to humanity, of course, but it changes almost nothing. It merely gives legal stature to social custom entrenched far deeper than any law, which declares: Black people, know your place.

Segregated housing's only a piece of the daily affront. Hospitals are segregated, and public schools, and restaurants and theaters, and public lavatories, and shaded grassy areas where you can escape the miserable heat of a summer afternoon, and cemeteries, too.

In the 1950s, when much of this is still unchanged and black people finally take to the streets and the courts and the legislative corridors, many puzzled white people will ask, "Why can't they just wait a little longer? Why does it have to be now? Why can't they move a little slower?"

Thus failing to notice that entire lifetimes have already come and gone.

Never mind this 1911 law that officially ghettoizes blacks—they needed no reminders. If they did, the *Baltimore Sun* was there to supply it. The newspaper called "the white race . . . the dominant and superior race" and applauded thugs who threatened violence against any black person appearing in a white neighborhood after dark. This happened most flagrantly in the south Baltimore community of Locust Point, where Francis Scott Key once gazed out from Fort McHenry and wrote "The Star-Spangled Banner."

The *Sun*'s view on violence just outside the birthplace of the national anthem? "It may not be an ethical position to take," the newspaper editorialized, "but it is successful."

And so, as Clarence Mitchell Jr. arrived in the world, ritualized racial segregation was fixed tightly into both law and public discourse, just in case anybody got any smart ideas.

At this time the Mitchell family lived on a narrow cobblestone block directly across from a lumber yard where braying mules did most of the hauling. When it rained, the street turned to mud. The father was a musician who worked as a waiter at the Rennert Hotel, at Saratoga and Cathedral. His big dream was that one day, with great luck and fortitude, his son Clarence might become a waiter. Thus were the borders drawn around human ambition. The mother took in laundry. She'd boil it in a pot over a fire and cook fish for dinner at the same time. Clarence Jr. hated the smell of fish for the rest of his life. He connected it with his mother washing other people's dirty clothes. He was the third of ten children. One died before him, and two died after him. The location was 1374 Stockton Street, the records say.

"Stockton alley," says son Michael Mitchell, correcting the record. He's a family historian. It's a summer morning in 2011 and Michael, beefy and his hair all over the place, is now sixty-five years old. "Dad always said he lived in an alley. And people would say, 'Here come them alley kids, they ain't gonna amount to nothin'.' That's the kind of place it was. That made him determined we'd have a decent life. It was the driving force for the whole family to have a decent life. Stockton alley. One of the narrowest streets in town, and no pavement. And then, from the alley, they moved to 553 Bloom Street."

Another mess. The house was a little bigger than the one on Stockton, but again had no electricity. Kerosene lamps kept the dark at bay. A coal-burning stove in the kitchen supplied whatever heat circulated through the house. Winters were awful. Young Clarence slept in a room euphemistically referred to as a "third bedroom." In reality, it was the bathroom. The Mitchells were happy to have the indoor plumbing.

In the middle of the block was a stable. Horses, mostly, but sometimes cattle and goats. But there was something else on the street: a rare mix of humanity.

"Dutch and Jewish and German," Michael Mitchell said, "so that prejudice wasn't so overt. Everybody was poor. That was the common denominator." A Greek family on the corner ran an ice cream parlor with a pool room downstairs. A German family lived next to a butcher shop. A Dutch family had a saloon, and a Jewish family lived above their grocery store.

To young Clarence Jr., it looked like America was supposed to look.

≈

When the innocent fifties arrive, Mitchell is still searching for such an America.

He awakens in that narrow row house on Druid Hill Avenue and takes the train to Washington, D.C., every day, to the NAACP offices, and then he walks up and down the halls of the U.S. Congress seeking help wherever he can find it. Everybody there gets to know him like a relative. He befriends John Kennedy before anybody thinks Kennedy's important. Once, Lyndon Johnson summons Mitchell to a meeting at five o'clock in the morning, and Johnson stands there in his underwear. That's how well they get to know each other. Mitchell learns to befriend people on both sides of the political aisle because this is the only way to win votes. Over the years he will testify more than one hundred times before U.S. congressional committees. His efforts will help desegregate every major federal agency in Washington. He'll convince Congress to pass the first civil rights act in eighty-three years, from which will come laws that ban housing discrimination and ensure the right to vote. One day, off in the distant future when his work is done, those on Capitol Hill will look back and affectionately dub him "the 101st senator."

But, for now, none of this matters. In America's eyes, Mitchell is a man with dark skin, and thus always a second-class citizen.

In the innocent fifties he still hears echoes of another time. Never mind the Ku Klux Klan or the White Citizens Council. Those people are knuckle-draggers. In allegedly civilized circles, such as the pages of the sophisticated *National Review* magazine, we have the brilliant William F. Buckley, the godfather of modern conservatism. In an editorial headlined, "Why the South Must Prevail," Buckley defends racial segregation and voting restrictions based on skin color because whites are "the advanced race" and "the claims of civilization supersede those of universal suffrage."

Thus marking the full distance covered in civil rights since young Clarence Mitchell's hometown paper was calling whites "the dominant and superior race."

Inches of progress, here and there.

In the post–World War II years, much of daily life remains unremittingly second-class for African Americans. Blacks and whites in Baltimore sometimes worked side by side during the war years. They were machinists and welders and riveters, and they worked on factory assembly lines and made bombers and ships that helped win the war. It wasn't sweetness and light. At the huge Bethlehem Steel plant, employing thousands, blacks were furious when initially denied training. When management bent and gave in to them, this enraged several thousand whites. But, given a chance, sanity prevailed. Workers stood there every day, ultimately putting aside skin color and trying to help the country survive, and it gave a lot of people hope that better days were coming.

But there they are, with the fighting done, and sometimes it seems the country has gone nowhere at all. The city of Baltimore now has roughly a million people, about one-quarter of them black. Never mind that the black population mushroomed during the war—they're still shoehorned into the same narrow ghettos. The crowding's gotten so bad, and the sanitation arrangements are so outdated and overworked, that the 1950 tuberculosis rate is now five times higher among blacks than whites. Infectious diseases are widespread. When the city's health department announces these conditions, the reaction among many whites is the usual: the colored must have brought it on themselves.

Thousands of their homes, mostly rented from whites, need to be condemned. Black people fill the old alley homes of West Baltimore or beat-up row houses left behind by fleeing whites. Many are still using kerosene lamps in the 1950s. Tar paper roofs are flimsy and leaky. Window sills are rotted. Stoves are obsolete, or they're broken and dangerous. A 1954 study says the average Baltimore slum dweller "carries his own stove with him, moving [it] in and out with the rest of his belongings whenever he changes his address."

Black children go to schools abandoned by whites. There's almost no place for kids to play—and hell to pay if they think they can use white kids' playgrounds or swimming pools. It's the same for adults. The city has a strict policy of no blacks and whites playing ball games together. Insane, of course. Jackie Robinson integrated big league baseball back in 1947 but, in Baltimore, this is seen as news from some distant planet. (Even after the Orioles arrive to play Major League baseball in 1954, and visiting American League teams need rooms for black players, the downtown hotels still refuse them.) When the Progressive Party of Maryland stages an integrated tennis match at Druid Hill Park, the cops are called in. They stop the match, disperse the crowd, and arrest thirty-four people. Beautiful—arrested for the crime of playing tennis. Seven are later convicted for "conspiring to riot," a marvelous euphemism for the playing of a country club sport. Later, police break up an integrated tennis match involving a team from Fort George Meade, the Second Army headquarters. A month later, they break up an integrated baseball game. Who's playing? Sailors from a visiting American naval vessel. As far as the laws of Baltimore are concerned, Jackie Robinson can go to hell.

The Maryland State Teachers Association remains segregated until 1952. The area's biggest drugstore chain, Read's, refuses to integrate its lunch counters until 1955. It's 1956 before the city removes "White" and "Colored" signs from all of its public buildings and 1957 before the city's bar association, in an embarrassingly close election, finally votes to admit blacks (and women). In the early part of the decade there are no black taxicab drivers, no black bus drivers, no black firemen in Baltimore.

And then we have black families begin to push as far west as Fulton Avenue. This is a few blocks west of Clarence Mitchell Jr.'s Druid Hill Avenue home, and it's one block east of Manya Leiber's little corner grocery store. History's in the details: Mitchell watching the beginnings of this drama, knowing it's a harbinger of battles to come all across America. And this kid Jerry Leiber, picking up the vagrant sounds to turn them one day into music that causes people to dance and laugh across color lines.

But now there are white people standing in their doorways, telling blacks: Go no further. Their homes are not exactly the palace at Versailles, but they're all they've got. In the war years, thousands of Baltimore families cashed in on the housing shortage by taking in boarders. Across the city, homes were cut up into boxlike units. People shared beds and slept in shifts. They stood in line to use the bathroom. Now they're living in these cramped little row houses, many of them already falling apart from wartime crowding and from age, but they stand there defending them like the gates of heaven—because here come the colored, and then come these telephone calls and letters from real estate speculators warning: Get out while you can.

The message is so relentless, and so unsettling, that the all-white Fulton Improvement Association takes out an ad in the *Sun*, in the closing weeks of the war, that warns real estate speculators not to "force us from our homes . . . The Right to Live in the Manner We Choose are the very things our boys are fighting for."

It's like the opening shots at Fort Sumter. A civil rights struggle, broader by far than any housing dispute, is about to commence. It will touch the public schools and the segregated restaurants and theaters and public drinking fountains, and it will last for years and change the country forever.

In Baltimore it starts right there on Fulton Avenue, where these black people arrive and whites immediately reach to the heavens for help. There they find it. Five white neighborhood churches, whose ministers must imagine God is on their side, rally to the cause. There's a big neighborhood meeting at Saint Martin's Catholic Church. Somebody stands up and blames it all on "the Jew realtors." Most just blame the blacks. The *Afro-American* newspaper jumps in: "Churches Lead Hate Crusade," the headline reads. No, no, the white ministers insist, you've got this all wrong, we've got nothing against the colored.

"We just don't want our people crowded out, that's all," says the Rev. Louis O'Donovan, pastor of all-white Saint Martin's. "We're just interested in keeping our people where they are."

The Rev. Benjamin Blubaugh, pastor of the all-white Franklin Street United Brethren Church, adds, "I approve of the action because the whites will move out."

The Rev. H. E. R. Reck, of all-white Garrett Park Methodist Church, adds, "I haven't got anything against the colored people because I was taught to give them a fair deal. But the day has not yet come for social equality."

Men of God, every one.

And each reflects the religious reality of the era. In the fifties a reported 96 percent of all Americans worship at racially separated churches. Sunday mornings are as segregated as any hour of the week. If these white people standing in their doorways leave West Baltimore, these white men of the pulpit will be speaking to empty pews. It occurs to no one that perhaps the answer is to bring people together in the very places where God wishes to embrace them all. Instead, we will soon see newspaper stories about the wonderful number of new churches going up in suburbia. White churches, every one. God's word, now reaching the hinterlands. But not so many stories about the abandonment of their former churches in the city, which will become black churches or empty, decaying shells signaling the dying of neighborhoods.

When Clarence Mitchell looks at Fulton Avenue, he sees a reflection of the entire city. Downtown movies are segregated, and most neighborhood theaters, too. If blacks want to see a live show at Ford's Theater, they have to sit in the distant second balcony. If they want to buy clothes from some of the big Howard Street department stores downtown, the way Mitchell's wife does, they're not allowed to try them on for size. Some consider this progress: for a lot of years blacks weren't even allowed to enter some of these stores. Now they can enter. They can even come in at Christmas time. But, if little black children want to sit on Santa Claus's lap at one of these stores, the kids are steered away by floor walkers.

When Clarence Mitchell goes to Pennsylvania Avenue, the commercial heart of black Baltimore, he sees stores that are owned by white people and completely staffed by white people, though virtually all their customers are black. When he reads the *Afro-American* newspaper, he sees the veteran columnist E. B. Rea, peering out from behind puffs of his cigar smoke, practically pleading, "The time is ripe along the Avenue, where 99.9 percent of the business comes from colored patronage, for bonafide colored managers in some of the business enterprises, representation in a bank, a desk sergeant at Northwestern, a colored magistrate, colored street car operators."

In 1950 Mitchell's younger brother, Parren, a future U.S. congressman, has to sue the University of Maryland to gain entrance into its graduate school at College Park. Mitchell's a World War II veteran who served with the 92nd infantry division and was wounded in Italy. The courts finally force open the school's doors and Parren Mitchell becomes the first black person enrolled at the college's main campus.

And when Clarence Mitchell comes home to Druid Hill Avenue each night and looks his four sons in the eye, he knows that their lives are only a variation of his. They are second-class children attending segregated, second-class public schools. And it takes Mitchell back to his own beginnings.

≈

In his Bloom Street youth, Clarence Mitchell Jr. went to the Carey Street Elementary School, where he got a lucky start. The kindergarten teacher there was Norma A. Marshall; her career would span nearly half a century. She had a son, three years older than Clarence, named Thoroughgood.

Thoroughgood, who could stand a name like that? Not this kid. He's still in elementary school when he takes it upon himself to change the name. He makes it Thurgood. Who gave him permission? "I didn't have nobody's permission," Marshall explained. "I just did it."

One day the city of Baltimore will honor both of them, Mitchell and Marshall. They'll name the city's main courthouse after Mitchell, and they'll put up a statue of Marshall outside the federal courthouse. But, for now, they're just a couple of black kids, like all others, regarded by law and by custom as municipal afterthoughts. So they do the best they can.

"The only relations [with white people] would be with the corner grocery store," Marshall recalls years later. It's the same kind of situation that still exists more than a decade later when Manya Leiber's running her grocery store—not far from Marshall's old neighborhood—and her son Jerry's making his deliveries to black families.

In Marshall's youth, though, *he*'s the one making deliveries for a local grocery store. He's seven years old when he starts. He gets ten cents a day plus whatever he can eat. The young Clarence Mitchell, meanwhile, delivers coal and ice during the school year. Summers, he works on the waterfront. When he gets home, he delivers the laundry that his mother spent the day washing.

He and Marshall both attended the Colored High and Training School, later named Frederick Douglass High School, at Calhoun and Baker. By this time, Mitchell's strapping on roller skates every evening to get to his nighttime job as an elevator operator at the Rennert Hotel, where his father's got the job in the dining room. The hours are eleven at night until eight in the morning. Then he heads off to school. Thurgood Marshall has his own job. On weekends, he and his father work for a local bootlegger. The job, and the neighborhood where he lived, toughened him up. Years later Marshall recalled,

> We used to have fights with the white kids, just on principle. There was a white Catholic elementary school two blocks from Division Street, and for some reason, we didn't get along very well . . . We used to have periodic fights—not too bad. Maybe a rock here and there. It was fists, and eventually [the white school] let them out fifteen minutes before we got out, so that they could get home.

But it was the high school that offered greater opportunities to both Marshall and Mitchell—even though the place was a wreck. It was the city's first public high school for blacks. It had no library, no cafeteria, no gymnasium. Overcrowding was so bad that students went only half a day in two shifts (doubling the number of students who could use the building) and hallways were crammed with bookcases. But they had teachers.

"You had teachers there with doctorates who couldn't get hired for a college job," said Michael Mitchell. "An incredible faculty."

A pretty incredible collection of students, too, and every one of them reduced to a municipal afterthought. Among them is Cab Calloway. He majors in street hustles. He shines shoes, he walks horses at Pimlico Race Course, he hustles newspapers. On Sundays he sings in church. At night, he performs in West Baltimore jazz clubs where he's tutored by the great drummer Chick Webb. Calloway goes on to a half-century career as a band leader and singer. He helps immortalize the Cotton Club of Harlem. He gives the world "Minnie the Moocher" and "St. James Infirmary."

Anne Wiggins Brown is another classmate. She comes from a pretty good family. The father's a surgeon. The mother plays classical piano while Anne sings in a voice to melt hearts. When the parents try to enroll Anne in a Catholic school, she's turned down for her race. Baltimore's Peabody Institute, a world-class conservatory, will reject her for the same reason.

Never mind, she goes to Julliard and learns that George Gershwin is writing an opera. When she auditions for a part, Gershwin falls in love with her voice. By the time he finishes writing the music, he's changed the opera's title to reflect Anne Brown's newly expanded title role. The opera will now be called *Porgy and Bess*.

And there's another member of that legendary Broadway *Porgy and Bess* cast. The role of Sportin' Life? That's Avon Long—also a classmate.

Who can tell a young person's potential? Thurgood Marshall's a bright kid, but he's a little short on self-control. Sometimes he plays the class clown. Nobody looks at him and imagines a future Supreme Court justice. Sometimes he's sent to the school principal. For the rest of his life, Marshall tells this story to everybody. The principal hands Marshall a copy of the U.S. Constitution, with orders to memorize a section of it. Then he sends him to the furnace room in the school basement. "You will stay there as punishment," he says, "until you learn the entire section." He does this every time Marshall gets into trouble, which is often enough to make its mark.

"Before I left that school," Marshall tells everyone, "I had that whole thing memorized."

He learned something else in high school. A second-floor classroom overlooked the Western District police station. From his window seat, Marshall could peer into the building. All officers were white. Most of the prisoners, black. Marshall remembered beatings. His teacher ordered him to close the window blinds. He could still hear the sounds, Marshall said, "of police beating the hell out of people, saying, 'Black boy, why don't you just shut your goddamned mouth, you're gonna talk yourself into the electric chair.'"

Clarence Mitchell saw some of the same things and saw them played out for years thereafter. He told his biographer, Denton Watson, "Blacks were herded into stations if they happened to be walking by when there was a lineup. Hundreds were arrested on 'suspicion' and held for days without bail. It was awfully easy to get arrested for nothing."

In high school Mitchell begins to notice Juanita Jackson. This is a courtship out of storybooks, including roadblocks placed by Juanita's mother, Lillie Carroll Jackson. For many, "Ma Jackson" was the godmother of the civil rights movement in Maryland. For three decades, she ran the Baltimore office of the NAACP and filed lawsuits right and left. She organized demonstrations against the various routine outrages. And she passed her passion to the daughter Juanita.

"An old-fashioned Methodist," her grandsons will call Lillie. No dancing, no boys, don't even think about kissing. Not even pretend kissing. When Juanita wins the starring role in Douglass High's production of *Sleeping Beauty*, the mother insists on rewriting the production: the prince must disappear off-stage while a girl, dressed in princely garb, takes his place and kisses Juanita's cheek.

"Boys and books don't mix," the mother declares when Juanita meets Clarence Mitchell Jr., two years her senior.

"And so," recalled Michael Mitchell, "my father became a book. That's what he told us. 'I became a book.' He knew how much her parents valued reading, and so he kept stopping by the Jackson house and dropping off books. That went on for four years. That's how he courted her."

Juanita graduated from high school at fourteen and went to the University of Pennsylvania. For the first time in her life, there are white students around her. In Philadelphia she can go to restaurants and theaters. She can go to department stores and actually try on clothes for size. When she graduates with honors in 1931 and returns home, her mother tells her, "We've given you what we could not get. You are not to come back and join the intelligentsia. You must share."

"She was that way her whole life," Keiffer Mitchell recalled. "Grandma Lillie used to say, 'Service to people is the rent you pay for your space on earth.'"

While Juanita went to Penn, Marshall and Mitchell went through Lincoln University, a small, all-male college with an all-white faculty. Some called it the black Princeton. The school was near Oxford, Pennsylvania. When Marshall and a few friends went to the local movie theater one Saturday afternoon, they ignored a sign saying blacks should sit in the balcony. They sat downstairs.

There they were, good as whites, when a voice called out, "Nigger, why don't you just get out of here and sit where you belong?"

"Bought a ticket just like everybody else," Marshall called back in the dark.

More words followed, until Marshall's group had heard enough. They tore down some curtains and walked out of the theater, breaking the front door as they left. No one followed them out, and no police ever followed up.

"The amazing thing," Marshall wrote home to his parents, "was that when we were leaving, we just walked out with all those people and they didn't do anything, didn't say anything, didn't even look at us . . . I'm not sure I like being invisible, but maybe it's better than being put to shame and not able to respect yourself."

This is Thurgood Marshall's turning point, a moment he recalled "started the whole thing in my life."

"Both of them," Keiffer Mitchell says, all these years later, "my father and Thurgood Marshall. They went after education like starving people."

The education went beyond classrooms, and it stayed with them, and one day in the fifties it will help change the color of America's public schools.

In the postwar years, Fulton Avenue was the city of Baltimore's west-side racial dividing line. Now, long-entrenched poverty, drug trafficking, and widespread neglect have turned the area into a depressing urban eyesore. (Courtesy Jim Burger)

Thrown Together on Both Sides
Fulton Avenue

The changes around Fulton Avenue have everybody rattled by the early 1950s. White families like Jerry Leiber's are moving out and black families like Richard Holley's are moving in. Leiber's out in California by now, where he'll knock on Mike Stoller's door with an offer to write music together. This new kid Holley's running the streets of West Baltimore with his buddies on a muggy summer afternoon when somebody says, "Let's go across Fulton Avenue and fight the white boys."

It's just something to do. It's an echo of Thurgood Marshall's street fights with the white kids over by Division Street maybe twenty years earlier. History's part of it, but so is distance. They've never known each other. They've never lived near each other or gone to school together, and a lot of their suspicions are based on folklore and stereotype. It's disdain built on mutual slander. And now, when these kids look up the street, they discover they've all been thrown together. It feels like forced intimacy. And so, having no one else to blame for the tension shadowing the neighborhood, they blame each other.

So let's go fight the white boys. They're sitting over there on the front stoops on the west side of Fulton Avenue or huddling outside the places like Manya Leiber's abandoned old grocery store. Evenings at the dinner table they hear their parents mutter about the arrival of the colored. They hear the neighborhood preachers on Sunday, caught between the healing words of the gospel and the anger of their congregants. A few of these men of God got their names in the newspapers. They said it wasn't quite time to talk about social equality. This meant black people were moving too fast. Such talk tends to give license to these white kids over on the other side of Fulton. Here's one of them saying, "Let's go fight the colored guys."

In a couple of years such kids will make history. After Thurgood Marshall has his triumphant hour at the Supreme Court, they'll be the first ones to sit in the same public school classrooms. Richard Holley will grow up and get his diploma from Morgan State College. And, instead of fighting the white boys around Fulton Avenue, he'll be teaching lots of white kids when he goes to work at a newly integrated Baltimore public school.

But, for the moment, it comes down to kids on both sides of Fulton Avenue saying, "Let's go across the street and fight those boys who don't look like us."

Why not? The grownups have been doing this in West Baltimore since the end of the war. The black families keep bulging out of their ghettos, obliterating the old racial dividing lines, and the white families are either digging in or bitterly moving out. The whites are furious at being forced (as they see it) from their homes. A lot of them have their life savings as well as their emotional security tied up in these places.

The blacks are just happy to be leaving behind their old homes where they had no indoor plumbing—or, if there was any, they had to use the bathroom as an extra bedroom, the way Clarence Mitchell's family did.

Richard Holley's family arrives on Fulton Avenue in 1949. He's fourteen years old. He was born in his parents' bedroom on Mount Street in 1935, when the issue of black people being welcomed at certain hospitals was still iffy. It's simpler to give birth at home than argue constitutional rights with some hospital guard while mom's writhing through labor contractions. Then the father took off when Holley was still a kid. It was Richard and his mother and grandmother after that. The two women worked as domestics and took home maybe sixty bucks a week between them.

In 1949 that was enough for a down payment on a house at 1312 Fulton Avenue. The place was fixed up pretty nicely and the cost was $5,980. The mortgage company was owned by Morris Goldseker. At the end of his life he leaves all his money to start a great charitable foundation to aid the poor. But Goldseker waits to die before he becomes a hero. In the fifties, and beyond, he's one of the biggest realtors capitalizing on every white person's fear of blacks and every black person's hunger for a better home. Goldseker knows people's naiveté about mortgages and financing and loopholes in contracts, and entire neighborhoods will come apart in the process.

≋

Sixty years later I find Richard Holley in his living room at 4207 Crawford Avenue. I had Holley for ninth-grade Spanish at Garrison Junior High back in the fifties. As it happens, I lived two doors away, at 4203 Crawford Avenue, when the two of us were teacher and four-teen-year-old student. In those years, when American cities were ethnic mosaics, Holley was still living on Fulton Avenue. In Baltimore, the blacks had West Baltimore, and the Jews had northwest Baltimore. Integration had reached Garrison Junior High, but it was still a few years away on Crawford Avenue.

"A great neighborhood," Holley says, glancing out his front window.

"Always was," I reply.

It was an all-white neighborhood as America's public schools were beginning to integrate, and it became an all-black neighborhood within a decade and forever after. On this summer morning in 2009, Holley's been on Crawford Avenue for about forty-five years. For about forty of those years, the neighborhood has had no white families. But it has trees and grass and a neighborhood elementary school. Fulton Avenue had cement and strife.

"When we went for the house down on Fulton Avenue," Holley remembers, "we had a problem right away. It wasn't just that we were black. They didn't want to sell to females. That's the way it was back then. My father wasn't there, so we used my Uncle Harry. Harry Day. We used his name on the mortgage. Uncle Harry didn't have a job, but he was a veteran. So that helped. And every month I'd walk the mortgage payment around to North Avenue and Fulton, up on the corner, where Mr. Goldseker was."

He smiles wryly at the memory. He's a kid in sneakers and dunga-rees, and there sits the mortgage holder Goldseker in a business suit, with his money and his lingering eastern European accent and his self-conscious formality.

"A very dignified man," Holley remembered, "and very tough. You knew you didn't come in late with his money. You did that, and you ran the risk of losing everything. That's the thing that everybody in the neighborhood knew. This man didn't mess around, and he didn't bend."

The dapper little Goldseker arrives here each day just after dawn and leaves after dark. He takes time off only for tennis or ballroom dancing. He never marries. He wears lifts in his shoes to pretend he's taller than five feet six. He came here from Russia but discovered how to make money the American way.

He started cashing in during the Depression. He convinced the big banks that he could handle hundreds of the properties they'd seized from people who'd lost all their money. He'd handle all the busy-work transactions with future renters. With the money he made, he started buying up properties. He bought by the hundreds and then by the thousands. Some of these row houses he picked up for less than a thousand bucks.

By the war years, he'd made a fortune buying these properties and renting them. By the postwar years, when the game's changing, Goldseker changes, too. The real estate boys are all making big money at this time, but he's smarter than any of them. They're all chasing the moving vans out to suburbia. Not him. Let 'em navigate their way out to sunny Towson and Owings Mills and Rosedale. It leaves him sitting there in the inner city with less competition. Somebody will need those old row houses left behind. Goldseker grabs with both hands. He buys these properties and spends a few bucks rehabbing them. Then he rents them. He uses the rent to pay off the loan, builds up his equity, and uses that to get another mortgage loan—which he uses as down payment for still more properties.

He transfers thousands of row houses from white families to black families. He sits there at the nervous heart of one changing neighborhood after another. He buys homes from all these white families frantic to get out while they can still make a buck or two, and he buys at auctions, and he buys five and ten or more at a time. Across the years he's got pieces of fifty different companies doing this business. In his landmark study of Baltimore housing, *Not in My Neighborhood: How Bigotry Shaped a Great American City*, Antero Pietila writes of Goldseker:

> Sales to blacks became his market niche. Of course, banks were not making mortgages to blacks at the time. There was not even a way for blacks to establish credit, because department stores neither wanted

their business nor sold them anything on time purchases. That was no problem for Goldseker. He conducted his own credit checks, reviewing wage records, rent remittances, electricity and telephone bills, and installment payments on stoves and refrigerators. If the results satisfied him, he sold a house for little money down and weekly payments.

Goldseker became a necessary middleman for lending institutions that had never dealt with blacks and did not want to begin doing so . . . He took a handsome profit each time. He sold thousands of houses that way in various parts of the city.

And sometimes he sold them more than once. Buyers bought the house, but Goldseker held onto the land beneath it. Purchasers had to pay him a fee twice a year. This is known as ground rent, and it supersedes the rights of the homeowner. You fail to pay your ground rent, you run the risk of losing the house. Brand new homeowners might have overlooked this little detail in their mortgage contracts—but Goldseker did not.

"Perhaps," Pietila wrote, "other real estate people were lenient or understanding. Not Goldseker. Anyone who failed to make a payment on time deserved to be put out. If that happened, those buying from him lost whatever money they had paid and whatever improvements they had made." An estimated 30 percent of Goldseker's land-installment buyers failed.

Piece by piece, neighborhoods failed as well. In a city whose housing stock included roughly forty thousand vacant, boarded-up, rotting homes by the twenty-first century, the deterioration begins right here, in the panic of the innocent fifties.

In the midst of this comes young Richard Holley with the monthly payment, always on time. The mother and the grandmother made sure of this. And there sits Goldseker, who will take the sixty bucks or so that Holley hands him, and from this he builds an empire, sixty and seventy bucks at a time from hundreds and then thousands of families.

It's only later, in the post-riot years of the late 1960s, that things begin to come apart for him when a group called Activists, Inc., accuses him of price gouging, of "unjust and inhuman practices perpetrated on the black community."

Goldseker was shocked, shocked by the accusations. A business associate says he always thought he was "doing good for people, providing an opportunity." Goldseker's accusers said he epitomized the "exploitative operation" linked forever with blockbusting and abandoned properties.

⇒

So there we are on a summer day, after the young Richard Holley has taken care of business with Goldseker, and he hears one of the neighborhood kids say, "Let's go across Fulton Avenue and fight the white boys."

"In those days," Holley remembers sixty years later, "nobody got stabbed or shot. You fought with your fists. You got in a couple of punches, and they got in a couple, and then everybody ran like hell."

"But why did you have to fight at all?"

"They wouldn't let us come over, that's all. That's why you have fights. They're on one side of Fulton Avenue; we're on the other. You know, 'They're not gonna tell me where I can't go.' We weren't gonna be like the old guys, shuffling their feet and staring at the ground. We're starting to fight back a little. And this one guy, Dirty Ida we called him, a light-skinned boy, brought a table leg this time. He said, 'I'm gonna hit a white boy over the head.'"

The fight didn't last long. Handful of kids on each side, some nasty words, somebody throws a quick sucker punch, and then a few more swings, and then everybody's running for cover with their hearts pounding before the cops show up. It's not like the rumble in *West Side Story* where somebody gets stabbed in the belly and then a Jerome Robbins ballet breaks out.

"A little tussle," Holley says, "and then we go back to our neighborhood. And everybody's looking for Dirty Ida. Finally he shows up. He can't believe what happened. Says, 'White boy hit me over the head with my own table leg.' We're all laughing our heads off, and he can't get over it. And then eventually we'd have more fights with the white boys."

Holley went to Booker T. Washington Junior High on Mount Street. Forty kids in his class, he remembers, "and thirty-plus went on to finish high school."

He says this with pride, as if no one back then could imagine such high graduation rates for black kids. He went to Douglass High and then Morgan State College.

"A totally segregated school life the entire way," he says. "It's the way it was for all of us."

At Morgan State he majored in Spanish and minored in French. He took ROTC and dived on the swim team.

"Every jock was a phys ed major," he says, "but I had a knack for languages. So I figured I'd teach. I was sitting in an education class at Morgan State the day we heard the Supreme Court integrated the schools. Oh, I remember that day."

"A great feeling?"

He shakes his head no. "A sobering feeling," he says almost in a whisper. "I can still see that professor looking at this room full of people. You know, we're on fire, we're gonna be the people who change the world. And now we've gotten the go-ahead from the highest court in the land. Man, you can feel your blood pumping through your body. And this instructor just looks at the guys in the room, and he's just staring. He says, 'You better understand something. They are never going to let you people in a classroom with any of those young white girls.'"

He could feel all the energy drained from the room. Never mind some legal bullshit over in Washington, it still came down to visions of colored field hands threatening innocent little white girls. Some things would never change.

Post-Korea, there was still a military draft, so Holley figured maybe he'd go into the army and forget about teaching. Harry Truman had finally integrated the armed forces a few years earlier. But a buddy, John Woods, told Holley, what the hell, take the teachers' test, see what works out.

"Woody and I stayed up drinking National Boh and studying for the test," Holley says. "Took it at Douglass, my old high school. And then I didn't think about it anymore, until I got a phone call from my mother. She said, 'You got a job offer.' I was up in Philadelphia with some friends."

He caught the next ride back to Baltimore and went straight to the old public school headquarters on Twenty-Fifth Street. They told him he'd scored 740 out of 800 on the teachers' test. They seemed impressed.

"We've gotta put you in somewhere," he was told.

They placed him at Hampstead Hill Junior High, in the autumn of 1958, in the heart of southeast Baltimore's white ethnic Highlandtown, an area bracing itself for a racial confrontation like Fulton Avenue on the west side.

There was a different kind of segregation on the east side. Practically block by block, it's a different white ethnic group. These are the descendants of those eastern Europeans who reached Baltimore with tags around their necks near the turn of the twentieth century, who settled with their own kind for a sense of security, who watched as their children took the first tentative steps toward the greater American mix when they entered the public schools, and played ball games over at Patterson Park, and went to the Patterson movie theater where John Wayne movies imbued them with the frontier spirit. In southeast Baltimore the embrace of America, the sense of patriotism, was overflowing. They showed it every year with a huge "I Am an American Day" parade.

But this business of black kids in their schools—or black teachers—this was something they hadn't exactly anticipated. Nobody warned them about such an American mix. They hadn't any blacks in their neighborhoods and hadn't even seen many on their TV sets or their movie screens. Blacks didn't play ball at Patterson Park. Around here, whites knew blacks mainly by agreed-upon slander.

Holley arrives at Hampstead Hill Junior High in September 1958, four years after the city's public schools have begun integrating. But it's a slow process around here. Unlike near Fulton Avenue, most of these white folks are sticking around. Their schools, public and parochial, are still overwhelmingly white.

These are the children of men who work the steel mills and the loading docks and the auto plants. A lot of their kids are already marking time until they're old enough to drop out of school and find some swell assembly line job where they can spend the next forty years. So who needs to learn some foreign language—especially from some colored guy who doesn't even belong in the neighborhood?

On his first day at Hampstead Hill, Holley's greeted by a white boy who eyeballs him and says, 'We just ran the last Spanish teacher out of here.'"

"You ain't seen me yet," Holley replies, eyeballing him back. "I got something for you."

He watches the kid back away, looking a little intimidated.

"That was a lesson for me," Holley remembers years later. "Turned out the kid was a leader. You get the leader, you got the crowd. Then somebody had a transistor radio in class when the World Series came on. Remember? They played day games then." It's October, about a month after his arrival. The radio's an electronic campfire, common ground where all can gather comfortably.

"I said, 'Leave it on. I like it, too,'" Holley remembered. And that was another turning point.

After taking ROTC at Morgan State he'd signed up for the Army Reserves. Now he had to go off to Fort Benning, Georgia, for a few months and then come back to Hampstead Hill. Feeling pretty good about himself. Feeling like he was getting his life in some kind of order. And, first day back in school, he's challenged again.

"Kid tells me, 'I'm gonna kick your ass, nigger.'" He chuckles lightly at the memory. "I said, 'You're gonna eat those words.' What the hell, I'm twenty-two, I'm right out of army training, I'm in good shape, and I'm feeling kind of hot-headed that this punk's challenging me."

"Meet me in the gym," the kid says.

"So I start going," Holley laughs. "And all these kids are following me. And there's a guy named Rink Williams, who taught gym. He says, 'What are you doing with all these kids?'"

"Kid over here wants to fight."

"Wait a minute," Williams says, "you don't want to lose your job over this. This boy gets in everybody's face."

This stops Holley in his tracks. He's not on Fulton Avenue any more. He's a schoolteacher now, not a street fighter. He's old enough to make distinctions. He's here to teach these white kids, not to hit one of them with a table leg like Dirty Ida.

Cooler heads prevailed. The following fall, Holley's transferred out to Garrison Junior High, at northwest Baltimore's Garrison Boulevard and Barrington Road. The school's about one-third African American. A lot of these kids still live down in West Baltimore, but they take the Baltimore Transit Company buses out to school every morning. Some have begun moving into homes on the streets near lower Liberty Heights Avenue and the Mondawmin shopping mall. Thousands more will follow.

The neighborhood around Garrison is still the city, but it's out near its grassy edges. This corner of town is where postwar Jews landed after leaving their old row-house neighborhoods. A lot of them moved up here from East Baltimore's Lombard Street area. Now they're out here above Park Circle, and they've settled around the area's three main corridors—Liberty Heights, Park Heights, and Reisterstown Road—trading one ghetto for another, trading the old ethnic gathering places for new ones, like the Hilltop Diner and Mandel's Deli, and new synagogues and Hebrew schools bursting with congregants. In the aftermath of the European Holocaust, the Jews are feeling a renewal of religious pride in safe America.

This is also where the first generation of a new black elite arrives now that the schools are officially integrated and some of the municipal jobs are opening up. Finally, a steady paycheck. And the black professional class, the doctors and nurses and teachers—finally, they can send their children to a first-rate public school.

The students at Garrison, black and white, are the children of upward strivers. They aren't imagining assembly line jobs, they're thinking about college. Maybe the parents didn't get that far—after all, they grew up during the Depression and went off to war—but this is 1950s America, when parents dream big dreams.

Holley arrives with built-in wariness but finds himself disarmed. When he stands in his first-floor classroom reciting irregular Spanish verbs, a lot of these kids are paying attention. They do their homework. They care about the day's vocabulary quiz. And he's knocked over by the faculty.

"One of the best staffs I ever saw," he says, "in all my years of teaching. And I remember thinking, 'I have to uphold myself. They're looking at me, and they're not just seeing a Spanish teacher, they're seeing a black man who happens to teach Spanish.' I knew I was on trial, that a lot of them were watching to see what a black man could do. But it was a learning experience for me, too. Teacher named Manny Velder, he taught me a lot. Taught me that teaching's not just a profession, it's a love."

When Holley wanders out to the boys' playground during lunch hour, he hears voices calling his name.

"Hey, Mister Holley. Wanta play?"

It's a pickup basketball game, and it's white kids and black kids. Come on, take a few shots, you're still a young guy. This becomes a lunchtime ritual. As he looks across the big blacktop playground every day, Holley sees punchball games everywhere. Every homeroom has a team, and every team's a racial mix. Nobody's choosing up sides by color.

The girls gather on the other side of the school, and they're doing their own mixing. They're talking about the latest fashions, they're talking about makeup, they're talking about boys. Color's an afterthought.

All of this looks like a pretty good start for school integration in America.

But it's only a start.

In June 1960, six years after the first black students arrive at Garrison, there are 290 white graduates and 159 black graduates. By the end of the decade, there are fewer than a dozen white graduates there. The rest have gone away: to suburbia, to private schools, to anywhere but the public schools of Baltimore.

It's the same all over the city. But, for a few years, Holley remembers now, he thought he saw a promising future. "No problems with the kids," he says. "Or the parents. Not to my face, anyway." Only with the school principal. An incident left Holley shaken with fear and anger. But the aftermath gave him hope.

"I'm on hall duty outside my room" when the principal comes up to him. "He's got a smirk on his face. He says, 'Isn't that a shame?' I said, 'What's that?' He says, 'I got a report that a foreign language teacher raped a white girl on the third floor.' Good lord! He's hinting that I'm some kind of suspect. I went right to Mrs. Hawkins, who taught French, and told her. She said, 'There he goes again. He did that to a colored science teacher who quit here in a hurry after that.'"

Holley went home to Fulton Avenue, where he still lived, and had a sleepless night. He was living in black America, and this was how white America was trying to keep him there. He had visions of White Citizens Councils, of men in white sheets demanding instant justice at the end of a rope. He knew he'd done nothing wrong, yet he felt completely alone and vulnerable. But, when he got to school the next day, he found something amazing: a small squadron of teachers, black and white, who'd heard the story by now and were rallying around him. He'd never in his life known such a moment.

And there was the African American vice principal, Dr. Elaine Davis, who asked Holley, "What did the principal tell you?"

"That some white girl was attacked up on the third floor. Dr. Davis,

I've never even been on the third floor." Such details remain with him even now.

"Who told the principal about this attack?" Dr. Davis asked.

"He said his secretary took a telephone call."

They went straight to the secretary, who was white. The secretary, furious, denied there was any such call. She rose from her desk and strode into the principal's office. Then, through a closed door, came the sound of the secretary's voice at highest pitch. Holley went back to his classroom, and minutes later he was summoned back to the principal's office. He sent word that he was busy teaching. The principal sent another teacher to pinch hit for him.

When Holley got to the office, the principal said, "Listen, you're doing a good job. I want you to stay here."

"What about that story?"

"Well," the principal said, "these are tumultuous times. Rumors get spread easily. The best way to stop a rumor is not to talk about it. So I think we should all stop talking about it, all right?"

Holley nodded his head.

"And this won't go any further? Do I have your word on that?"

"I didn't start it," Holley said.

Sitting in his living room half a century later, he still cringes at the memory. But there were times of delight at Garrison, as well. Holley's students were learners. The kids playing basketball on the playground made him feel welcome. He'd do cafeteria duty at lunchtime, with the smell of freshly baked sticky buns in the air, and one day the air was filled with music, as well.

A black kid named Claude Young had climbed up on a table and was singing a Ray Charles number out loud: "What'd I Say." Young's father was Buddy Young, who'd played halfback for the Baltimore Colts football team. All around him now, black kids and white kids were not only listening but surrounding Young and chiming in.

"Hey," Young sang out like Ray Charles.

"Hey." The crowd sang back like the Raylettes backup group a hundred strong.

"Hey."

"Hey."

"Ho."

"Ho."

"Hey."

"Hey."

"Ho."

"Ho."

"Oh, baby, one more time . . . "

Holley let the singing go on. It was too noisy, too anarchic, for a school atmosphere, but so what? This was chanting back and forth across the American color line. They were obliterating it for a few joyous minutes, getting past the invisible wall that blocked their parents and grandparents from finding any kind of common ground.

And it wasn't the only place where such things were happening.

You can go to Kenwood High School, on Stemmers Run Road, in eastern Baltimore County. It's 1956, and the cafeteria's filled with more music, which comes from forty-five rpm records played by an eighteen-year-old senior named Jack Edwards. He'll go on to a fifty-year career as a radio disc jockey around Baltimore.

Now, in the summer of 2011, he's still at it. He's the morning man at WTTR in Westminster, Carroll County, still playing music of the fifties and sixties—and still remembering how it all started for him at Kenwood, where all but a handful of students were white.

"I played music in the cafeteria every morning for the kids who came in on the bus," he recalls, "and after school, too. I just loved the music." He'd buy records at Yeager's Music Store, on Eastern Avenue near the old Haussner's Restaurant.

"This was an era," says Edwards, "where Joni James and Patti Page and Kay Starr were still big. And Doris Day and June Valli. Rock and roll was just coming in. But these kids in the cafeteria were all asking for songs by black performers. That's what they had to have. 'Crazy little mama, come knockin' on my front door . . . ' The Turbans, groups like that. At first I didn't know where they were hearing it."

Johnny Dark has the same story. He sits there now, at the studios of WTTR, where he follows Jack Edwards on the air every day. Half a century earlier, they were both on WCAO when it was the biggest rock-and-roll station in town and caused consternation among parents and newspaper editorial writers everywhere.

"I'm playing record hops all around the state of Maryland," says Dark, now seventy-seven. "You can't name an armory, or a high school gymnasium, that I didn't play. And I'm putting on Perry Como, I'm putting on the Four Lads. But that's not what the kids want. These are all white kids, yeah. There were no integrated dances back then. And they want Fats Domino, they want the Drifters, they want the Coasters. So that's what we're playing on the radio—and that brings on the backlash. The parents. They didn't want to hear black music. 'You shouldn't be playing that race music.' That was the polite term. But the kids wanted it. They wanted rock and roll, and it didn't matter who was performing it."

"I'd play songs by black groups back then," Edwards says, "and the phone calls start coming in. 'Hey, nigger lover, quit playing that stuff.' But it was the parents making those calls, not the kids."

This was an era where the White Citizens Council in the South was putting out material that said, "The screaming, idiotic words and savage music of these records are undermining the morals of our white youth in America."

All of which meant nothing to Jerry Leiber. He and Mike Stoller were about to link arms and become a twin American cultural bridge: the musical bridge between Rodgers and Hammerstein and Lennon and McCartney. And the racial bridge between black and white music.

By the early fifties Leiber's gone from West Baltimore, but the music of Fulton Avenue remains in his head. He's in Los Angeles now, where he and his mother moved to be near his two older sisters. Leiber's graduated high school by now. He's studying music and working in a record store. He's scribbling lyrics in a notebook every day but needs somebody to put his words to music. A pal mentions some guy named Mike Stoller. This guy, says the pal, writes a little music.

Stoller's a native of Queens, New York. In 1940 he's eight years old when his parents send him to an interracial summer camp in New Jersey. Real left-wing stuff. For its day, practically subversive. Paul Robeson and Woody Guthrie show up to sing to the kids. One day Stoller wanders into an old barn on the campgrounds and hears a black musician playing boogie-woogie on the piano. The music knocks him out, like it did to Leiber hearing the same stuff a few years earlier around Fulton Avenue.

Stoller's father's an engineer and his mother's a former dancer. On weekends they take the subway into Manhattan to see Broadway musicals. Young Mike starts taking piano lessons. By his early teens, he's sneaking into Manhattan bebop clubs.

In 1949 the family moves to Los Angeles, where Stoller studies music with James P. Johnson, a pioneer in the stride style of jazz piano. Johnson, all but forgotten today, was a role model for Count Basie and Duke Ellington and Fats Waller and Art Tatum. And now for Stoller, who's begun to see himself as a kind of musical sophisticate. One day the telephone rings, and it's Leiber on the other end, following up on a friend's tip.

"Are you Mike Stoller?" he asks.

"Yup."

"You play the piano?"

"Yup."

"Do you write notes on paper?"

"Yup."

"My name is Jerome Leiber. I write lyrics. How would you like to write songs with me?"

"Nope."

Stoller said he didn't like pop music, he liked bebop and jazz, Charlie Parker and Thelonius Monk. Hell, he'd studied with James P. Johnson. Who was this strange kid on the phone to compare with that?

"I think we ought to talk about it," Leiber said.

Minutes later there's a knock on Stoller's door. Stoller stands there for a moment, focusing on this disheveled, yacking, energetic mess standing before him.

The two of them started writing songs that afternoon.

"Mike would sit there jamming at the piano," Leiber remembers sixty years later, "and I'm pacing around the room. Both of us smoking cigarettes. He's jamming, I'm pacing. Smoke filling up the room. That's how it went, from that very first day."

Neither one's certain where they're going with this. They don't even have a name for it. Alley music, they call it at one point. Hell, rock and roll's just beginning to invent itself. Nobody's even heard of Elvis Presley or Little Richard. The two guys just know what they don't want— that 1950s pap that calls itself pop music. And they know in their bones what moves them: not just bebop and jazz, not just rhythm and blues, but comic bits on the radio, street sounds, the stuff of school-yards and classrooms, parents hollering at kids.

"We're just shouting out lines to each other," Leiber remembers years later, "and seeing what sticks."

One day Stoller's noodling at the piano and Leiber's making tea. Stoller picks up the beat. A line comes into Leiber's head, which he hollers from the kitchen: "Take out the papers and the trash."

Stoller hollers back, "Or you don't get no spending cash."

It's an echo of Manya Leiber hollering from the grocery store on Fulton Avenue. What the hell, it's an echo of every mom and dad in America hollering at a teenage kid—and, when the kid tries to respond, the old man in a basso profundo voice declaring, "Don't talk back."

All of which becomes not only the stuff of comic lyric but of common ground. Millions of kids, black and white, will listen to this group of black guys called the Coasters sing "Yakety Yak" and embrace their singing as a riff on their own home life. "How do you like this?! The colored kids' folks holler at them the same as white folks!" And, together, we can all laugh at our predicament, and cruise around in somebody's beat-up car late into a summer night all over America with the radio turned up full blast and everybody singing along.

This beats a lecture on the brotherhood of man any day of the week.

Leiber and Stoller make up a character named Charlie Brown. Again, it's the Coasters performing this comic musical play. Charlie Brown calls the English teacher daddy-o. He shoots dice down in the boys gym. He throws spitballs in class. He asks, plaintively, "Why's everybody always picking on me?"

A generation of teenagers hears this cry and knows Charlie Brown in their bones: he's that cut-up in everybody's newly integrated home-room at school—and it doesn't matter what color he is, only that he's funny, and he's bucking authority—and, therefore, he's cool. He's everybody's imaginary friend—*Who wouldn't want to be this guy's friend?*—and because he's cool, and he's black, then at least on some subliminal level maybe this means black is starting to look cool.

Decades later Leiber tells *Rolling Stone* magazine, "I felt black. I was, as far as I was concerned. And I wanted to be black for lots of reasons. They were better musicians, they were better athletes, they were not uptight about sex, and they knew how to enjoy life better than most people." He nodded toward Stoller. "We used to argue between the two of us over which one was the blackest."

"Who won?"

"We did," Stoller said.

In 1953, when they're still scuffling, they write a song called "Hound Dog" for a rhythm and blues belter named Willie Mae "Big Mama" Thornton. The guys aren't even twenty-one yet, so they need their parents to sign the contract.

"Took about eight minutes to write it," Leiber says nearly sixty years later.

"Are you serious?" he's asked.

"Maybe ten," he says, laughing.

The song does pretty nicely on the rhythm and blues charts and then fades away. Three years go by. Stoller marries and goes off on his honeymoon, on a ship called the *Andrea Doria*, which collides somewhere in the Atlantic with a Swedish liner called the *Stockholm*. The *Andrea Doria*'s sinking into the sea with its passengers on deck praying that a nearby freighter will reach them in time.

When Leiber learns that his partner's among the survivors, he rushes to the dock.

"There's a story about this moment. Is it true?" Leiber's asked half a century later.

"Completely," he says.

As Stoller and his new bride finally reach dry land, Leiber embraces them and says, "Guess what? 'Hound Dog' is the number one hit in the country."

"Big Mama Thornton?" Stoller says.

"No," says Leiber, "some white kid. Named Elvis Presley."

"Huh?" Stoller says. "Who?"

As written for Big Mama, the song's about a freeloading gigolo. In Presley's version, a few of the lyrics are moved around.

"The new lyrics didn't even make sense to me," Leiber says sixty years later.

But the new version sold seven million records.

"When they started sending me checks," says Leiber, "I decided to start liking it a lot."

It's another bridge across the American divide: a couple of urban Jewish guys authoring a song for a black woman out of rural Alabama, and a white kid out of Tupelo, Mississippi, and Memphis, Tennessee, hearing it one night and turning it into a rock-and-roll romp for the ages.

But "Hound Dog" is just a beginning. Leiber and Stoller will write hundreds of songs that bring a hip, comic, urban sensibility to the airwaves. They write "Jailhouse Rock" and "Loving You" for Elvis. They write "Poison Ivy" and "Searchin'" and "Along Came Jones" for the Coasters and produce "Stand by Me" and "Spanish Harlem" and "This Magic Moment" for the Drifters. They write "Love Potion Number Nine" for the Clovers and "Is That All There Is?" for Peggy Lee. They enter the Rock and Roll Hall of Fame, and Broadway stages a huge hit show at the turn of the new century, "Smokey Joe's Café," built entirely upon their music.

Such songs were first heard at Hampstead Junior High in nervous East Baltimore, where the lyrics started to take a little edge off racial uneasiness; and at Garrison Junior High out in northwest Baltimore, where Richard Holley watched kids singing to each other across the school cafeteria; and at Kenwood High in Baltimore County, where all these white kids discovered the Coasters and the Drifters and the Turbans; and in all these old jalopies cruising through the streets of mid-century America late into the night, with their radios turned up loud, and all these voices singing along so happily, and so loudly, that you could hear them clear across the great racial divide.

That's the future Speaker of the U.S. House of Representatives, Nancy Pelosi, when she was young Nancy D'Alesandro. She's with her dad, Thomas D'Alesandro, and her mom and five brothers. Nancy's dad was mayor of Baltimore, but her mom was the power behind the throne. (Courtesy D'Alesandro family)

Time and Opportunity
Nancy Pelosi and "Big Nancy"

African Americans weren't the only ones struggling to find their place in the 1950s.

So were female Americans.

Nobody raised Nancy D'Alesandro imagining she would make history. Everybody knew that history was made by men. It said so in all the schoolbooks young Nancy read at the Institute of Notre Dame, located on Aisquith Street across from East Baltimore's Latrobe Homes housing projects. Presidents and prime ministers were always men, and so were big-city mayors like Nancy's father. As were priests. The girls at Notre Dame took religion classes every day, and their teachers were nuns in starched black-and-white habits who knew their place in the world. Second to men, always. The girls all said daily prayers in chapel. They went on retreats for three days at a time. Some days everybody ate lunch in enforced religious silence. Nobody even suspected this little dark-haired girl would become Nancy Pelosi, the first woman Speaker of the U.S. House of Representatives.

"My brother Tommy was raised to be mayor," Pelosi says half a century later. "I was raised to be holy."

It's a sunny afternoon in the autumn of 2011 and Pelosi, sitting in her congressional office in Washington, D.C., gestures to a couple of old black-and-white photographs sitting atop four television sets always tuned to cable news channels. The old photos show Pelosi when she was a little girl. She's watching with big saucer eyes as her father is sworn in as the first Italian American mayor of Baltimore in 1947. Tommy D'Alesandro Jr. spent three terms at City Hall. Later his son, Tommy the Younger, succeeded him. He was raised for it. Nancy wasn't. She was supposed to be a nun.

In the innocent fifties, the choices for half the population are criminally narrow, only nobody seems to notice this. Generations of parents unthinkingly shortchange their own daughters. Most little girls are raised to become housewives. And if the right guy never comes along, maybe a brilliant girl in America becomes a nurse or a schoolteacher. Or some executive's private secretary, so the big shot can pat her on the head and tell everybody, "Miss Mavis here is a genius. I don't know how I'd get along without her." If these are beyond her reach, maybe she becomes a crossing guard at the neighborhood elementary school or a cashier at the A&P. That's about it. But nobody could imagine some little girl becoming the third most powerful person in America. According to all the cultural dictates, a woman was never even the most powerful person at a duckpin bowling establishment.

"In our home," says Pelosi, as though reciting a familiar litany, "we were devoutly Catholic, proud of our Italian American heritage, fiercely patriotic, staunchly Democratic. That was the program. Those twelve years at Notre Dame, it was about being Catholic and emulating the lives of saints. Holy things. My mother wanted me to be a nun."

"Do you remember that conversation?" Pelosi is asked now.

"Do I remember it?"

"Yes. The one where your mother told you she wanted you to be a nun."

"Sure I remember it," says Pelosi. "It lasted about fifteen years."

She laughs delightedly at the memory. "My mother was always saying it would be the most wonderful thing in the world. 'Isn't it wonderful how Sister so-and-so does this, how Sister so-and-so does that . . . ' I think it was her way of saying, 'I'm going to protect you from all of the world's ills. By putting you in a convent.'"

"Isn't there a story about you telling her you'd rather be a priest?"

"A priest, maybe," Pelosi says, trying to retrieve a wayward memory. "More power."

Halfway into a smile, her expression changes abruptly. She looks across the room again, toward the four television sets. On one of them, she sees a video news clip of herself.

"Oh, there I am," she says, "doing something, and I don't know what. Was this yesterday?"

Two political aides, sitting nearby, turn their heads to look.

"It's on Fox," one of them says.

"Then it can't be anything good," says the other.

"Fox, Rush Limbaugh, the whole Republican Party mechanism," somebody says. "There have been times when they've really demonized you."

"Oh, really?" Pelosi says. "I didn't know this."

This is her little deadpan joke.

She's been the Republican Party's designated punching bag ever since 2008, when she became the first female Speaker of the House. She immediately took on Wall Street and the big oil companies and the insurance industry. She faced a Congress so split that she couldn't count on a single Republican vote. She had to hold the fractious and frightened Democrats together in ways nobody imagined she could.

"According to many historians and political scientists," *Ms. Magazine* remarked in the winter of 2011, "Nancy Pelosi was probably the most successful House speaker in U.S. history."

Under her leadership, the magazine recounted, landmark legislation was passed in a couple of frenzied years: health care reform, financial reform, the Lilly Ledbetter Fair Pay Act, student aid, ethics reform, a minimum wage hike, a $787 million stimulus package, and the repeal of Don't Ask, Don't Tell.

"And these," the magazine reported, "are just the bills that were made into law . . . The 111th Congress is now considered to have been the most productive since the 89th Congress during Lyndon B. Johnson's term—and through most of it, Speaker Pelosi didn't lose a single vote."

In 2010 the Republicans spent roughly seventy-five million dollars to win back the House. Much of it was spent demonizing Pelosi, the poster child for all that was deemed politically progressive and therefore dangerous for America. When the party wasn't ripping her, its puppet network, Fox News, was. Even her outmatched opponent in San Francisco, with no shot at winning, spent two million dollars and compared Pelosi to the Wicked Witch of the West. This was considered one of the milder smears.

"To have the stomach," somebody says to Pelosi, sitting in her office on this sunny afternoon, "to stand up to this barrage, day after day, had to come from somewhere. That kind of toughness. Where does it come from?"

Begin with the mother.

Annunciata Lombardi D'Alesandro preceded her daughter at the Institute of Notre Dame, and when she graduated she did something considered by her family to be an act of certifiable insanity. She got a job. It was 1923, and Annunciata had been raised in Baltimore's Little Italy, twelve square blocks of narrow row houses a few blocks north of the city's harbor, in circumstances her children later called "Sicilian cloistered."

Annunciata wanted no more of that. She went to work for Billig Auctioneers. She still lived with her parents on Albemarle Street, number 204. Across the street, at number 215, lived Tommy D'Alesandro Jr., who still lived with his parents. He was twenty-five, Annunciata was nineteen. They'd lived in these row houses, on this little street, all their lives and never laid eyes on each other. Tommy was a state delegate starting to make some political waves. For Annunciata, politics was a foreign country. She was anchored to the house. She knew nothing about Tommy, including his name. When he spotted her coming out of Saint Leo's Roman Catholic Church one Sunday morning and asked her for a date, she said she'd have to clear it with her family, including the grandmother.

After they married, he spent twelve years as mayor of Baltimore, and many say it was this woman, her name now Americanized from Annunciata to Nancy, who was the true power.

"When she met my father," says Tommy D'Alesandro III, who followed his father as mayor of Baltimore in the 1960s, "my mother didn't know anything about politics. But she wound up knowing more than him. They weren't afraid of my father, but they were terrified of my mother. You cross her, you're dead in the water. She'd get you. With my mother, there was no forgiving. Oh, she was vicious."

He laughs with high-pitched delight at the memory. He is past eighty now, white-haired, retired from careers in politics and the law. Across a dozen years Tommy the Younger watched his father run the city of Baltimore. The old man was a pretty tough guy, sometimes prickly, sometimes profane. One day, when a *Baltimore Sun* reporter said to him, "My desk wants to know . . . ," Tommy the Elder leaned down and put his ear to the top of his desk, as though listening to it.

"And my desk," he told the reporter, "says to tell your desk, 'Go fuck yourself.' "

And yet, compared to the wife, he was a cream puff.

"My mother," says Nancy Pelosi, laughing aloud, "thought my father was a pushover. She'd tell him, 'Don't forget, they're doing this. Don't forget, they're doing that. Don't forget . . . ' You know, it's a lot easier to forgive than to forget. And my mother never forgot."

From her earliest days the daughter, Little Nancy, took all of this in.

When she's born, her father's newly elected to the U.S. Congress. Her entire run at Notre Dame, first grade through twelfth, across the 1950s, he's serving his three terms as mayor of Baltimore. Other little girls spend hours playing with dolls in their rooms. Little Nancy dutifully writes names of voters on yellow pads of paper. Other little girls examine *Modern Screen* magazine for the vital details of Tab Hunter's love life. Little Nancy learns how to put people in touch with the welfare department of the city of Baltimore when these penniless souls arrive seven days a week in Little Italy looking for help.

They line up every morning and evening outside the D'Alesandro home on the corner of Albemarle and Fawn. Some are looking for jobs; others seek a place to live or a meal or the cleaning of a neighborhood alley. Some are immigrants who speak no English. Annunciata speaks to some of them in Italian.

"They were poor, they were patriotic," Nancy Pelosi reflects years later, "and they built America. They were told the streets were paved with gold, and when they got here they discovered *they* would be paving those streets."

They sit at a little desk in the D'Alesandro home beneath portraits of Franklin Roosevelt and Harry Truman. Political material lays about— bumper stickers, buttons, pamphlets—any time there's a campaign going on. When young Nancy's thirteen, she takes charge of the desk.

"I knew," she says now, "by osmosis, or by watching my mother, how to do almost anything. How to get into the projects, or get on welfare. I heard her say it so many times. I would tell these people, 'This is what you have to say.' I was a little girl. People would come to the door, and they wanted help getting a bed in a hospital, or a place to live in the projects, or a family member out of jail. They didn't know where to go for medical help or food. As a teenager, I started getting on my way. But, as a child and a young teen, yes, I was doing all that stuff. But it's not that I saw my future in politics. I mean, I've seen stories that I wanted to be in politics ever since I was five years old. That's nonsense. I didn't want to have anything to do with politics. It's not that I was rejecting it. But I thought I had done that already."

In her school days, she left home each morning in the back seat of her father's mayoral limousine but arrived at school on foot. The limo took her to Aisquith Street by the housing projects, and then Nancy insisted on getting out of the car so there couldn't be any sense of privilege in front of the other girls.

"What I really wanted to do," she remembers, "was take the bus to school. I wanted that more than life itself. Because all my friends were on the bus. I wanted to be with my friends. I didn't want to advertise that I wasn't allowed to take the bus." Getting out of a limousine implicitly declared: You're not one of the gang; you're not like the rest of us.

Years later, when she became Speaker of the House, Pelosi paid a visit to her old family home to celebrate the moment. The city named a street after her, and the choir from the Institute of Notre Dame sang. She told people gathered for the occasion the obvious: No one of her generation could have imagined such a life in politics for her—or for any woman—and no matter that two men in her family had run the city of Baltimore.

"My parents," she said, "didn't raise me to be a politician. They raised me to help people do the work of the angels." She said these words without the slightest tone of self-righteousness. She was talking about a way of life, a way of seeing women, that slowly began to change after her generation.

She was a very good girl in an era populated by good girls and good boys. She wore a white dress and gloves when she accompanied her father to political speeches. When the family vacationed in Ocean City, her brother Tommy remembers, "she was prim and proper, not a hair out of place." In those days a sign hung in the vestibule at Notre Dame that said, "School is not a prison, it is not a playground. It is Time, it is Opportunity." Young Nancy took this to heart. Sixty years later, sitting in her congressional office, she spontaneously recites the sign, word for word. When she graduated from the Institute of Notre Dame, her grade point average was 93.22. The grade point average, she did not commit to memory.

Postwar America expected such wholesomeness from its young women. They went to school, and then millions put away their books and put their brains on automatic pilot. And this, too, the country expected, although they called it by a different name. They handed women a broom and told them to wave it like a baton.

This is the last era when women are expected to be satisfied with their fullest potential on permanent hold. Most are housewives. Pelosi's mother quit her job with Billig Auctioneers and a few years later went to law school. But she gave it up for family, which came first. Sometimes Big Nancy had shrewd investment ideas but her husband wouldn't go along. So the investment ideas went no further, since husbands of that era still had to sign off on all financial arrangements.

Of those American women who worked outside the home in the fifties, three-quarters had female-only jobs. Maybe they worked in the typing pool. But most had service positions. They worked the cash registers at the Read's drugstore. Only about 3 percent of all U.S. doctors were women, and only about 4 percent of all attorneys. Virtually every member of the U.S. Congress was male.

The political women of the fifties are trained to be artifacts. They stand there just off-camera, like Mamie Eisenhower or Bess Truman, who smiles and says, "A woman's place in public is to sit beside her husband and be silent and be sure her hat is on straight." Or they bring charm and beauty to a moment and then disappear when things get serious, like Jackie Kennedy. Women's magazines are still filled with articles on pie recipes and not power politics.

In Baltimore that rare female political figure, Mary Burgess, Republican executive of the city's twentieth ward, says women have only themselves to blame. "They're too emotional," she says. "They can't subordinate their personal feelings." Few of either sex rise to challenge her.

In the spring of 1953 a *Sun* newspaper story carries the headline "Marry 'Em Dumb, Boys; They're Less Inhibited." The story quotes a marriage expert, Dr. Mary Macauley, who says, "Girls who read too many books make the worst wives. Intellectual wives are too repressed. The girl with horn-rimmed glasses and a college masters degree? Outlook for marriage is poor." Male editors run the story on page 1.

It's 1961 before Shirley Jones becomes the first female judge on Baltimore's Supreme Bench. It's 1963 before Jacqueline McCurdy becomes the first female prosecutor in Baltimore County. At the Union Memorial Hospital School of Nursing, all students (female, of course) have to stand at their desks any time a doctor (male, of course) enters the room.

Girls are raised to know their place.

At midcentury we're a nation where many adults still recall the good-natured teenage role models of the war years, such as pint-sized Mickey Rooney playing Andy Hardy to Judy Garland's Polly Benedict in the movies. They're Good Teens before the term's even invented. If Andy's a little troubled, there's Lewis Stone as his dad, the wise and dignified Judge Hardy, offering advice as though dispensing stone tablets in the Sinai.

Big Nancy D'Alesandro is Little Nancy's Judge Hardy.

On Sunday mornings, Annunciata and Tommy D'Alesandro walk from their home on Albemarle Street to Saint Leo's Roman Catholic Church two blocks away, and their sons and little Nancy are always with them. But Annunciata is much more than a housewife who puts down the broom only to praise God.

"Nancy," her brother Tommy reflects years later, "is the reincarnation of my mother's ambition."

"Well, my mother was my mother, first and foremost," Pelosi reflects all these years later. "That door closed behind us, and they were Mommy and Daddy. But she was a very strong woman. To raise a big family, you had to be." There were five boys and Nancy.

"My brother Tommy, she practically grew up with. Me, she was delighted to have a girl," says Pelosi. "But I was never raised in the female stereotype of that era. What you have to know about my mother is that she was a feminist long before she ever heard the word. She didn't think young girls should be getting married, she thought they should have their career and be self-sufficient, take care of themselves."

Many college girls of the fifties performed a useful charade, understood by all. They weren't aiming for a career, they were aiming for a husband. The familiar joke was that men went to college for a BS and women for an MRS. College was a place to meet a better class of contender.

When she graduated from high school, young Nancy decided to go to Trinity College, an all-female Catholic school in Washington, D.C., dedicated equally to public service and education. This meant leaving Baltimore, leaving home. No one in the D'Alesandro family had ever left home. They didn't even leave the neighborhood. Big Nancy, who understood feminism before it had a name, broke the news to Big Tommy, the mayor.

"Nancy's going to Trinity," she said.

"Over my dead body," said the mayor.

"That could be arranged," said the mother.

"My mother," says Pelosi, "was the complete opposite of the era. In college, the girls I knew, their mothers wanted them to meet some nice young person from Georgetown or something and get engaged and then married. My situation couldn't have been further from that reality. She just wanted young girls to reach their fulfillment.

"When I told her I was getting married, she was, like, 'What? Why would you do that? You're young.' She was not happy. As happy as her marriage was, she was not an advocate for getting married so young. Reach your own fulfillment. It wasn't about politics. It was about being whatever you wanted to be."

Big Nancy took care of the housework and the family, and she loved an afternoon at Pimlico Racetrack, where she knew how to read a racing form like a catechism. But politics gave her purpose. She told her husband how to run the precincts. She had her own political army. There were scores of women, many from the neighborhood but lots of them from around the city, doing volunteer work for Big Tommy. They were like the CIA. They'd hear all the gossip, and they'd bring the messages. Big Nancy would tell the mayor, "You can't trust this one, we had bad dealings. This other one, he's OK, you can trust him."

These women worked the phones and sent out letters and put together rallies. In fifteen minutes, Big Nancy could put a couple dozen of them together. They were tough ladies. Sometimes they worked out of the basement of the D'Alesandro home. "That's where the power was, down in that cellar," says Tommy the Younger, laughing out loud. "About a hundred of the most vicious people you'd ever see in your life. I mean, they would go out and tear wild dogs apart. It wasn't a ladies group, it was like a pack of wild animals. They controlled precincts. They worked year 'round. They went out with a vengeance from that cellar."

Night after night during campaign seasons these women cooked spaghetti and ravioli for fund-raising dinners. This was a time before politics was played mainly on television, when the midcentury campaigns routinely went into the neighborhoods, where there were parades and bull roasts, and then everybody went back to the D'Alesandro basement to figure out what to do the next day, and the day after that.

This was Nancy Pelosi's home schooling.

"What I remember most," Pelosi says now, "is that those women came from all over the city, not just the neighborhood, and my mother was a friend to them. It became more than political campaigns. If a daughter was having her first communion or there was a christening, that became part of our lives. We're all in this together. The nurturing of relationships. People have to feel you're important to them—and they are. That's what I learned from my mother and all those women down in the basement."

"But your mother," she's asked, "was a pretty tough cookie, no?"

"Oh, God, yes," Pelosi laughs.

When Ronald Reagan was president, he offered to meet the D'Alesandros at their house in Little Italy. The White House was reaching for Democratic political support.

"My mother told them, in her inimitable way, that the president should not come to our house," Pelosi remembered. "And so they called my brother Tommy and said, 'Gee, we called the house and somebody was very unfriendly to the president, and almost threatening the president if he should come to the house.' That was my mother. Hard core stuff." Pelosi winces at the memory.

Once, when she was eighty-three, in a gesture of high political honor and long family friendship, Big Nancy invited William Donald Schaefer to sit at her table for a neighborhood spaghetti dinner at Saint Leo's Roman Catholic Church. Schaefer, who was governor of Maryland, accepted. Then Big Nancy changed her mind.

Days after her invitation arrived, the Democrat Schaefer made the colossal political blunder of endorsing a Republican, George Bush the elder, to be president. The earth slipped its axis. The next day, Schaefer received a letter from Mrs. D'Alesandro. He was informed, in language most vivid, that he was no longer invited to the dinner. He was now considered a traitor to his party.

Three years later, on the day Nancy D'Alesandro died, there was Schaefer remembering the incident.

"She never talked to me again the rest of her life," he said. "All those years we were friends, and that was the end of it. You want to know where Nancy Pelosi gets her toughness, there's your answer."

"If she'd been born later, God knows what my mother would have done," her daughter says now. "But she was confined by the culture of her time, and the Italian American culture even more so. As progressive as they were in their politics, the personal side was very conservative."

"The Italian American culture?" she was asked.

"Elements of, shall we say, protection. Protection of girls. I won't say chauvinism."

"There's a story that your brothers were ordered to tail along whenever you went on a date."

"No," says Pelosi. She looks appalled at the thought.

"It's been written."

"No," she says again. "I would never have even gone." The possibility seems to rattle her. "They may have gone and I didn't know about it. Hah! Because I was very protected, and I was resisting it. My father was clinging to the old ways, and I'm gonna live my own life. You know, 'Give it up, it's over.' But that was the conflict."

So much of the country was trying to hold onto that vanishing world of Norman Rockwell and his *Saturday Evening Post* sensibilities, trying to live their lives like that nice Anderson family on television's popular *Father Knows Best*.

Millions of midcentury Americans watch this show and learn from it. The Andersons are a Rockwell painting come to life and transplanted to suburbia, the country's great TV role model nuclear family. The parents sleep in separate beds. There are no racial or religious minorities around to make anybody uncomfortable. The D'Alesandros probably notice there's just about nobody on TV identifiably Italian. The Jews at least have Molly Goldberg. The blacks have Amos 'n' Andy, considered a mixed blessing. But 1950s TV's almost all packaged white bread. Forget ethnics. And there's not a hint anywhere of any oddball counterculture until the goateed beatnik Maynard G. Krebs shows up in a sweatshirt at decade's end on *The Many Lives of Dobie Gillis*.

Such shows set a standard: this is what an American family is supposed to look like. Archie Bunker (too outspoken) will have to wait a while to make his debut, as will Roseanne Barr (too working class) and Bill Cosby (too black.) Here in the fifties, TV dads dress for dinner. Moms have the latest kitchen appliances, the better to legitimize sponsors' products. The kids do nicely in school, and nobody's yet heard even a whisper about drugs.

Maybe Nancy D'Alesandro's brothers didn't tail her on Saturday night dates. But on *Father Knows Best*, Jim Anderson's ready to do the next best thing. When he finds out his teenage daughter Betty's got a new boyfriend, he suggests they need a chaperone—or, he tells her, she should bring him by the house one evening.

"And do what?"

"We could pop corn," says Father. "Play records. Get up a rousing game of hearts."

Never mind popcorn, never mind a rousing game of hearts. Sixty years later Nancy Pelosi's still wondering if her brothers were quietly trailing after her when she started leaving the neighborhood on dates with teenage boys.

In midcentury Baltimore the newspapers run stories about good, wholesome kids all the time, as if assuring themselves in the face of a gnawing uneasiness. "Recreation Center Molds Hamilton Teen-Agers' Life," an *Evening Sun* feature headline says. The kids have "improvised a lively program" of dances and healthy after-school activities, the story says.

A photograph shows about thirty of these youngsters gathered at the Hamilton Recreation Center, Hamilton Avenue and Harford Road, a white working-class neighborhood in northeast Baltimore. Everybody seems to be playing dress-up for the occasion. The boys wear white shirts and neckties, like government tax accountants, and the girls look like the advance team for Future Housewives of America. But this is a teenage after-school hangout. Everybody should be wearing T-shirts and ponytails, shouldn't they?

It's the last time in American history when the kids still want to look like grownups, and not the other way around.

In the fifties parents see such comforting mass media images and heave sighs of relief: "The kids will be all right." "Girls Reveal Strategy on Dating and Kissing," says another *Evening Sun* headline. The story includes this bit of insight from some South Baltimore kids:

Sophie approved of "kissing on the first date," she told the local Youth Board. "Why not?" she asked. "If the girl likes the boy well enough and she's been dying to go out with him and finally gets the chance, why shouldn't she let him kiss her?"

"Horrors," retorted the other girls with strong disapproval.

"I've known kids," said one girl, "who've gone out for as long as seventeen days without kissing one another."

Such thinking will soon go the way of the crinoline. But the newspapers run more stories in this vein: "Eastern Girls Like Neat, Humble Boys." The story says the girls at Eastern High go for boys who are "neat and tidy" and know how to get along with parents. Down at Southern High the girls give a rousing ovation to the visiting syndicated advice columnist Ann Landers when she tells them, "Sex is like dynamite—it makes all the difference in the world what you use it for."

In the fifties, standards must be kept. In Brentwood, New York, thirty-seven girls are suspended from school for wearing their skirts too short. Their knees are exposed. In Baltimore the newspapers run big stories when a thirteen-year-old girl is sent home from Franklin Junior High because her skirt is too short. The skirt touches the top of the girl's knee. She sewed it in her home economics class.

"I was a typical 1950s teen," Nancy Pelosi recalls now. She wore blouses with Peter Pan collars and circle pins. She loved cinch belts, crinolines, charm bracelets, and matching sweater sets. The girls all wore ponytails or pixie cuts.

"And we had sleepovers at our house," says Pelosi, "and danced to Billy Haley and the Comets, and Elvis Presley. Oh, how I loved Elvis."

Elvis begins to change everything.

In the early evening, American families gather around the one television set in the home and watch *Father Knows Best* and its mirror images—*Ozzie and Harriet*, *Donna Reed*, *Leave It to Beaver*—and take their cues. This is what a family looks like, this is what America looks like: happy, intact, and white. The droll Kurt Vonnegut will call this "the Golden Age of White People." All three networks carry programs to reinforce the image evening after evening.

And then comes the great cultural disconnect. The kids say their polite good nights, like those nice Anderson kids, and go to their bedrooms. They put behind them the television set, which is watched with parents in the light of the living room, and turn on the radio, which is heard in the dark, alone, under the covers, in the middle of the sweaty night. None of this business of popping corn, or playing hearts, while the grownups scrutinize their dates. The kids will make up their own minds. The music on the radio gives them permission. In the dark, they move from a TV set recycling old and suffocating rituals to songs on the radio that subvert so much of the old culture.

For this is where they find Elvis singing "Hound Dog" and the Coasters doing "Charlie Brown" and the rest of that first generation of music that is distinctly not their parents'. Nor is it their parents' ethos. It's not Perry Como in his cardigan sweater crooning "It's Beginning to Look a Lot like Christmas" or Rosemary Clooney in pearls singing "Come on-a My House."

These rock-and-roll singers on the radio are kids, and their music is all about heat. It's not about doing some old-fashioned minuet, it's about pressing your hot, hungry body against somebody else's and hoping your partner will press back. The music's louder, it's faster, and the beat is insistent. The music's about urges, which the old folks in the living room watching Lawrence Welk probably can't even remember. So don't share the big secret with them, or it might embarrass everybody. This is about sex. Nobody listens to "Sixty Minute Man" and mistakes it for a guy punching a time clock.

Naturally, this terrifies the grownups. Some Catholic schools warn students that attending an Elvis Presley movie is considered a mortal sin. Clergy of every religion launch sermons from the pulpit. It's the music of the devil. At the Lord Baltimore Hotel, Maryland Gov. Theodore McKeldin is asked by the jittery State Council of the Daughters of America to issue official condemnation of the music.

To his credit, the governor urges calm. "Let us go back in memory to the disgust with which some of our elders expressed their opinions of jazz," says McKeldin, "and in some cases, of those who danced to its tunes. Now jazz is quite respectfully defined as melodious and subtly syncopated. Some teachers have told me that rock-and-roll fans are among their best students."

Sixty years later, Nancy Pelosi sits in her congressional office and strikes a rapturous pose. "Elvis Presley," she says. "Oh, I adored him. Bill Haley and the Comets. The girls would come to our house and we'd have slumber parties in the basement and dance all night to Elvis Presley. Oh, we loved him. Oh, my."

The kids aren't waiting for any grownup's benedictions. They're listening and dancing, and they're singing along on their newly invented transistor radios, which they carry with them everywhere and hold up to their ears whenever the reception gets fuzzy. The new radios mean they don't have to fight with mom or dad for possession of the airwaves.

It also means the people who run radio stations, and the people who run record companies, and the people who run TV networks and think obsessively about ratings have to begin considering the growing power of the teenage dollar.

And, ultimately, the power of the teenage hormone.

Andy Hardy and Polly will fade from memory, followed by the *Father Knows Best* kids. James Dean and Natalie Wood arrive in *Rebel without a Cause* and send a shiver along all teenage spines. It's the public unleashing of the previously squelched adolescent id.

In the fifties young people begin to create headlines that scare their parents to death when they read their newspapers. Half a century later, thanks to computers and cable TV, we can scare ourselves twenty-four hours a day. No wonder we miss the old days.

But, in the fifties, America still held onto fading images of its innocent self. We were still contentedly watching *Father Knows Best*. Some of the high school girls were still holding off kissing until the seventeenth date. The kids at the Hamilton Recreation Center dressed up like grownups for a picture in the daily newspaper, which everybody still read religiously. Families went to church on Sundays. Smart little girls like Nancy D'Alesandro prepared for a life of holiness.

But a new kind of young person was beginning to arrive to alarm everyone, and the image would be reinforced on screen and stage, in fear and in laughter.

Baltimore's midcentury "drapes" were the inspiration for Ken Waissman and partner Maxine Fox to produce *Grease*, the hit Broadway show that became the biggest movie musical of all time and helped create a nationwide nostalgia for the 1950s. (Hearst Newspapers LLC / Baltimore News-American)

The Original Cast of *Grease*
Kenny Waissman

The line outside the Forest movie theater stretches along Garrison Boulevard past the firehouse to Liberty Heights Avenue, catty-corner from Read's Drug Store and Knocko's pool hall up the street. On this Saturday afternoon in the summer of 1955, something special's on the bill. Usually on a Saturday, the Forest shows monster movies. *I Was a Teenage Werewolf* was very big here. So was *Creature from the Black Lagoon*.

This is bigger.

This Saturday the Forest has *Blackboard Jungle*. Everybody can't wait to find a seat inside since the word of mouth has been terrific. Already the U.S. ambassador to Italy, Claire Boothe Luce, has demanded the movie be withdrawn from the Venice Film Festival. She says it gives "an unflattering and unrealistic view of American school life."

As if anybody at the Forest Theater cares about Claire Boothe Luce's opinion. The movie's all about modern teenagers misbehaving in school. It's got every PTA president in America sputtering with outrage and anxiety, which naturally adds to all kids' viewing enjoyment.

The previews of coming attractions, shown all week, got everybody at the Forest worked up. There on-screen was that nice Glenn Ford, showing up for his first day as a schoolteacher with his astronaut crew cut and his gentle smile and his good-guy idealism. He will lose all but the crew cut. It starts when Ford notices the hysterical panorama spread before him: teenage boys in the schoolyard, one of these geniuses banging at trash can lids, a few of them ogling a woman walking past in a tight skirt, and some of these lads wearing dungarees and dancing.

They're jitterbugging to the sound of Bill Haley and the Comets doing "Rock around the Clock" while an announcer with a stentorian March of Time voice declares, "Many people said this story could not . . . must not . . . dare not be shown . . . 'Blackboard Jungle' deals with an explosive subject—the teenage terror in the schools . . . It is fiction—but fiction torn from big-city modern savagery. It packs a brass knuckle punch in its startling revelation of those teenage savages who turn big-city schools into a jungle."

Yeah, sure.

Inside the Forest, reaction is great. As Bill Haley and his guys sing the opening number, a couple of teenage boys grab girls and start dancing in the aisle. The music's cool, so why not? Other kids are throwing those hard little Jujube candies at the screen. In the whole history of the Forest Theater, nobody can ever remember kids dancing in the aisles, although throwing Jujubes at the screen is something of a Saturday afternoon house tradition.

The other reaction is a kind of muffled laughter. It's a movie, but it certainly isn't real life. This is why parents are getting so worked up? This melodramatic nonsense, which has nothing to do with mainstream life anywhere within miles of the Forest Theater?

This is northwest Baltimore, a fifteen-minute walk from Forest Park High School, where Kenny Waissman's a student, and it's ten minutes from Garrison Junior High, where Barry Levinson's a student. One day Waissman will produce a Broadway show called *Grease*, which will turn these *Blackboard Jungle* kids into singing and dancing huggy bears. The show will set off a nationwide nostalgia for the 1950s and lead to a movie called *Grease* that makes every teeny bopper in America fall in love with John Travolta for about six months and makes more money than any previous movie musical in history.

Levinson, meanwhile, will go on to write and direct no less than four movies about midcentury Baltimore, which will make everyone yearn for the era's return.

Most American youngsters in the fifties don't realize how innocent and protected they are. They take security for granted. In northwest Baltimore, teenage boys hang out at the Hilltop Diner that Levinson will later make famous, and they walk all the way home at three in the morning without parents fretting that some cretin with a switchblade's lurking in the bushes. The Boy Scout and the Girl Scout meetings fill up places like the Howard Park Methodist Church every week, and all baseball diamonds over at Leakin Park and Conlon Field are filled with amateur teams on spring evenings. Every boy imagines he's the next Brooks Robinson.

That's the youth culture in places like northwest Baltimore, not this business about "teenage terror" and brass-knuckle punches and blackboard jungles. Those things are a sidelight, an aberration.

"My generation out there in the suburbs," Kenny Waissman recalls his sense of rebelliousness, "every Friday night you'd go out and crash parties. Girls would have them. They never invited boys, but they'd let the word out. When I was fifteen our big necessity was to hook up with a sixteen-year-old because they could drive. And these parties, the girls had 45 rpm records they'd play, and everybody would dance. We didn't take rock and roll as rebellion. But it was ours. I was conscious of that. In the fifties the music was different, and the teenage styles were different. Button-down shirts and Ivy League pants with buckles in the back that parents hated because the buckle would tear up the upholstery. The Joe College look. Hummers (those low-cut, white sneakers) and three-button sports coats. It was unthinkable not to have those things. You had to fit in."

Those *Blackboard Jungle* types were different; they didn't want to fit in. When you see these so-called juvenile delinquents at school, you're caught between an instant's shock and a muffled, lingering laugh. Those kinds of kids are mostly down in the working-class neighborhoods where Jerry Leiber grew up, where those hanging out on street corners all day are beginning to suspect the American dream isn't going to work out for them, that the game's been fixed. They're starting to pop up over in Hamilton, where all those kids at the recreation center posed in neckties and dresses for their big newspaper photograph. Now *there's* an image that's about to fade. Or you see them in some of the cramped row-house neighborhoods in white working-class neighborhoods closer to downtown. But, in America's grassy outer-city neighborhoods such as northwest Baltimore, it's a different story. It's a wonder Kenny Waissman remembered those kids when the fifties were so far behind us. They're the ones America called greasers. But Baltimore called them by another name.

They were drapes. They wore black leather jackets with the collars turned up, and they greased back their hair to a duck's ass finish. They were midcentury America's working-class rebels without a cause. Or, anyway, a cause they could articulate. If they bothered to show up at school they took a lot of shop classes and boasted about making zip guns while the sheet metal teacher had his back turned. Maybe they took up glue sniffing until somebody in the neighborhood discovered marijuana was cooler. By then the real sixties were arriving. When they passed a cigarette around, they warned each other, "Don't nigger-lip it." (This was softened to "Don't Bogart it" when everybody started getting self-conscious about race.) A lot of these kids dropped out of school the moment it was legal. They weren't headed for college, they were headed for the steel mill or the loading dock. Or a probation officer. They hung out at gas stations on Saturday afternoons hoping to get visiting privileges in the grease pit. The grease would match their hair.

The original drapes were the lingering remnants of the zoot suiters of the forties. An *Evening Sun* piece, in January 1950, headlined "Zoot Suiters Unwelcome at Many Rek Centers," tells some of the story:

> If you're a zoot suiter, you're unwelcome at many of the city's teen-age recreation centers. A sixteen-year-old youth, Donald Greeley, 109 South Tremont Road, rigged out in a blue-gray "drape" suit, blue suede loafers and a dark overcoat, got the old heave-ho at one city recreation center the other evening for that very reason.
>
> According to the boy's mother, the ticket-taker at the door took one look at the boy's attire and pronounced his verdict: "You got pegs on, son—you can't come in. That's a drape suit you're wearing." It seems there's a rule at the center prohibiting trousers that measure less than 17 inches at the cuffs. Sometimes, when it looks like a photo finish, the supervisors measure the cuffs. The youth, it is said, knew about the rules and had his pants let out to 17½ inches—just to make sure.
>
> Asked about the "drape" incident, H. S. Callowhill, director of public recreation, said: "The young people at the center decided they didn't want extremes in dress and made the rule against peg trousers themselves. We have had some unpleasant experiences with people who dress in that fashion. They seem to have a different kind of dancing, which is not acceptable in ballroom circles."

Wonderful. Some kid wants to twirl his way around a dance floor at a teen recreation center, with adult supervisors all over the place like wardens, and he's turned away for tight pants.

And this is what frightens midcentury Americans about their children.

The newspapers of the era cover these kids as though dealing with an alien culture, complete with foreign language. Every middle-aged reporter assigned a feature on these kids reflexively locks into images of potential carjackers.

They're doing what a foolish society always does: creating The Other. Stigmatizing a class of people whose mere attire or their style of speech marks them not only as outsiders but as potentially dangerous. Such as these drapes.

The typical drape, reports a 1950 *Evening Sun* story,

> lives in a "pad" instead of a house. When he leaves for a party in an automobile he "cuts out." The things he likes are "solid" or "real cool." Those he doesn't are "square." A drape is likely to greet a friend with "What do you say, Daddy? Gimme five." Whereupon the others may extend three fingers, slide them across the friend's open palm in lieu of a handshake, and reply, "Owe y' one." The natural habitat of a great many drapes is the ice cream parlor.

Here's another *Evening Sun* headline from 1950: "Fourth of Juvenile Crime Linked to Gangs." The story decries "hoodlumism and vandalism in the city. Most spectacular in recent months have been the 'drape' gangs, made up chiefly of white boys."

At this time the population of the city of Baltimore was just under one million. There were twenty-four hundred kids who landed in Juvenile Court that year. That means, figuring five court days each week, about nine kids each day. In a city of nearly a million.

Sixty years later, with the city's population barely more than six hundred thousand, the number of Juvenile Court cases will be ten times the 1950 figure. No wonder we remember the fifties as an innocent time.

That same year a headline reads, "Drapes Branded as Wild, Detrimental to Youth." It's a round-table discussion with a bunch of Good Teens, another of those attempts to separate the good kids from the bad, to reassure adults that most teens are fine, that the center holds. We're imposing innocence upon ourselves, *willing* it, attempting to reinforce values that we suspect are slipping away. And why do we suspect this? Because of the considerable attention we give to those we brand as deviants, such as these dangerous drapes who dare to smoke cigarettes in the shadow of school grounds.

So here we have this round-table discussion with a so-called Youth Board of high school Good Teens who meet each week at the Sunpapers building to enlighten everyone with their mature take on life. Their views are reported five days a week by the *Evening Sun*.

You want assurance, you got it right here.

"Down with drapes!" declares the opening paragraph. "The members of the youth board were vociferous in their denunciation. All but one don't want drapes at dances. They wouldn't date drapes. And furthermore, they think it's the duty of every parent to prevent their children from 'going drape.'"

For the uninitiated, it's explained that "drapes are different. Their vocabulary is unique. Drapes say 'gone-dad' for wild, and call policemen 'fuzzes.' They hang mostly on street corners. And there are girl drapes, too. They pull back their hair, wear slacks outside school, bebop glasses—and jitterbug even to a slow number."

"A girl turns drape when she dates a boy drape," said Dick Lejk, of Baltimore Polytechnic Institute. "I've seen it happen. Parents shouldn't allow a girl to date a drape."

It all seemed so scary then and feels so innocent and vaguely endearing now. Also, it feels like the adults of America committing a serious mistake, which will be repeated endlessly: making a big deal out of a little deal, stigmatizing a small subculture that's restless but not yet particularly dangerous—and, in the process, unwittingly creating the social outcast and the miscast.

Ken Waissman remembered all of it, though he wasn't a part of it. In his world, the drapes were strictly a supporting cast, noticed during brief cameo appearances. At Forest Park High, drapes took auto mechanics so they could learn to soup up the jalopies they bought for a few bucks. They were part menace (especially if they caught you mocking them) and part comic relief if you just looked at their outfits.

These kids knew something they were unable to express very well but understood in their bones. The world is changing quickly, and they're getting passed by. They come from working-class families who have done all right since the war. The country's factories are humming, and Baltimore's are singing a sweeter song than many others.

But the ground has begun to shift. The world's getting more automated. The new jobs require new skills. Some of them demand schooling. These kids whose fathers have worked the steel mills out at Sparrows Point, who assumed they'd go there, too, since jobs are handed down like legacies—why do they have to suffer through tenth grade English where some four-eyed nerd's trying to make them memorize lines from freakin' *Julius Caesar*?

By 1962, the government says 40 percent of school kids will not finish high school. But the jobs once grabbed by dropouts are disappearing. In New York City alone, brand new automatic elevators have now displaced an estimated forty thousand operators. In Detroit, factory jobs formerly filled by teenage dropouts are disappearing by the thousands each year. In one auto plant, a manufacturing operation that previously required scores of workers is now handled by a handful of humans and nine machines.

Then there's Bethlehem Steel's operation out at Baltimore's Sparrows Point. As Deborah Rudacille writes in *Roots of Steel: Boom and Bust in an American Mill Town*:

> Year after year, the ovens, furnaces and finishing mills of the great works on the Chesapeake belched fire and smoke, crafting the ships and armaments that helped win World Wars I and II and churning out the raw steel and finished products that were the backbone of postwar America. In 1959 Sparrows Point claimed the title of the largest steelworks in the world. By then, Bethlehem (known locally as "Bethlem") employed over forty thousand Maryland residents at its steelworks and shipyards, and the fortunes of thousands of small businesses through the state were tied to Sparrows Point.

But there were rumblings of trouble even then. The big war contracts were drying up. Jobs were cut, layoffs made permanent. Consolidation arrived, then globalization. All but a few thousand jobs would disappear altogether.

"In little more than a generation," Rudacille wrote in 2010, "an industrial economy that enabled people without much formal education to create stable families and communities has become a technocratic one in which most of the nation's wealth—in the form of both wages and investment—flows inexorably to best-educated, most affluent Americans."

In their bones, and in their dinnertime family conversations, and in their street-corner gripe sessions that reinforced all resentments, the drapes saw it coming. Their disdain for mainstream culture didn't come from nothing. Feeling they had nowhere else to go, they withdrew into themselves and created their own sullen culture.

≈

Kenny Waissman knew where he wanted to go. But he never imagined he'd bring these drapes along with him, twenty years into the future, where he could help make America fall in love with them retrospectively and picture them as the comic and cuddly embodiment of the fifties.

Waissman came from a different world. He was a child of the theater from the beginning and a student of the fashions of the day. In the fifties, when he's into Joe College khakis and button-down shirts, the drapes are into their black leather jackets with the collars up, and cigarettes dangling from lower lips, and eyes at half-mast like Robert Mitchum on a particularly moody day.

The memory of these losers stays in a tiny corner of Waissman's brain as the years go by, until a telephone call ultimately recalls a lost 1950s that Americans in the 1970s think they'd like to have back.

The phone call comes from Phil Markin. "You gotta come out and see this show," he says. He's calling from Chicago, years after he and Ken went to school together. Markin's out there to take a course in advanced orthodontics. Waissman's in New York by now, where he's already in theater production.

"What show?" says Waissman.

Actually, it was more like the starting point for a show. It was half a dozen songs about these kids from the fifties. Only now, instead of being felonious and threatening, they were lovable.

It's the show that converts the menace of a *Blackboard Jungle* to a musical comedy called *Grease*.

"Just come out and take a look at it," Markin said. "It's songs like we used to have. You can take this thing to Broadway."

The theater out in Chicago was a dump, a converted trolley barn with no seats, where everybody sat on newspapers on the floor. There were drip marks on the scenery from a bad paint job and a five-piece band. The moment the actors came out, Waissman looked at them and fell deeply in love.

"These people," he thought instantly, "are drapes and drapettes."

Welcome back to 1950s high school, 1970s America.

So now, forty years since the premiere of *Grease* on Broadway, here was Waissman at one of his regular hangouts, Joe Allen's Restaurant, on Forty-Sixth Street in the heart of Manhattan's theater district, surrounded by big marvelous posters for Broadway shows of the past half-century. They covered all available wall space: *Pirate Queen* and *Rags* and *Rosa*. And *Laughing Room Only* and *Home, Sweet Homer* and *Mata Hari*.

Every single one of them (and dozens more) a complete flop and a testament to the sheer long-shot odds facing every show with dreams of success.

And here sits Waissman, the man who produced *Grease*, the long-running Broadway show that became the biggest hit movie musical of all time. Also the man who produced Broadway's *Agnes of God* and *Over Here!* and *And Miss Riordan Drinks a Little* and *Torch Song Trilogy*. All of them, not only covered in financial gold but resounding critical acclaim.

"All of these shows that failed," a man says, pointing to the nearby posters. "Each one represents a theatrical cautionary tale. How did you know *Grease* would work when so many shows don't?"

"Because of what happened in between," says Waissman. "*Grease* opened in 1972. It was only a dozen or so years since the fifties ended, but it might as well have been fifty years. The sixties was assassinations, riots, wars. It was another lifetime. The fifties was completely different. You didn't have fights. It was all bravado. Somebody'd say, 'The kids from Cold Spring Lane are coming over to fight us.' They never came. I don't even know if there *was* a gang from Cold Spring Lane. And there were very few fist fights in those days, and nobody carrying weapons."

Waissman sounds like Richard Holley, who couldn't believe his pal Dirty Ida carried a broken table leg to a rumble.

"It was all bravado back then," Waissman says. "And so I took one look at these people on stage in Chicago and thought, 'My God, drapes and drapettes. I haven't thought about them in a hundred years.' And right away I knew every one of these characters on stage. From Forest Park. Rizzo was Arlene Sinsky, who had a bleach blond spot in the front of her hair, and tight skirts, and was probably a nice girl but looked tough. It was like my high school yearbook had come alive. And there was a heavy girl who was the blind date. I looked at her and immediately thought of Cass Elliott."

She was Ellen Cohen then. In the sixties when she changed her name, she and three others would make up the Mamas and the Papas. At Forest Park High she was a transfer from Washington who arrived with braces on her teeth and some kind of spinach caught in the braces and an attitude. She wasn't exactly a drape. But she was linked in Waissman's mind with that actress on the little Chicago stage, and she helped spark memories of a time and a type.

These kids were part of a postwar disillusionment. All over the country, newspaper stories were popping up about these weird teenagers. First it was just about attitude and outfits. Later, when they had to live up to their public image, they were fighting and shoplifting and swiping cars. There was talk of brass knuckles and zip guns. And nobody was imagining any comic Broadway melodies about them.

In the fifties, in his elementary school days, Waissman was already smitten by show business. Like Jerry Leiber, who is seven years older, he's a Jewish kid whose family knows the music of Irving Berlin, of Rodgers and Hammerstein, of Kern and Gershwin. If you can hum a Broadway melody, it tells you you've got a little sophistication. Unlike the street urchin Leiber, who's dazzled by rhythm and blues, Waissman embraces the music of the legitimate theater.

In 1947, his parents took him to New York for a long weekend. One night he saw *Finian's Rainbow* with the great Ella Logan. The next night, the lovable waif Judy Holliday in *Born Yesterday*. More than sixty years later, Waissman can still recite the show's opening lines. On the third night, he saw *Oklahoma*. At age seven, he knew his life's course.

"I was already obsessed with being the boss," he says. "I said to my father, 'Who's the boss in the theater?' He said the producer, the director. That was in August. In September we went back to school." The old elementary school no. 69, Mordecai Gist, around the corner from Forest Park High.

"The teacher asked the class, What do you want to do when you grow up? The usual answers: policeman, fireman. I said, 'I want to be a Broadway producer.' The teacher called my mother. She said, 'I've been teaching for twenty years and never heard this.' My mother said, 'He'll get over it.'"

The mother was wrong. Three years later, Waissman was building primitive stages in his parents' basement on Penhurst Avenue. He put in dressing rooms. He had seating for seventy-five. He put on shows every summer. He was a kid entering junior high.

"All on my own," he says. "We'd get chairs from National Chair Rental, and curtains and lights and scenery. We had a tool room in the basement. The tool room became the lobby. Laundry cardboard became theater posters. Every tree in the neighborhood had a poster."

America was entering the golden age of the long-playing record album. Stereophonic sound was coming in. In the fifties Broadway was bursting with *My Fair Lady* and *Pajama Game* and *West Side Story*. In Baltimore middle-class families reaching for a patina of sophistication were rushing to Luskin's appliance stores and buying up these LPs. The Waissmans had all the shows and movie soundtracks. Down in the basement Kenny would play the records and neighborhood kids would lip-synch the lyrics while their proud parents watched from their National Chair Rental seats.

"Four days and four nights every summer," Waissman says. "Adults a dollar, kids fifty cents. We sold out every performance. We did *Show Boat* and *Calamity Jane* and *Cinderella*. We'd donate the proceeds every year to the Maryland Cancer Fund, and they'd get us on TV to present the check."

By the time he got to high school, Waissman was practically a Broadway pro. He was producing, and he was performing. He'd sing at weddings and bar mitzvah parties with a local orchestra. And, at Forest Park High, he co-directed *Ballad for Americans*.

One weekend he went back to New York, where *West Side Story* had opened: the Jets and the Sharks, black leather jackets all over the place. Broadway with an early touch of social conscience.

"The scene that stays with me," says Waissman, "is the rumble. One of the kids gets stabbed—and the kids on stage were as stunned as we were. Those things didn't happen back then. It was like kids in my neighborhood hearing that some gang from Cold Spring Lane was coming over to fight us. It was all talk. There were no real fights. And here you had somebody getting stabbed. It was the end of innocence."

≈

When Waissman got his call from Chicago, to see the show that became *Grease*, he remembered those drapes from Forest Park. They stood around in little bunches, trying to look menacing. Big deal, they smoked cigarettes. Who didn't? Big deal, they tried to look sullen. What teenager didn't? Nobody took them seriously. They were so out-numbered by good kids, they seemed sort of comical. Those were the images Waissman recalled.

"When I saw that first production," he said, "it was only about a dozen years since the fifties had ended. But it seemed like half a century. The sixties had created a real separation. This had the same distance as *Gone with the Wind*. That's how far back the fifties seemed at that moment."

Waissman, without fully realizing the national yearning for the return of the fifties, decided to roll the dice. He told the show's writers, Jim Jacobs and Warren Casey, "If you make this into a full musical, we could make it work on Broadway."

Returning to New York, he headed straight for Greenwich Village, to a place where they sold records from the dawn of rock and roll, compilations of the era's big hits. He was listening for the musical rhythms and the teenage yearnings in the lyrics. The fifties, he figured, didn't actually start in 1950.

"It was 1954," he said, "because that's when rock and roll really came in. You heard 'Hearts of Stone.' You heard Bill Haley. You heard 'Sh-Boom' and 'Sixteen Tons.' This was *our* music, not our parents'. It wasn't rebellion, exactly. But it was music that was ours."

For the drapes, though, the music did represent part of their rebellion. They knew they didn't fit in with the era's conformity, and so they stopped trying. They understood they were being written out of the squares' game, so they started their own culture—all posture, all attitude. When they were typecast, they started living up to the type. They knew what was expected of them.

In Waissman's world, the kids were still more cautious about sticking to the old rules. It was safer that way—until it became suffocating.

"We were still stuck in our Victorianism," he said, "until the pill changed everything. Up to then, everybody worried about a girl getting pregnant. I remember my mother hollering, 'You get a girl pregnant, you'll never be a doctor. Look what happened to your friend Myron. He wanted to be on Broadway. He had to give it all up.' Mom always used that—'He could have been on Broadway.' Myron became a teacher."

Waissman became a Broadway producer. Then he brought the drapes along with him.

Baltimore Police Capt. Alexander Emerson, scourge of dice rollers, numbers runners, and striptease artists, peers from behind his glasses and holds aloft the legendary maul he used on gambling raids. (Hearst Newspapers LLC / Baltimore News-American)

The Vice Man Cometh
Captain Alexander Emerson

$\mathcal{O}n$ the $\mathit{afternoon}$ of September 12, 1954, officers of the Southwestern District, Baltimore City Police Department, gathering up all courage and professional expertise and all desire to squelch the great criminal acts plaguing their city, swooped down upon two dozen men conspiring in an alley behind the nineteen hundred block of Wilkens Avenue.

It was, as police described it, a remarkable thing to behold. The two dozen men "exploded in all directions" when the cops suddenly announced their presence. One suspect tried to escape by climbing halfway up a telephone pole. He got no farther. Another was chased three blocks and then stopped, tired of the pursuit, and informed police they never would have caught him because "I used to be a Poly track star."

Six of the men were captured and taken into custody. Naturally, the story made all the daily newspapers, since it concerned such a major piece of criminal enterprise and such a threat to the daily lives of all who lived in Baltimore. The captured men were handcuffed and locked behind bars. The charge? Taking part in a game of craps.

For their great initiative the police officers were able to seize six dollars and forty-five cents and a pair of dice.

Thus, another crime wave is staunched.

The midcentury police departments are marvelous at such crime busting. Day after day the newspapers carry stories of the big gambling raids of the era. Here are the Eastern District police in Baltimore breaking up a pinochle game at a Lyndale Avenue row house. "Disturbing the peace" this is termed to make it sound dangerous. Then the cops out of Southeast are nailing a bookmaker at the Oldham Street Pleasure Club for taking bets on the afternoon's horse races at Pimlico. Or the vice squad's barging through a row-house door on Harlem Avenue to grab brown paper bags suspected of containing three-digit numbers bets. But—whoops! It turns out there aren't any numbers slips inside these brown paper bags, just large amounts of hamburgers and onion rolls gathered for hungry persons by members of a neighborhood organization—with the full cooperation of the city's Department of Welfare.

Well, what's a little mistake like crashing in the front door of somebody's home when it comes to fighting crime? In his charge to a 1958 Baltimore grand jury, Supreme Bench Judge Anselm Sodaro calls the playing of illegal lottery games "vicious." Vicious! Sodaro doesn't foresee the day when the state itself will run such "vicious" games. The *Sun* newspaper, quickly mouthing its amen echo to the judge's missionary cry, calls gambling of all sorts "evil." Evil! But they're apparently not referring to church bingo, which gets a heavenly pass. The cops take their marching orders from such pronouncements. Year after year they're pouncing on gamblers all over the city of Baltimore, mirroring many more cities across the nation.

America suffers from a kind of postwar cultural schizophrenia when it comes to its gambling habits. Broadway gives the country *Guys and Dolls*, with its lovable rogues singing "Luck Be a Lady" while they roll the dice to win Miss Sarah from the Salvation Army. Television offers Phil Silvers as Sergeant Bilko, with his platoon of scruffy misfits seeking subversive poker-game action while conning all military brass. Their popularity reflects a spirit of anarchy, the half-squelched national desire to cut loose a little in such an orderly, uptight time. But the official keepers of morality are still out there chasing down those considered outlaws, such as dice shooters and off-track horse players and bettors on three-digit numbers.

And the first hints of the legitimate crime wave that will ultimately stain the entire country, based on the spread of narcotics, go all but unnoticed as it emerges from the shadows.

In Baltimore, midcentury police arrest so many suspected gamblers that Criminal Court judges regularly set aside entire days to hear nothing but cases involving lottery bets and horse race wagers and crap games and, of course, dangerous pinball machine cash payoffs. Here we have a typical such day in Criminal Court, in the summer of

1950, which the *Evening Sun* describes as "crowded with defendants, most of them Negroes." Nice of the *Sun* to make its usual racial distinctions when it comes to crime. "63 Negroes Arrested in Pearl Street Raid," reads a routine headline of the era. Such days prompt E. B. Rea, in his *Afro-American* newspaper column, to note that black neighborhoods "bear the brunt of most of the holdups, yet there are more arrests for numbers writing. Numbers writers don't take people's money at the point of guns. The people just give it to them to satisfy an urge to get easy money. Gambling is only a pleasurable vice. Robbery and robbery-murder are criminal premeditations."

These blacks now standing trial will take the fall for those who actually run the numbers rackets in Baltimore—mostly Jews and Italians, later jokingly termed the Kosher Nostra—who will then pay off fines for any of their employees who happen to get busted. What transpires on this day in court is the usual carefully choreographed charade—Henry Ford's assembly line as envisioned by Oliver Wendell Holmes. The cases move rapidly. Not a single defendant bothers to take the witness stand. A man named William Brown is summoned.

"Has the witness been here before?" asks Judge Michael Manley.

"No, sir," assures Brown's attorney.

"Well now," prosecutor Charles Orth points out, eager to characterize this Brown as a multiple offender, "one William Brown *was* here in 1946."

"I meant this year," says the judge. "Not four years ago."

"Yes, sir," Orth replies meekly.

"One hundred dollars and costs," says the judge.

And that's it. Next case, please. There are too many yet to be tried to waste precious minutes on details. Everybody knows the routine. The cops make the arrests; the defendants (or their secret bosses) pay the fine. Attorneys on both sides make a living. And the newly released defendants rush back to the streets as quickly as possible to take the remainder of the day's action.

From this comes a roster of career gambling figures who are familiar headline names to a generation of Baltimoreans: Julius "Lord" Salsbury and Louis "Gus Funk" LeFaivre, Phillip "Pacey" Silbert and William "Little Willie" Adams, Robert "Fifi" London and Louis Comi.

Comi runs a highly profitable numbers operation out of the city's east side. All that separates him from these other characters is a suitable Runyonesque nickname. But this is rectified one historic Saturday night when Comi's arrested on gambling charges.

In the *News-Post* newsroom that night, amid a clacking of typewriters and wire service machines, an acting city editor named Jack Ryan leans over a young rewrite man and tells him, "We're running Comi out front for Sunday's paper. Make it sing."

When Ryan looks over the rewrite man's opening paragraph a few minutes later, he says, "Your lead's no good."

"What's the matter with it?"

"Make it Louis 'Boom-Boom' Comi," says Ryan.

"But that's not his name," says the rewrite man.

"I know," says Ryan, "but it reads better that way."

Thus, a name is attached to a front page headline, and the name is criminal. "Boom-Boom," indeed. Not only does Comi become part of a colorful cast of gambling characters—he joins a kind of outlaw repertory company, a Guys and Dolls road show played with real handcuffs.

The cast comprises men who came of age during the hardscrabble Depression years, who survived World War II, and who, in the post-war era, figure out they're about to be left behind again by a society that didn't give them much of an education, that now offers dreary jobs barely lifting them out of poverty—and so they've taken up a profitable profession that the law calls criminal but nobody knows exactly why. These men aren't choirboys—but they've been added to the criminal class without serious cause.

It's the lingering aura of the country's Puritan ethic—"the fear," as H. L. Mencken put it, "that someone, somewhere, might be having a good time." Comi and the others are thus created by the forces of the self-righteous imposing their values upon the simple human desire to enjoy a fling with a few bucks. It's an impulse that creates an American outlaw class that's bloated beyond reason. And it's an attempt to prop up a perception of human innocence that never existed in fact.

Years later, realizing the tremendous profits to be made from gambling, the State of Maryland itself will turn this into a multi-million-dollar government enterprise. Such state-run games spring up all across America. Suddenly, there's nothing immoral or criminal in betting on a three-digit number. Now it's practically a public service to place a bet.

In the innocent fifties, though, in a time when Baltimore has an estimated three hundred illegal horse-wagering emporiums, there are scores of corner barbershops and saloons, pool halls, and dry-cleaning establishments that take numbers bets on the sly, and the city's three daily newspapers regularly carry stories of police cracking down on gamblers. And they all but ignore this thing that has begun seeping into neighborhoods, known as narcotics. It touches the young people first, and soon it will devastate families everywhere.

In the meantime, the most legendary city cop of the era is Capt. Alexander Emerson. He's the complete True Believer. He thinks he's cutting into real crime every time he takes up his eight-pound maul and leads his vice squad on a gambling raid.

Once, he has to batter his way through nine different doors to get to a numbers operation. This takes three hours. He uses his famous maul, which he calls "an eight-pound pass key," and a heavy crowbar. When he finally gets inside the ninth door, all incriminating evidence naturally has been destroyed, and several men lounge lazily around a card table.

"Why didn't you knock?" one of them inquires pleasantly. "We'd have let you in."

Emerson is undaunted.

Once, he goes to Maude Avenue, in South Baltimore, and enters the home of Mr. and Mrs. Ashley Wood. Emerson picks up a garbage pail containing the usual kitchen trash. Believing that it contains numbers slips, he spreads out the smelly contents—across Mrs. Wood's living room table.

"I just cleaned this house," Mrs. Wood cries.

Emerson shoves her into a chair. Then, fearing that she might be swallowing numbers slips, he sticks his fingers into Mrs. Wood's mouth. She bites him. Emerson grasps his leg with both hands and shouts, "Call the patrol wagon. I've got to go to a hospital. She stomped on my foot."

At this time, Mrs. Wood is not wearing shoes.

In court, Emerson denies none of this testimony. Through much of it, he snickers. The snickering ends when Magistrate Herbert Franklin asks Emerson, "Did you really put all that garbage on the living room table?"

"Yes," Emerson says.

"Case dismissed," Franklin says.

Emerson remains undaunted.

He goes after ordinary citizens whose gambling arrests attach them to a name: racketeers, disturbers of the peace. In 1950 he and his vice squad arrest 3,119 people. One day he raids a Frederick Avenue pool hall and arrests seventy-six men. It's the West End Veterans Social Club. These are guys who survived World War II, dodging enemy fire at Normandy Beach and Anzio, shivering through the Battle of the Bulge, only to be confronted by this crazy person with a gun wearing a Baltimore police badge. In a corner of the room is a large tub filled with Coca Colas and ice. A radio plays racing results from tracks around the country. Three men are charged with bookmaking. The other seventy-three are charged with disorderly conduct. A joke, of course. As the men are led from the pool hall, scores of neighborhood residents stand along the sidewalk heckling the police, who will later complain that citizens are somehow losing respect for the law. Go figure.

Emerson is still undaunted.

He comes off of Maryland's Eastern Shore, the son of a kind-hearted father who became belligerent only when drinking, which was often, and a deeply religious mother. Emerson has a wife and six children. He never misses mass on Sundays or holy days and never takes a vacation.

In his early days he serves in the army at Fort Meade and gets a taste of police duty on special MP assignment. He likes it. He spends some time out west as a cowpuncher. When he finally joins the Baltimore police, he discovers that Prohibition has created a crime boom and a grand opportunity for young men with high professional ambition and low tolerance for immorality.

One Saturday night he single-handedly rounds up 147 people in a crap game. Then, since the evening is still young, he takes part in five more raids, bringing the total number of arrests to nearly five hundred.

In a single night.

All this, for games of chance—while the business of real crime is changing all around Emerson, and it sneaks up on every oblivious police department in the country, and nobody in the fifties—not the cops, not the prosecutors, not the judges or anybody else—knows what to do about the dawning of the era of narcotics in America.

Some of the parents notice it first. Their kids leave the house for previously innocent dances in the local church basement or at the neighborhood rec center but come home acting half drunk—and there's no smell of liquor on their breath. When the parents start asking questions the kids get belligerent. Doors are slammed, voices raised. The parents stand there in the darkening hallways, scratching their heads.

"Kids today, what are you gonna do with 'em?"

Here and there you find newspaper briefs. Some loser arrested on a drug charge—what the hell's that all about? The stories seem out of context, almost comic: narcotics, isn't that the stuff they smoke in Chinese opium dens?

The game's so new, those writing about it for a living still don't know which drugs are addictive and which ones aren't. Among them is the *Sun*'s William Manchester. He'll go on to write respected biographies of John Kennedy and Douglas MacArthur and Winston Churchill. But for now he repeatedly refers to "marijuana addicts," and the phrase slips right past editors who also don't know the difference. They're like everybody else in the early fifties: clueless and in denial.

Some of this sense of denial comes from distance. It's only the colored, isn't it? That's what the newspaper stories keep saying every time they report an arrest.

Levi Acion, also said to be known as "Lee White," "Crips," "Whitey" and "Hop," a 50-year-old Negro poolroom operator . . .

Richard W. Cockey, a ten-year-old Negro who, for a 25-cent profit, acted as a go-between in the heroin sale . . .

Virginia Thomas, 19-year-old Negro girl who stole a suit to raise the $3 price of a heroin capsule . . .

Ernest Harding, 30, Negro, who pawned the suit stolen by the Thomas girl . . .

Then, in August 1951, this story in the *Evening Sun*: "Charges against a 28-year-old Negro laborer, accused of giving dope to three teen-age white girls, will be heard today in District Police Court. The man was identified as Charles Richardson. He was arrested after residents of the Pimlico section reported white girls getting into an automobile with a Negro."

Never mind heroin traffic—in 1951 America, whoever heard of white girls getting into a car with a black man? Now you have your newspaper headlines, boy. In Baltimore Criminal Court Judge Joseph

Sherbow presides over the case against this Richardson, identified in the *Sun* as "a Negro race-track follower."

Prosecutors bring in a small parade of white teenage witnesses. A seventeen-year-old girl says she started using heroin at Forest Park High School. A Saint Ambrose Parochial School girl says she was fifteen when she "smoked her first 'reefer' in the infield at Pimlico during the race meet when thousands of persons were around." Another, sixteen years old, says she "took shots of heroin melted in a teaspoon in Richardson's room."

Judge Sherbow does two things. He finds Richardson guilty, and he declares "a plague loose" in northwest Baltimore, "a plague that has hit that area as terribly as any plague of the dark ages."

This kind of language will never do. It's one thing to report drug traffic down in the colored ghettos, but now you're talking about white kids, and everybody knows white kids are playing happily at the rec centers and the baseball fields, too busy running their after-school paper routes to ruin their lives at the end of a needle, aren't they?

Aren't they?

"Not one case has come to our attention," Wendell E. Dunn, principal of Forest Park High School, tells the newspapers. "No evidence of narcotics," adds Mildred Coughlin, principal of Western High School. And on and on in this vein, statements of denial from community elders who have investments in the status quo, unshakeable beliefs in American values holding as they've always held.

These people are whistling past the future, in which graveyards will replace neighborhoods.

Mayor Tommy D'Alesandro suggests mandatory medical care for addicts. The problem's starting to feel a little close to home for the mayor; he's heard whispers about kids in his neighborhood, Little Italy, getting into trouble. But D'Alesandro's about forty years ahead of his time on this notion of medical treatment instead of punishment. These junkies want to break the law, let's throw 'em all in jail.

From all the years of failed Prohibition, America has learned precisely nothing.

As a gesture of concern and respect for the veteran Judge Sherbow, the Baltimore police establish a drug enforcement unit, headed by Sgt. Joseph Carroll. It's composed of three officers. Wonderful, three cops assigned to stop drug traffic in a city of nearly one million people.

Eight months later, in May 1952, a triumphant Carroll announces that the city's narcotics traffic is "pretty well under control." In the first four months of the year, Carroll declares, his guys arrested thirty-nine narcotics traffickers—and, the *Sun* reports comfortingly, thirty-two of them are "colored people."

The words read like a warning cry to whites: Keep your distance from blacks, and leave everything to the police and the prisons.

Meanwhile, wake-up calls begin sounding around the country in the early fifties. Detroit police estimate fifteen thousand addicts. Chicago police cite "booming" drug traffic. New York police report about thirty thousand users. Half, say the police, are teenagers.

And nobody knows what to do with them.

In 1956 the Senate Judiciary Committee spends seven months looking into drug traffic. They interview five hundred witnesses and produce more than eight thousand pages of testimony. They announce that the United States now has more addicts than all other Western nations combined—thirty thousand known addicts, they estimate, mostly young people, and many of them responsible for the nation's growing crime rate.

When did this happen to our innocent postwar America? It's too mind-boggling to imagine—and so we don't.

In Baltimore the drug traffic is thought to be somewhere else. Maybe it's just in those faraway cities; maybe it's just in those faraway colored neighborhoods. Maybe, if we don't think about it, it won't exist at all.

But reality keeps intruding. In Maryland in the mid-1950s, officials declare that the number of drug-addict inmates in state prisons has increased fourfold in the past decade. The only bigger upswing is the number of inmates imprisoned on gambling charges. For which everyone can thank the marvelous Capt. Alexander Emerson. Through it all, he goes his merry way. The newspapers continue to make this guy a hero, since he gives them good copy. He makes certain all reporters are informed whenever he's about to go into action. He even alerts them when he stages his 250th gambling arrest.

Nobody stopped to wonder what these hundreds of arrests each year were all about. Why were gamblers being arrested for crimes where there were no victims?

The arrest numbers went up, and the raw numbers made it look as though serious law enforcement was being done. The police could then go to government officials and declare: Look at all this crime. We need more men and more money to fight it.

Thus bureaucracies grow and political power bases grow. A criminal class is created. The bookmakers and the numbers operators, seeing themselves classified as career criminals, branch out into other low-rent endeavors. Julius "Lord" Salsbury—he got the nickname by giving it to himself—opens a striptease bar on The Block. Louis "Boom Boom" Comi—we know how he got his name—drifts into stolen goods and prostitution. Mr. Salsbury, meet Mr. Comi. Maybe we can do a little business together. And, by the way, meet some of my friends.

And these kids everybody calls drapes—the ones barred from recreation centers because their pants cuffs are too tight, the ones considered dangerous because they wear black leather jackets and smoke cigarettes on school grounds—they learn to live up to their images, too.

Meanwhile, the things that will cause real crime to explode in the coming decades—the intractable poverty and the explosion of drug traffic—go ignored by all those who might have stopped it or put it into some sensible perspective early in the game. In 1951, the entire prison population of Maryland numbers less than four thousand. Sixty years later, about thirty thousand are behind bars. The vast majority of inmates have years of drug violations behind them. And years of poverty. It's the prison-industrial complex, and it's become a marvelous growth industry.

But let's not leave the good Captain Emerson too soon, for he is a creature of his inhibited era, a comic martinet who postures himself as the last man standing between Judeo-Christian values and the forces of barbarism. When he's not breaking up dangerous games of dice, he's attempting to put bloomers back onto strippers. When he's not arresting those who bet a few off-track bucks on the action at Pimlico Race Course, he's putting his mark on the great literature of his time, deciding which books are fit to read and which ones fail to meet his particular literary standards, such as *From Here to Eternity*.

Emerson has a problem with sex, particularly as enjoyed by others. Whenever he strides along the city's neon row of East Baltimore Street striptease joints known as The Block, the captain finds it infuriating to see posters of young ladies, such as the famous Blaze Starr, Irma the

Body, and Virginia Belle and her Twin Liberty Bells, wearing little more than low-cut theatrical bras and fishnet stockings.

One night he presides over the arrests of an entire burlesque troupe. He confiscates their lingerie as evidence. When the case comes to criminal court, Emerson demonstrates how flimsy the lingerie is by holding it up—and reading a book through it.

He makes headlines after glancing at a nudist colony photo magazine he finds on a Baltimore Street newsstand. In the photos, deemed pornographic by Emerson, some people are playing volleyball. Others, shuffleboard. That's as racy as it gets. But you can see their bare bottoms, Emerson cries. And he hauls the newsstand dealer off to jail. So once more we widen the so-called criminal class. Once more the law steps in to inhibit consensual adult behavior. And once more we attempt to enforce innocence where no one's asking for it.

In fact, much of the country's eager to throw off suffocating Puritan sexual strictures—but most are reluctant to say so out loud. These are the sexual dark ages, which the comic Richard Pryor will recall as "the Great Pussy Drought of the Fifties." Hopeful high school boys of the era purchase condoms and carry them in their wallets as badges of sophistication. The condoms remain in the wallets. They remain there so long that they leave indented circles in the leather. We still have the last, lingering notions of Emily Post propriety, of brides who are still virgins or claim they are to their mothers, who insist they remain chaste lest "no man will want you." In his 1957 book, *The American Sexual Tragedy*, Albert Ellis laments that a woman is obliged "to make herself infinitely sexually desirable, but finally approachable only in legal marriage."

A nation of TV watchers tunes in to a sexual wasteland. In 1951 the National Association of Radio and TV Broadcasters sets forth a code that they hope will satisfy government bluenoses. Among the provisions: no jokes about the traveling salesman and the farmer's daughter; no camera angles "emphasizing anatomical details indecently"; the banning of profanity, including a word like *broad* unless it means width or a state of mind, and total avoidance of the words *hell* and *damn*.

In the 1950s sex without marriage feels like a distant rumor or a secret outlaw act chilled by the likes of Captain Emerson. It's a dirty joke shared at the office water cooler or a whisper passed on like a furtive prayer. Sex is the newest issue of *Playboy* magazine, where this month's centerfold might let a towel slip enough to bare a little cleavage. When young men compare notes on a weekend's dating triumphs, they issue front-line battle reports heavily embellished by imagination, like Vietnam body counts.

The midcentury marriage manuals present a kind of sex-by-the-numbers list of instructions. This goes here, and that goes there. Meanwhile the Boy Scouts are still passing out handbooks condemning masturbation and declaring sex harmful to athletes. And there are street-corner rumors that excessive masturbation can lead to hairy palms or blindness. (The standard joke: "Can I just do it until I need glasses?")

In the fifties no couples are "living together" before getting married. On college campuses young men stage panty raids, which the writer Dan Wakefield calls "demonstrations of post-adolescent frustration which were the Fifties version of the orgy—where boys stormed girls' dorms and demanded not sex but the symbol of it, panties and bras and other female undergarments, which damsels dropped from the windows of their walled fortresses." Even this clumsy horseplay was considered so unbecoming that college presidents threatened disciplinary action for any young men involved: loss of student deferment from the military draft. Not a good idea when they're sending kids off to frigid Korea.

When Barry Levinson makes *Diner*, his first Baltimore movie about life in the 1950s, one of the guys bemoans "six years of a platonic relationship." Another, approaching his wedding night, is asked if he's "still a virgin." "Technically," he replies. That figures. A 1955 study by the American Sociological Society says that, among engaged couples, only 33 percent of the men and 14 percent of their fiancées have had "full sexual relations" before marriage. Dan Wakefield writes, "Ours was the last generation for whom foreplay was accepted as an end in itself."

In 1961, when the fifties are beginning to be over, First Lady Jacqueline Kennedy draws flak for wearing skirts that reveal her kneecaps. Mamie Eisenhower never did that. Fussy civic groups in such places as Rehoboth Beach fight to bar women in two-piece bathing suits from the boardwalk. Colleges impose evening curfews on female students until they reach the age of twenty-one—and, even then, they mustn't wear shorts or slacks to class. Some radio stations ban the novelty song

"I Saw Mommy Kissing Santa Claus" because, as a station executive in Tennessee puts it, "It violates a provision against songs in which children describe parents' misconduct, and implies an insult to Santa Claus and the sacred occasion of Christmas."

The generation just coming of age will seize upon each of these insanities, and more, as evidence that the country's sexual glands are in lockdown and must be set free when the sixties arrive.

In 1948, when the nation's sexual census taker, Dr. Alfred C. Kinsey, releases the first of his famous reports, *Sexual Behavior in the Human Male*, a quarter-million copies are sold. When *Sexual Behavior in the Human Female* comes out in 1953, sales are even higher. We're a nation hungry to know what's going on beneath the covers.

Kinsey tells us. He declares that a sexual revolution has arrived while everybody was taking cold showers. He says half of American women and more than 80 percent of American men are having sex before marriage. True, most of the action's with their future spouses, and, true, most of it's in the final months before the wedding, but still . . . He says half the men and one-quarter of the women have extramarital affairs. He says almost everybody does some petting before marriage. He says that about three-quarters of married women reach "sexual fulfillment" in their first year of marriage "at least once."

When Kinsey's *Sexual Behavior in the Human Female* appears, explosions are heard. New York Rep. Louis B. Heller immediately demands a congressional investigation. "Kinsey," says Heller, "is contributing to the depravity of a whole generation, to the loss of faith in human dignity . . . to the spread of juvenile delinquency, and to the misunderstanding and confusion about sex."

"It was," says Joann Rodgers, "a culturally repressed and stodgy time. If you were young you learned whatever you learned from your friends—and who knew what kind of information they had?"

On this autumn afternoon in 2011, Rodgers has her own information. She came of age in 1950s Baltimore and became chief medical writer for the Hearst newspapers, based in Baltimore at its *News-American* newspaper. Later she was a voice of the Johns Hopkins Hospital. She also wrote a book, *Sex: A Natural History*.

"Sexually, the 1950s was the silent generation," says Rodgers. She's a seventy-year-old grandmother now, an elfin, twinkly woman who looks as if she could still go out for college cheerleader. Sitting in her

Baltimore County kitchen, sipping a diet soda, she glances back with a social scientist's insight and a sense of humor.

"There was," she says, "the same desire for sex that there is today. But you didn't talk about it. In the fifties the concept was: You have to teach people to be sexual. And teach them to do the things that had always been natural. There was Dr. Spock teaching us how to be parents. There were books on how to be 'appropriately' sexual. And the Kinsey reports. Suddenly it became an education industry. People worried about doing it 'right.' Making the woman happy, making sure she had an orgasm, and 'Should it be simultaneous?' That had to create even more anxiety, laid over all this other stuff going on at the time. In the fifties you had to have 'the talk' with your priest or rabbi or your doctor before you got married. Go to your gynecologist. Everything became a checklist of things you had to think about. You know, people have been reproducing since time immemorial, and nobody had to hand them a book to do it."

The culture dampened down all sexuality, and the law tried to mute all hints of it. But, the human sex drive being what it is, the hunger never went away. The guys were reading *Playboy* (the faux sophisticates claiming, "I only look at it for the articles"), whose centerfold girls were billed as "the girl next door." If only, if only. But each come-on photo, each sexually teasing story, seemed a testament to change: the pasties are off, and the bloomers are being lowered. One fine day, gentlemen, we won't have to rely on magazines, or panty raids, either, for our sexual thrills.

Meanwhile, women had a few dozen publications, known as "confession" magazines, each of them heating up the room. Take any newsstand in the spring of 1957. There's *Modern Romances*, whose April cover announces, "I Sneak Out at Night for Thrills." Or *Secret Confessions*: "I Committed Adultery," says the cover headline. Or *True Life Stories*. Here a teenage girl recounts rape by a giggling maniac, seduction by her boss's stepson, addiction to "sex pills," and confinement in a home for delinquent girls. All of this was advertised as fact, and some of it almost sounded like it.

In the fifties the boys talked about sex a lot, mostly lies, but the girls didn't. Instead of sex, the girls talked about romance, about being in love, about having a crush. Some of this was lying, too, but mostly to themselves. They got their ideas from the romance magazines that created myths suitable for fourteen-year-olds. The mainstream movies and TV weren't much more sophisticated.

"We had a lot of pajama parties and sorority parties," Rodgers recalls, "but we didn't talk about sex. We talked around it. There were a few girls who were considered 'in the know,' who were sexually active and knew the stuff the rest of us didn't know. We either envied these girls, or we thought they were nuts. One of the two. But, when I got to college in 1959, practically every girl—my roommate, my dormitory friends, everybody—sex was all they talked about. That was a big eye-opener. They were treating it matter-of-factly. This was the dawn of feminism to an extent, as we reached the early sixties."

But, in the innocent fifties, for every tentative step forward, there are authority figures looking to chill all expression of this frustrated American lustiness. And no one is trying harder to hold back the dark night of sexual freedom than the good and noble Captain Emerson.

Sometimes he and his vice squad boys raid parties where "smokers" are shown. "Indescribable movies," he calls them. More headlines, more indication to newspaper readers of a link between activities sexual and activities criminal.

Once, Emerson drops into a nightspot on The Block where a young lady begins a languid professional undressing. The captain sits at a table near the stage. As this woman removes her clothing, bit by bit, and others are roused to prurient thought, Emerson is roused to action. He jumps onto the stage.

"Put your clothes on, and never do this again," he cries.

The audience takes unkindly to this interruption.

"Throw the bum out," somebody yells.

"I don't know who made that remark," says Emerson, "but I'd like to inform you that everybody at his table is guilty of disorderly conduct. We have a dozen wagons at Central"—city police headquarters, conveniently located half a block away—"and if it is repeated, we'll be glad to take you all up there and hold you until we find out who said it. Now just let me hear one more remark, and see what happens."

Nobody says a word.

When the city's bluenoses complain that there are obscene books being sold at bookstores and newsstands, Emerson's assigned the duties of municipal censorship.

"Have you read many books?" he's asked.

"A lot," he says.

"Can you name a few?"

"I can't remember any names offhand," he says.

"Then how do you know what's obscene?"

"I don't like things too raw," he explains. "And, of course, no dirty pictures. If it's suggestive—and that's the sort of thing people want to read—let 'em go down to Mexico."

In Washington in this era, a special House committee investigates "cheesecake girlie magazines, salacious pocket-sized books and 'flagrantly misnamed comics,'" such as *MAD*. The committee declares a national epidemic of unhealthy literature. Included in the epidemic are works by John Steinbeck, James T. Farrell, and Alberto Moravia.

In Baltimore the mayor forms a Committee for Decency to examine books and magazines for obscenity. They set Emerson and his boys loose on *From Here to Eternity* and *Nana* and *Mr. Roberts*.

The country's sex drive goes underground in the postwar years—not people's desires, just the long-shot odds that they'll see human sexuality openly reflected in the culture. There's violence in movies? Cool. There's a woman's bare breast? Somebody call the vice squad.

In Baltimore, members of the Maryland State Board of Censors issued a 1954 report despairing over "the moral quality" of the year's films. "Many of them," the report declared, "emphasized marital infidelity, seduction and betrayal of girls, illicit love, gangster and underworld life. Trashy sex-dramas likewise made their appearance." Fortunately, the report noted, the board was there to protect the public—deleting scenes from more than fifty movies over the year and killing about a dozen movies entirely.

In 1950 there were great public debates over the strapless evening gowns and bare shoulders displayed on national TV by actress Faye Emerson (no relation to the ever-vigilant Baltimore vice cop). Public opinion sided with Faye.

Ten years later, on Baltimore television, girls on the Buddy Deane dance program model strapless outfits for Etta Gowns commercials. A Catholic priest protests their bare shoulders, citing "rampant sexuality." The bare shoulders are thereafter covered with a piece of net.

And so-called vice? It continued, of course. By the end of the innocent fifties, when the striptease shows on Baltimore's Block were getting increasingly risqué—some of the ladies were actually removing their pasties now—one brave man stepped forward and offered to hold back the night of depravity.

"Give me two good policemen and in a month—no, a week—there won't be any Block," he said. "It's worse now than it's ever been. Keep tormenting them, and they can't stay in business."

The man was a retired Baltimore policeman—our former vice captain, Alexander Emerson.

And he was crying into the wind.

Madalyn Murray, the woman who drove organized prayer from the public schools and became "the most hated woman in America," displays a rarely seen puckish sense of humor as she turns thumbs-down on a Baltimore religious billboard. (Hearst Newspapers LLC / Baltimore News-American)

The Most Hated Woman in America
Madalyn Murray

In the innocent fifties, the angriest person in Baltimore becomes the Most Hated Woman in America. She takes the title and waves it triumphantly, like a beauty pageant crown. She wins it when she helps silence all organized prayer in the public schools. Now and forever, God will hang out strictly with the private school kids. Half a century later, people across America still curse Madalyn Murray's name for this. And Murray, long since dead and not likely to be singing hosannahs with any angels in heaven, would surely relish all the anger.

"Oh, America still hates her," Leonard Kerpelman says one spring afternoon fifty years after Murray first surfaced in the American consciousness. She arrived in the midst of God's Decade. On school mornings, teachers everywhere stood with Bibles wide open in front of their students, and all voices intoned, "The lord is my shepherd, I shall not want . . . "

They did this five mornings a week through all of the years of schooling, and hardly a parent or child anywhere complained out loud. Everybody understood: This is the way America raises its children. Even if we don't pray at home, we display our piety by having our kids bow their heads in school. Look at us, we're raising our kids to be reverent! Even those with qualms went along with it. The kids stood at their little desks and recited the morning prayer, whatever their religion (or lack of one), and then they said the Pledge of Allegiance to the flag, thus uniting God and country. And now in the pious fifties, the pledge included the newly inserted words "under God," thus reinforcing that psychological binding of church and state. Many of these children recited the words with reverence, and many others muttered them numbly from so much daily repetition, kindergarten through twelfth grade, day after day, and then Madalyn Murray arrived to stop all of this religious business without another syllable uttered.

"Even now," Kerpelman says, "they hate her for this."

And never mind the vanished decades. Kerpelman knows there's anger. But, edging toward ninety, he leans on his wooden cane and happily recalls days when he and Murray went to war with the whole country.

"Madalyn's probably still laughing about it," he says.

He should know. He was Murray's attorney, even when she called him bad names. He shrugs off the insults. He felt sorry for Murray's son Bill, who was getting bullied every day at school after the story hit the newspapers. Kids shoving him around, spitting on him, pushing him in front of a bus. That's how Kerpelman got involved. One morning he read about Murray in the newspaper and showed it to his wife Eleanor.

"Go see these people," said Eleanor. "Look what they're going through."

That's how it starts, though Kerpelman doesn't know the half of it when he gets in. This is a woman at war with the whole wide world. She keeps a diary, categorizing all of her bitterness. She's broke, her two sons have no visible father, she feels isolated from people. She hates most of them, anyway, and calls them morons. She fumes about American hypocrisy. She consigns herself to the quixotic loneliness of the crusader. All she needs is a cause, something where she can unload all this pent-up rage.

In the final months of the Eisenhower era, she finds it. She enrolls her son William at Baltimore's Woodbourne Junior High School and sees children bowing their heads in prayer. Such morning rituals have been going on for generations. On this day, though, Murray decides to make it an issue. When she reaches the guidance counselor's office a few moments later, she unburdens herself, but good.

"This praying," she says. "It's un-American and unconstitutional. I don't want my son praying."

"No one's ever complained before this," says the counselor. "It's really not about religion, it's just a recitation. It sets a nice tone for the day."

Murray believes this man to be an idiot. He obviously knows nothing about constitutional law, about separation of church and state. So she gets nasty. And he gets nasty back.

"If you don't like it," he says, rather dismissively, "why don't you sue us?"

Famous last words. For that's Murray's son William on the front of the morning newspaper a little later. The headline says, "Boy, 14, Balks at Bible Reading." Everybody can't get over this. First it's the *Sun*, then quickly the wire services, the broadcasting networks, and national magazines. Followed by months of young Bill getting tormented regularly. And Kerpelman arriving on the scene.

When he meets Murray, Kerpelman sees a family in all kinds of trouble: legal, financial, psychological. But he likes the issue itself. He charges Murray a thousand bucks for three years of work. Even in the fifties, this is considered cheap. In Murray's version of gratitude, she calls him "the dirty little attorney" behind his back.

And Kerpelman takes her case against prayer in public schools all the way to the U.S. Supreme Court, where Murray will stand on the sunlit front steps in front of television cameras and happily take all credit for pushing God out of the classroom.

In the fifties, the whole country couldn't imagine such a thing. God was on America's side back then. He got the whole country through the war, didn't he? His churches overflow on Sunday mornings when people wear dress-up outfits to express their full devotion and respect. In the fifties God has his own prime-time television show where Bishop Fulton J. Sheen with his purple cape delivers half-hour religious sermons. These are watched by millions and sponsored by corporations that can't wait to link their products with the good bishop's heavenly branding power. Meanwhile, the new Christian evangelists like Billy Graham and Oral Roberts are filling ballparks with rapturous followers. They will call themselves "born again." The phrase will stick forever.

So what was Madalyn Murray's problem?

"It takes," says Kerpelman, so many years later, "a little bit of intellect to be an American. And Madalyn was many things that were not particularly likeable, but she was smart and she was tough, and she was never going to back down to anybody."

"Including God," he's told.

"Especially God," Kerpelman says, "since she didn't believe in him anyway. She had this idea to make a big thing out of religion and prayer, and the church-and-state conflict, and she did. She liked the pressure. That was her métier. And, listen, she was right. She was right about organized prayer in schools and not afraid to say so. And this was a time when very few people would say it, even if they felt it. It was her, and me, and a lot of people hiding in the bushes."

In the fifties, nobody's challenging God or religion—nor any of its pop culture manifestations, which are everywhere. You turn on TV for that *Father Knows Best* program, and there's nice little Kathy Anderson, played by Lauren Chapin, kissing her doting dad, Robert Young, good night.

"Don't forget to say your prayers," says dad. "I'll say 'em twice," Kathy assures him.

Why twice?

"Forgot 'em last night," says Kathy.

This is a generation that came of age watching movies where men of God are always wise and trustworthy and would never cast a leering eye toward any children: Spencer Tracy in *Boys Town*, Bing Crosby in *Going My Way* and *The Bells of St. Mary's*.

In the movies it's not just the holy men we hold in esteem. There's angelic Audrey Hepburn, in *The Nun's Story*, shocked when she learns she'll have to work with "a man, a bachelor—and, I'm afraid, a non-believer."

Then there's Deborah Kerr, gazing upon the half-dressed Robert Mitchum on an island in the Pacific. They're all alone, except for some Japanese troops who eventually drop in since it turns out there's a war going on. The picture's called *Heaven Knows, Mr. Allison*. Mitchum's a U.S. Marine. He has sleepy bedroom eyes and a bare chest. But Kerr seems not to notice, for reasons immediately clear: she's married to God.

And the vows of the faithful shall trump all fevers of the flesh.

Across the decade, there are songs with religious themes that top the pop charts. You can't turn on a radio without hearing them: "I Believe" and "Three Bells" and "Little Jimmy Brown" and "He's Got the Whole World in His Hands."

In 1950, the number 1 fiction in America is *The Cardinal*. In '52, it's *The Silver Chalice*. In '53 it's *The Robe*. Affirmations of faith, every one. From '52 through '54, *The Holy Bible* is also the number 1 seller. It's listed under "Non-Fiction." In the fifties, nobody's questioning the good book's historic authenticity—not openly, anyway.

On September 30, 1952, two million people in three thousand communities attend meetings across America and Canada. They gather to celebrate the appearance of a book. It's the Revised Standard Version of the Bible. Within two months, roughly one and a half million copies are sold.

God's everywhere in the fifties. *Newsweek* declares, "Americans have become one of the most churchly people in the world," and later the *New York Times* notes that nonreligious people are "loosely regarded as something less than 100 percent patriotic." After all, the communists are godless, and we're locked in a cold war with those commie Russians. To believe in God is implicitly to support the country. A *Catholic Digest* national survey says 99 percent of Americans of all religious backgrounds are "absolutely certain" or "fairly sure" they believe in God.

In such an atmosphere, who could hear Madalyn Murray's voice crying against the national hallelujah chorus? "Religion," she declares, "has caused more misery to all of mankind in every stage of human history than any other single idea." That's an argument worth having—but nobody in America's having it in any kind of public setting at midcentury.

The National Council of Churches reports that nearly 60 percent of the U.S. population belongs to a church or synagogue—"an unprecedented high." Around the country, seminaries and theological schools have doubled in size since the prewar years; in 1955, there are more than 150,000 women in religious orders and more than 25,000 men in religious orders. They're so packed that some of them are forced to turn away applicants.

The daily newspapers are devoting a huge amount of space to religious features. Every Monday in Baltimore, readers of the *Evening Sun* get a full page of inspirational excerpts from area church sermons. Here's Hampden Methodist, here's Saint Paul's Episcopal, here's the Cathedral of the Assumption of the Blessed Virgin Mary. You read these newspaper pages, column after blessed column, week after blessed week, and find thousands of words about the glories of God and the joys of religious belief. Platitudes, every one, words of faith delivered as if taken straight from some ancient weathered parchment, connecting with the modern world's problems only by implication. But it's all right, that's their job. They're reinforcing the eternal verities, cementing them into place while the national mood's right. We haven't quite reached that time when white clergy lift their eyes from the holy scriptures and notice there's virulent racism in America, and some of them begin talking about it from the pulpit, and some belatedly join the civil rights movement. And we're still a decade away from those of the cloth challenging American war policy in distant Vietnam.

Anyway, lest anyone lose their way before next Sunday's sermons, at midweek there's another full newspaper page—"From the Choir Loft," it's called—devoted to dozens of churches' musical events. It's the full congregational choir set in linotype.

Give it to editors, they know their readers. In the fifties, new churches and synagogues are going up miraculously fast. Especially in the suburbs, the brand new Promised Land. Here we find all those white people who have bailed out of city neighborhoods. The churches follow their flocks. So do the newspapers. They run lovely stories about the new suburban churches while ignoring the empty cathedrals in the fretful neighborhoods left behind.

The great thinkers of the era connect the new religiosity to modern anxieties. God offers comfort. We're still suffering aftershock from the war and wondering about the arms race with the Russians. The Associated Press runs a big series on religious trends in America—"a phenomenal upsurge," says the AP—and senses "the insecurity of our time" behind much of it.

All of this, every bit of it, makes Madalyn Murray crazy with anger. She's been wrestling with notions of God since she was a Presbyterian teenager back in Akron, Ohio. The family had two books at home: a dictionary and a Bible. One long weekend Murray read the Bible from cover to cover.

"Shocking," she calls it later. "The miracles, the inconsistencies, the improbabilities, the impossibilities, the wretched history, the sordid sex, the sadism. I remember I looked in the kitchen at my mother and father and thought, Can they really believe in all that?"

Murray recounts this in 1965, two years after her Supreme Court case, when she's still being vilified by most of the country. She's lying in a hospital bed in Honolulu, where she's recovering from nerve injuries suffered in what she claims was a beating delivered by God-fearing police in Baltimore. She unburdens herself to *Playboy* magazine, which headlines the interview "a candid conversation with the most hated woman in America."

Recalling that distant time when she was still a believer, Murray says, "In church, my first memories are the minister getting up and accusing us of being full of sin, though he didn't say why. Then they would pass the collection plate, and I got it in my mind that this had to do with purification of the soul, that we were being invited to *buy* expiation from our sins. So I gave it all up. It was too nonsensical."

At twenty-two, just before Pearl Harbor, she marries a fellow named John Henry Roths. They separate shortly thereafter. He joins the U.S. Marines and she joins the WACs. The marriage essentially ends right there.

One night an army buddy calls her an atheist. She's never heard the word before. "So I looked it up," she said later, "and found out the definition fitted me to a tee. Finally, at the age of twenty-four, I found out who—and what—I was."

Madalyn's stationed in Italy as the war's winding down. Two things happen there: She takes her first poke at religion. And she has an affair with an army officer named William J. Murray Jr. One night their little gang gets drunk. Three in the morning, they slip into Saint Peter's Basilica by bribing a Swiss guard. What the heck, they're American military, the war's almost over, what could it hurt?

Champagne glasses in hand, they make their way to a glass case and find the three-tiered crown used in papal coronations. The moment carries not an ounce of reverence. They slip the crown from its case. They place it on Madalyn's head. They declare her the first female pope.

Anyway, that's the story Madalyn tells for the rest of her life. What's true beyond denial is this: she discovers she's pregnant. And, Vatican or not, female pope or not, this is no immaculate conception.

"We could get married," Madalyn tells William Murray Jr.

"Oh, no, we couldn't," says Murray. He's already married, and he's Catholic. Divorce is out of the question. It's not what Catholics do in the fifties.

And so are planted some more seeds of discontent with the power of religion. Who is this guy to leave her all alone? What is this religion to keep him away from their child? She begins calling herself Madalyn Murray. Along with the name, she takes on a new bitterness.

Home from the war, she goes to court and forces Murray to give her fifteen bucks a month in child support. But that's it. She's broke, she's living in squalor, and she's pregnant by a married guy whose religion makes Murray look like some tramp.

She goes to Ashland College, in Ohio. It's a religious school where she has to take two years of Bible study for graduation. Those two years confirm all her doubts about God and religion. Now, she figures, she's entitled to refute with authority.

In 1946 she gives birth to son Bill, graduates from college, and three years later receives a law degree from South Texas College of Law. But she never practices law. Later Bill will say his mother failed the bar exam, but Madalyn claims she never took it—because it required a religious oath.

Two years later comes another son, Jon Garth Murray, again without benefit of wedlock. She lands in Baltimore, with her parents, the two sons, her diaries full of misery, and a home life not exactly out of Norman Rockwell.

The Murrays, son Bill will write years later, were

not the typical American family, where a mom and the kids cuddled up on the couch with hot chocolate and popcorn to watch *Father Knows Best*. At my house we argued about the value of the American way, whether or not the workers should revolt, and why the pope, Christians, Jews—anybody who believed in God—were morons . . . Instead of talking and playing games, we cursed each other and screamed.

As Bill reaches adolescence the screaming's sometimes so bad that he spends the night at the Kerpelmans' house. But sometimes his mother makes sense to him when she talks about God. So, as Madalyn tells the story, her son confronts her.

"I don't believe in God, either," he says, so why must he say prayers in school? His mother has no answer.

And so comes the day when Madalyn Murray walks through Baltimore's Woodbourne Junior High, sees the morning prayers recited in every classroom, and decides she's ready to do battle with church and with state over what she deems their unholy alliance.

And this will send the whole country reeling.

By 1959 Murray looks at her life and decides she hasn't got a prayer. She has a law degree but never passed the bar. She has a social work job that pays her wages she considers insulting. And she lives in a nation where she's surrounded by people she considers idiots because they go to church and pray, and send their children to schools where they pray, and all of them worship a God who does not, in Murray's opinion, hear a single syllable of any of their entreaties.

She's a beefy woman with the heft of an Olympic shot-putter. Also, the demeanor. She throws her weight against the immediate world: her parents, her kids, her neighbors, school officials, and most especially a God she considers nonexistent and a religious culture she considers overbearing and unconstitutional.

Don't get in this woman's way.

"A tough, tough woman," the attorney Kerpelman recalls from the shelter of fifty years of distance, "and angry all the time. Oh, jeez, she was angry. And slovenly looking, didn't care how she dressed. And always fighting."

Mutual affection, this is not. In her diary, Murray calls Kerpelman "Sammy Shyster."

But he's the one who takes on Murray's fight against organized prayer in the public schools. He arrives when others have bailed out on Murray. She goes through two previous lawyers and makes them crazy. "Go fuck yourself," the last one told her as he walked out the door. She's embraced by the American Civil Liberties Union but makes them crazy. Kerpelman hangs on when he learns about Murray's son Bill getting beat up by classmates. The classmates' delicate sensibilities are offended because nobody's supposed to criticize religion in the fifties, and these kids have overheard their parents fuming about it. So the kids, thinking they're doing somebody a favor, become vigilantes. Atheism? It's not just sacrilegious, it's unpatriotic, isn't it? So it's Kerpelman who will put up with Murray for three years and take her fight all the way to the U.S. Supreme Court.

He might never represent a human being who is more impossible to like.

In 1953 she writes in her diary, "I am frustrated and bitter and full of hate . . . I am impossible to live with." All of the religious misgivings she's harbored since adolescence have now solidified in her mind. It's not just prayer in schools that bothers her. She's ticked off by "In God We Trust" on her money and "under God" in the pledge to the flag. Each night at dinner she goes into a familiar harangue. Anyone believing in God must be nuts, she tells her family.

But, all around her, American culture insists otherwise. There in the fifties, with the arrival of television, there also arrive God's surrogates, such as Bishop Fulton J. Sheen and the reverends Billy Graham and Oral Roberts, each raising his voice to full volume on heaven's behalf.

Whenever Murray turns on the television and sees such men, she becomes crazy with rage. She finds the show called *Life Is Worth Living*, starring Bishop Sheen, America's first nationwide televangelist. He's there in prime time every Tuesday like a night class, complete with blackboard and pointer.

The good bishop wears the vestments of his office, including the full cape and gold crucifix gleaming on his chest. He speaks without notes or TelePrompTer and always finishes his half-hour sermon precisely on time, like a miracle out of scripture. When the show first hits the airwaves, it's carried by three stations. Within two months, seventeen. A few months later, he's got a TV congregation of millions.

His point of view, says the *New York Times*, "reflects the doctrines of the Roman Catholic Church, but he is not using television for proselytizing or sectarian ends. His purpose is merely to induce the television viewer sitting at home to have a love of God." Also, a disdain for those the bishop does not love, such as Darwin and Freud and Karl Marx, and those ideas of theirs deemed dangerous by the good bishop.

Madalyn Murray practically has a coronary over this program.

For five years Bishop Sheen is so popular, he brushes aside a series of network competitors. When he wins an Emmy, Milton Berle cracks, "He's got better writers than me—Matthew, Mark, Luke, and John." Sheen is so popular, the Advertising Club of New York names him "Television Man of the Year" in 1953 for stressing "the great spiritual value of the American way of life" and for being "an implacable foe of communism."

Since communism is godless, it's the job of the church to fight it. The bishop is America's celestial weapon in the Cold War. One night in 1953 he devotes the show to a reading of the death scene from Shakespeare's *Julius Caesar*. But he substitutes the names of Joseph Stalin and his Soviet henchmen for Caesar, Cassius, Marc Antony, and Brutus.

"Stalin," Sheen proclaims, "must one day meet his judgment." A few days later the Russian dictator suffers a stroke. He's dead within the week. In 1950s American television, that's entertainment.

"I only want to help my sponsor, the good lord," Sheen modestly tells reporters.

Actually, God is only one of his sponsors. Others, wishing to sell television sets and cleaning products and vitamin candy for children, spend millions to sponsor the show. It's history's first nationally televised collection plate. This sets off a small storm of reaction—from other clergy.

"Religion is not an adjunct to the selling of commercial products," a New England pastor tells the *New York Times*. "And whoever consents to placing it in such a position has failed to express the basic integrity of faith . . . which is far too great to allow for any cheapening of its appeal, any subservience of it to the materialistic motives of anyone."

Clearly this pastor understands nothing of the power of the marketplace. Here in the fifties, Bishop Sheen has merely given us the opening vows in the marriage of money and television and all those purporting to speak for God. For soon there arrives a young preacher out of Oklahoma named Oral Roberts.

He mounts "healing crusades." He starts out in a traveling tent and winds up, with his florid hell-fire delivery, preaching on prime-time television. He takes Christianity, once the gospel of "blessed are the meek, for they shall inherit the earth," and drives it in a fancy limousine all the way to the heart of capitalism.

Roberts is the godfather of the "prosperity gospel." It's the linking of money and theology. Wealth is a sign that God is smiling down upon his most favored. Send your donations to me, Roberts tells the faithful, and God will repay every dollar seven times over. As anyone can see, this beats the stock market by a lot.

"His genius," writes Michelle Goldberg, author of *Kingdom Coming: The Rise of Christian Nationalism*, "was to market faith like an investment, one that would pay predictable dividends to true believers. Thus wealth became a sign of piety, and poverty a spiritual, rather than a material, condition."

Roberts takes in hundreds of millions of dollars across the years. In the summer of 1956 he says God has personally asked him, in audible tones, to win a million souls within one year. He claims to have a "healing" right arm through which the power of God flows like a current of electricity. Worshipers gather in a prayer line and pass before Roberts, who sits there like a sultan on an elevated stage.

Madalyn Murray goes apoplectic at such displays.

The young Rev. Billy Graham has his own lines of the faithful. He's an ordained Southern Baptist minister who initially gets mostly sneers from the media sophisticates. They call him a hillbilly holy roller.

Time declares, "He takes his listeners strolling down Pavements of Gold, introduces them to a rippling-muscled Christ who resembles Charles Atlas with a halo, then drops them abruptly into the Lake of Fire for a sample scalding. His language is a strange, original blend of farm-boy idiom, Shakespeare, the New Testament and the latest slang."

Graham tells a packed ballpark crowd, "Heaven is a literal place. Christians go there the moment they die, and there will be wonderful reunions as loved ones are recognized up there . . . What a glorious place it will be—with streets of gold, the gates of pearl . . . and the tree bearing a different kind of fruit every month. Think of that—you farmers—twelve crops a year!"

Graham produces his own radio and TV shows. He leads month-long crusades where he draws thousands to outdoor prayer sessions, his sermons backed by a choir of seven hundred voices.

By 1957, when Graham arrives in sophisticated New York to preach to a packed Madison Square Garden, the sneer has been removed from press coverage. The *New York Times* treats his arrival as a moment of historical significance, publishing the entire forty-five-minute text of his first sermon. Hearst's *Journal-American* sends its star reporter Dorothy Kilgallen out to cover Graham. She writes a five-part series that sounds almost biblical: "Billy has come to save the city from sin," she writes, "but the city knows him not."

He's gotten too big to criticize. He's part of that midcentury American full-bodied embrace of religion—the huge church attendance across the country, the swelling of religious schools and seminaries, the TV shows and movies and songs—and all of this pop culture reverence is driving Madalyn Murray absolutely nuts.

And then, in Murray's version, comes her son Bill telling her, "I'm like you, mom. I don't believe in God, either. So why do I have to go to school and pray with the other kids every day?"

As Madalyn tells it, Bill's challenge is her final impetus. As Bill tells the story years later, when he's become a born-again evangelical, it was mom pushing reluctant son. "My family," he tells the *New York Times*, "was the mother of all dysfunctional families . . . On a scale of normality from a zero to a ten, my family was a minus three."

Never mind who sets the final spark, Madalyn goes to war with Woodbourne Junior High in North Baltimore. She goes to war because school officials make her son listen to organized praying every morning, and in three years this will take not only the Murrays but all of America to the U.S. Supreme Court.

Murray first pulls Bill from class on October 12, 1960, and declares for all to hear that her son will not return as long as he's required to sit through the traditional morning Bible-reading ritual. The newspapers run stories about the protest—about this crazy mother who doesn't believe in God and about her son who inexplicably doesn't, either. And then angry Baltimoreans begin practically running the Murrays out of town.

Madalyn loses her social work job. She discovers nobody else wants to hire her. She gets endless telephone calls and letters from strangers—abusive, obscene, threatening. Her house and car are vandalized. Neighborhood kids throw bricks against the house.

God's got a lot of friends committing vandalism in his name.

When Bill gets bullied at school, Madalyn hauls some of these kids into court, but the courts repeatedly dismiss the cases. So Madalyn fights openly with judges, creating more headlines. Nobody comes out of this with clean hands. When neighborhood kids refuse to play with her younger son, Jon Garth, Madalyn buys the boy a kitten. A few weeks later the cat's found on the porch with its neck wrung.

Leonard Kerpelman still cringes at the memories. "This is why you get into the law," he says. "You want to help the underdog. And here was this boy, Bill, getting beat up by these other kids. His mother's the ultimate underdog, trying to take on God in his God-fearing postwar America. And Madalyn wasn't easy. I mean, sometimes she was cordial and fun, and a lot of the time she was very difficult to get along with. She was disrespectful of everybody, and she tried to use everybody, including me, and I resented that.

"But she was right about the issue. She was absolutely right. The constitution said so. Nobody stopped school kids from praying. To this day, they can still walk into a classroom and pray. They can fall down on the floor and pray, if that's what they want. Anybody can. You just can't have the schools say, 'This is when we will pray, because this is a Christian nation, and this is how we do things.' You know, this was not a tough case on the merits. Fact is, almost any case I ever had was tougher than this one."

He means "on legal grounds." But it sent America into emotional convulsions. It would take its toll on Kerpelman, too. Years later he's disbarred for allegedly overcharging a client. To this day Kerpelman believes it's retaliation for his fight against school prayer.

When the Murray case arrives in his life, Kerpelman's thirty-six, a man with a reputation for handling unpopular civil liberties cases. He had developed an outsider's identity early. He went through the public schools of Baltimore and remembers, "When I was big enough to start thinking about things, I'd wonder, 'Why are they talking about Jesus Christ in school?' They were doing this every day. It was very disturbing." And it helped him understand Murray's case.

But her case wasn't about specific religions, or one religion versus another, or one set of beliefs versus another. It was about the right not to believe at all and not to be challenged by the government because of it.

The country doesn't talk about such things in the fifties. In Cold War America the word *atheist* is attached instinctively to another word, *communism*. The Russians are coming to get us, and religion is what separates and protects us from the godless commies. If God is removed from the schools, then America's children will be left crouching out there in the hallways during their pathetic air raid drills, while Russian bombs fall from the unprotected godless heavens.

And all of this is Murray's in-your-face challenge to a nervous nation.

In the fifties, says Kerpelman, "If you were an American, you were made to feel you had to agree with the majority. Or else you weren't an American. But millions didn't agree. And they felt they had to remain silent. And we shouldn't ever be silent when it comes to the First Amendment."

So now we have young Bill Murray's protest over praying, and the next day's *Evening Sun* making a very big deal out of it, which is just what Madalyn wants. "Pupil in Bible Row Kept Out of Class," says the headline. Then Madalyn ups the ante.

"Mother Lists Text Objections," says the next morning's *Sun* headline. She's not just protesting compulsory Bible reading, she's going after any religious references in textbooks. Such as Bill's history book, *The Story of Nations*, which carries a painting by the Spanish artist Velázquez. Jesus's head is illuminated by a halo.

"I know of no historical evidence," Murray tells reporters, that Christ ever lived. Listeners cannot believe such blasphemy. She calls the resurrection "myth." She calls it contrary to all known science. Her words are printed in the newspapers.

Deal with it, America. This is only the beginning.

One day later the American Civil Liberties Union (ACLU), acting on Murray's behalf, formally asks the Baltimore school board to discontinue the reading of the Bible and reciting of the Lord's Prayer in school classrooms.

In Baltimore, people don't know what to make of all this. This woman's obviously crazy. In the fifties, who doesn't believe in God? And who doesn't believe in the Lord's Prayer to open the school day? The morning prayer is part of each day's comforting rituals, not only a religious gesture but a signal to parents that the eternal verities of school life still exist—even in this jittery time when the godless commies are practically at our door and, just as threatening, the courts have foisted racial integration into the schools and created anxieties that never before existed.

Murray doesn't care. She's finally found her reason for living. She writes a letter to the *Sun*:

Anybody in America can worship this alleged God in his own way, organize a church, publish religious books or magazines, operate a religious school and preach to his heart's content. This is fine, but please, "Include us out." We atheists and agnostics want only the freedom of our opinion. We desire to be excluded from your collective madness.

We desire not to have this forced upon us against our good conscience and our considered convictions.

Madalyn appears to be taunting the entire culture. When Bill goes to school, the other kids call him names. They tell him he should move to Russia. He gets pushed around in the schoolyard, in the hallways. One day outside a shopping center, some tough guys shove him in front of an approaching bus.

Six months after Murray files suit to bar organized praying, Baltimore Judge J. Gilbert Prendergast turns her down. Never mind Madalyn's claim that Bill's "religious liberty" is violated, says the judge, he cannot understand "just how the religious liberty of a person who has no religion can be endangered."

You can hear the sigh of relief around Baltimore: the center is holding; the old institutions are keeping the crazies from taking hold.

But such perceptions are wrong, for this is only the beginning of three years of Murray and Kerpelman working their way through their legal appeals. And politicians weighing in. And clergy weighing in.

And Bill moving up to high school at Baltimore Polytechnic, where he tries so hard to fit in, to find a friend, that he joins the United Nations Club, and the Chess Club, and the Ham Radio Club, and the Debate Club.

And continues to get beat up all over the place.

To say that Madalyn Murray drove God from the public schools isn't strictly accurate, but it certainly sounded good to Madalyn.

There were a couple of similar cases in that same era. In 1962 the ACLU brought suit on behalf of five families in New Hyde Park, New York, who objected to a prayer composed by state officials for daily recitation. The Supreme Court, in *Engel v. Vitale*, ruled that even a nondenominational prayer was religious and that "it is no part of the business of government to compose official prayers for any group of the American people to recite."

A year later came two separate suits challenging Bible reading. One, *Abington School District v. Schemp*, out of Philadelphia, was brought before the Supreme Court at the same time as Murray's suit.

But it's Murray who's out there taking bows on the front steps of the high court when the verdict's in and reporters and photographers gather. And it's Murray happily taking credit for expelling God from America's schools and Murray who's glad to absorb America's wrath for the remaining decades of her life.

"The odd thing," Leonard Kerpelman says now, recalling January 26, 1963, when the Murray case finally reached the Supreme Court, "is that I felt no pressure at all." He smiles wryly at the memory. Analysts around the country were calling it the most important, and certainly the most emotional, Supreme Court case since school integration nearly a decade earlier.

"Don't get me wrong," he says. "I was nervous. Hell, I got nervous handling parking ticket cases. And this is the Supreme Court, and the whole country's watching. I'm as nervous as anybody in the history of nervousness. But I started to give my brilliant oration, and I no sooner opened my mouth when the justices started throwing stuff to each other. And I just sort of stood there. And it became fun."

Later, Murray will write that the justices were clearly on her side, their questions "so leading, so obvious . . . that I thought I was Snow White in the friendly cabin of the Seven Dwarfs."

It's as though the justices have been waiting for this moment. Americans will be outraged—but they'll have to get over it, because as the fifties begin to die, just months before John Kennedy goes to Dallas, God in the public school classroom also begins to fade away.

First Kerpelman offers a few words about the separation of church and state. It is unconstitutional, he says, to have organized prayers led by public school teachers. It is unconstitutional to have Bible reading in class. It's been condoned for so long, he says, that its supporters claim it's traditional—but anything unconstitutional in the first place doesn't become constitutional just because it's become traditional.

Justice Potter Stewart interrupts. "If we strike this prayer down," he says, "we are interfering with the majority's right to free exercise of their religion. You are entirely free. Why not just walk out? You are not required to participate."

And here the argument goes beyond the mechanics of the law. You walk out of a classroom when others pray, Kerpelman tells the court, and you mark yourself. You're no longer like the others. Now you're an outsider, you're an unbeliever. You're a target. Never mind the intricacies of the legal system; this is about the laws of human nature.

"This boy was spat upon, insulted, actually assaulted," Kerpelman says.

Then he's cut off again. This time it's Justice Hugo Black. He's talking directly to Justice Stewart, addressing this notion of the freedom to simply walk out of a classroom full of praying students. The two of them go back and forth on it. Then comes Justice Arthur Goldberg. He wants to talk about constitutional issues. Where do we draw the line on free speech?

Kerpelman's very careful here. He says he has no objection to teaching the Bible as history or as literature. He's not even objecting to prayer itself. Let students get together voluntarily, he says, and say the Lord's Prayer each morning before school starts. Let them have a moment of silent devotion. But there has to be a separation of church and state and, thus, a removal of organized praying.

Francis B. Burch, the Baltimore city solicitor, argues the other side. "The wall of separation between church and state," he tells the justices, "is not an absolute, finite, unyielding wall." And the morning ritual is not strictly religious, he says. Rather, it has a "sobering influence" on students.

He's gone too far on that one.

"You could just give them tranquilizer pills if that's the purpose," says Justice Stewart.

Burch counters that he's referring to discipline and moral ideals. The morning prayers might be framed as religious observances, but they're really about secular ideals.

Again he's gone too far.

Chief Justice Earl Warren drolly asks, "Wouldn't an entire religious service in a school instead of this brief exercise serve these same moral purposes even better?"

Thomas Finan, Maryland's attorney general, sees Burch getting nowhere, so he pipes up. Individual states, he says, should be free to decide the issue.

"Even if it means Mormon prayers in Utah?" one justice asks. "Even if it means Buddhist prayers in Hawaii?" asks another.

"Yes," says Finan.

But, like Burch, he's gone too far.

"Then the big contest," says Justice William O. Douglas, "would be which church gets control of the school board."

In March 1963—midway between the legal arguments and the court delivering its decision—*Life* magazine vents its emotions but good. The magazine is a powerful voice in mainstream American culture, with millions of readers, and its editors wish to advise the justices about the difference between right and wrong, in case they're having any trouble making the distinction themselves.

Outlawing prayer in schools, *Life* declares, would "offend the nation's natural piety and sense of its own past . . . The Bible is better in school than in court . . . [Removing prayer would be] a radical break with the American past [and is more likely] to lead us into darkness than into light."

That's all Madalyn needs to see. Nobody gets the last word with this woman. A lifetime of rage pours out of her, and never mind any sense of diplomacy. For Madalyn, talking back to *Life* magazine is like talking back to America. It's as if she's been waiting her whole life for this very moment. Her atheistic position, she writes, is

> founded in science, in reason and in love for fellow man rather than in a love for God . . . we find the Bible to be nauseating, historically inaccurate, replete with the ravings of madmen. We find God to be sadistic, brutal and a representation of hatred, vengeance. We find the Lord's Prayer to be that muttered by worms groveling for meager existence in a traumatic, paranoid world . . . This is not appropriate dicta to be forced on adult or child. The business of the public schools, where attendance is compulsory, is to prepare children to face the problems on earth, not to prepare for heaven—which is a delusional dream of the unsophisticated minds of the ill-educated clergy.

Life is flooded with letters, as anticipated. Unanticipated, however, is this: according to *Life*, the letters are "evenly divided, pro and con." Something is beginning to shift in parts of the American religious consciousness.

On June 17, 1963, the court releases its opinion in both the *Murray* and *Schemp* cases. The vote is eight to one. The justices say the laws requiring Bible reading and prayer recitation violate First Amendment rights. Only Justice Stewart dissents—and even he admits conflicted feelings.

Justice Tom C. Clark, writing the majority opinion, declares,

> The place of religion in our society is an exalted one, achieved through a long tradition of reliance on the home, the church and the inviolable citadel of the human heart and mind.
>
> We have come to recognize through bitter experience that it is not within the power of government to invade that citadel . . . In the relationship between man and religion, the state is firmly committed to a position of neutrality.

Notice the language:

—"Exalted" religion.
—Religion in the "citadels of home and church."
—And the "inviolable citadel of the human heart."
—The government—that is, the schools—aren't worthy of invading such lofty places.

The justices, knowing their verdict will send convulsions through the whole country, are attempting to turn the argument on its head. It's not that the kids shouldn't pray in school—it's that schools aren't a worthy place for prayer! They're trying to soft-peddle the fact that they've just thrown a bomb into the center of America's religious customs and comforts, and they're trying to show America that religion isn't being attacked here, it still has a special place and, in fact, it belongs in a place more holy than a scruffy school room.

Well, let the justices choreograph their decision any way they want—millions of Americans are outraged and will remain so over the coming decades.

And Madalyn Murray doesn't care. She's out there on the courthouse steps moments after the decision arrives. She's talking to everybody, posing for photos with family members, taking full credit for sending God home from school. And she's declaring herself happy with the triumph, and happy with the court, and she can't wait to pack up her family and get them the hell out of Baltimore.

The feeling is mutual. She'll be vilified by millions for the rest of her life, and her name cursed, and Madalyn will revel in this. She'll spend the next several decades fighting organized religion, fighting organized prayer, asking why the churches are tax-exempt, filing lawsuits hither and yon.

In 1980 her son William has a change of heart about God and religion. He takes up work as a Baptist preacher. He calls his mother an "evil" person. Madalyn, never one to yield the last word, describes their parting as a "post-natal abortion . . . I repudiate him entirely and completely for now and all times."

All of this woman's wars end in 1995. Madalyn, her younger son Jon, and granddaughter Robin Murray O'Hair are kidnapped and murdered by a man who had worked for Madalyn's American Atheist office.

But Murray's work lives on, for better or worse. In the wake of the Supreme Court ruling—just months before Dallas and the end of the innocent fifties—organized prayer was forever removed from morning classroom rituals in America's public schools.

Disorganized prayer—the kind that flourishes among frantic students just before exams—remains forever.

Nobody at Forest Park High School imagined Barry Levinson would go to Hollywood and immortalize midcentury Baltimore's Hilltop Diner. But here's Levinson, in an Orioles cap, directing *Diner*, the film *Vanity Fair* called "the most influential movie of the last 30 years."

The Diner Guy
Barry Levinson

Barry Levinson in his teens is every teacher's best bet to go nowhere. He hides his intelligence as though fearful it could lead to respectable grades. The comic credo, in his high school crowd, is that studying's considered a form of cheating. Most of these guys get by on natural smarts. Nobody wants to crack open a book when there's Elvis deep into the night on the radio, and Sergeant Bilko and Sid Caesar on the TV, and occasional girls who might let you get all the way to second base even though it's only the 1950s.

At Forest Park High School in northwest Baltimore, Levinson finishes last in his class of June 1960 and doesn't know if he'll graduate until the final day of his senior year. The kids who dutifully memorized all their irregular French verbs and their kings of England will traipse off in the fall for brainy Harvard and Yale, or at least the University of Maryland, assured that they have a promising future in the American professional class if they just keep cracking the books for another four years. Levinson's headed for Baltimore Junior College, sometimes known as thirteenth grade.

It's impossible to believe this kid will make some of the most admired movies of his generation, including those which become anthems of life in Baltimore in the fifties. He is a sponge. He soaks up all the pop culture of the era and makes it his professional inventory. He'll make his way to California and write for TV programs such as the *Carol Burnett Show*. He'll write movies with Mel Brooks. When they chat between shots, Levinson tells Brooks about this crazy place where he hung out as a kid, called the Hilltop Diner.

In the postwar years the diner's the central meeting place to kibitz for that first generation migrating from the inner city out to the inner suburbs of northwest Baltimore. They're the people who previously gathered by their little front stoops to escape the confines of narrow row houses. They sat there waiting for a summer breeze to cool them off. They caught up on the business of the day with their neighbors. They watched their kids play in the street and hollered at them to watch out for small annoyances, such as Baltimore Transit Company buses bearing down on them.

But those row-house neighborhoods are behind them now, and everybody's spreading out. So the diner's a new front stoop. The place is open all night. It's people talking to each other in a crowded room, and staying up as late as they want, and creating an energy instead of the isolation that will come one day with twenty-four-hour cable TV, and computers and video games, and air conditioning in every new home. At the diner, people arrive after the drudgery of the day: aluminum siding tin men and racetrack junkies and parents who arrive after their kids' PTA meetings. Or those who bowled a couple of duckpin games at the Hilltop Lanes around the corner or gathered at one of political boss Jack Pollack's Trenton Democratic Club meetings, where they'd ask Pollack to get their traffic tickets fixed by a cooperative downtown judge.

And the teenage boys like Levinson would drive past with their Saturday night dates to check whose cars were parked out front. If their buddies had arrived, they had the awful dilemma: Which is better, the potential for a make-out session or hanging out with a bunch of funny guys?

So, figuring the odds in the 1950s, they dropped off their dates and went back to the diner, whose stories Levinson relates years later to Mel Brooks. And it's Brooks who tells him: This place has *movie* written all over it.

Thus, Levinson makes *Diner*. On the cover of its March 2012, issue *Vanity Fair* magazine calls this "The Most Influential Movie of the Last 30 Years." Then Levinson goes on to make *Rain Man* and *Good Morning, Vietnam* and *The Natural* and *Bugsy*, and he'll capture the media insanity of the Bill Clinton sex scandal with *Wag the Dog*, and along the way he'll add three movies about midcentury life in Baltimore: *Tin Men* and *Avalon* and *Liberty Heights*.

But now in the fifties he sits in this crowded high school classroom, in the midst of some essay test on *Silas Marner*, maybe, or *Ivanhoe*, and refuses to put pen to paper. Forget it, he's just not in the mood to participate.

Around him, all these earnest college-bound kids are scribbling madly away. Levinson writes his name at the top of the paper, and then he puts down his pen. He's sixteen years old, and he's declared all that he wishes to declare: name, homeroom, and date, nothing further, like he's a prisoner of war who knows his rights. Let the others regurgitate all that literary bullshit about symbolism in *Beowulf*. Levinson's staring out the window toward puffy clouds. He's got larger matters on his mind, such as who might show up Friday night at the diner, or maybe Mandel's Delicatessen across the street, where the local jargon consists entirely of slices of wry.

More than half a century later, he recalls this little classroom rebellion of his with gentle affection. He likes that kid back there. "I had no problem putting my name on a piece of paper and not filling out anything," he says, chuckling at the memory. "Just don't fill it out, whatever the subject. Pass or fail, that's the only thing I was concerned with. Some people would fret over grades. To me, grades didn't matter at all. I didn't see any difference between a C or a B. My main thing was avoiding summer school. That gave me my adrenaline. There was a little drama connected to that line between passing or failing, you know? I kind of liked the drama."

The couldn't-care-less attitude punctuates his Baltimore movies. In *Diner*, the smart-ass Fenwick smashes some windows and explains: "It's a smile." He isn't a bad kid—he's just a kid. In *Tin Men*, wise-guy aluminum siding salesmen scam the uptight system anywhere they can spot an opening. They're boys forced by time into impersonating men. A Jewish kid in *Liberty Heights* gives his family heart failure when he dresses up for Halloween—as Hitler. Then there's little Michael, in *Avalon*, whose teacher banishes him into the hall because he isn't paying attention. She thinks she's punishing him. When the old lady turns her back, the kid does a happy little dance, thrilled to be liberated from the maximum security confines of a second-grade classroom.

They're all oddballs, out of step, testing society's calcified midcentury boundaries, and dancing out there on its edges because the safe postwar center's so crowded that it's suffocating in there.

So now Levinson sits in class, a laconic high school kid allowing nothing out of distant, irrelevant nineteenth-century literature to violate his brain. Let the others write their hearts out about Silas Marner; let the brown-nosers impress the teacher with their terribly insightful recitations about Ivanhoe. On this particular day, who knows what's going through Levinson's head?

This is the generation that's just beginning to shake off the expectations of their elders. Rock and roll's part of it, but there's more. One night in 1953 Levinson's in his parents' living room watching TV's *Goodyear Playhouse*. It's an original play by Paddy Chayevsky called *Marty*, later an Academy Award–winning movie, about a middle-aged Italian American butcher trying to break loose from his mother's apron strings.

The dialogue that stays with Levinson is the simplest stuff of everyday discourse between a couple of guys. It will become a pop cultural refrain.

Angie: What do you want to do tonight, Marty?
Marty: I don't know, Ang, what do you want to do?

Nearly sixty years later, Levinson says, "I thought that was the greatest dialogue I ever heard in my life. It was conversational. It was like you talked with your friends. What it was about didn't actually matter. It's not about story, it's about behavior. It was the simplicity of it. And that's what leads to *Diner*."

Modell: You gonna eat the rest of that sandwich?
Eddie: You want it?
Modell: No, I just thought, if you're not gonna eat it . . .
Eddie: You want it? If you want it, just say so.
Modell: No, I just . . .

"It sounds," says Levinson, "like they just made it up."

Controlled improvisation, it's now called. He wants characters to talk like people, not people talking like movie characters. When Levinson started casting for *Diner*, he sat down with actors such as Daniel Stern and tried something new. He didn't have a script reading, he had a conversation. It was just two guys kibitzing instead of saying lines. Levinson wanted a sense of who his prospective actors were. Could they ad-lib? Did they have the right conversational rhythm? Could they make it sound like real-life patter from the original diner days?

When Levinson showed the rough cut to studio executives, they didn't get it. They wanted the kibitzing scenes, the scraps of dialogue that didn't advance a story line but added texture to his characters, cut from the movie. Levinson said, "No cuts." The studio suits backed down.

In *Diner*, the veteran film critic Michael Sragow would later write, Levinson "crystallized the 'observational' humor that would dominate American comedy for decades, whether in TV series like *Seinfeld*, Larry David's *Curb Your Enthusiasm* or Judd Apatow's stream of big-screen hits." It wasn't just reaching for the joke, it was guys shooting the bull and things happening based on character.

There's another moment out of the fifties that stays with Levinson through the decades. It's the Gwynn Theatre on Liberty Heights Avenue one Saturday afternoon, and he's watching something he'd never previously witnessed on a movie screen: an image of real life.

The movie is *On the Waterfront*, with Marlon Brando as the longshoreman Terry Malloy. Levinson's bowled over. As is the rest of America. The movie's about naming names, about turning on your friends when you think they've gone wrong. It's about exploitation of the working class. Also, to the discerning watcher, it's about manner.

"The behavior," Levinson says, thus echoing the fundamental instruction of Brando's acting teacher, Stella Adler. "Don't act," she told her postwar students. "Behave."

This isn't Lawrence Olivier, previously considered the great role-model actor, with his perfect elocution and his chiseled theatrical features, it's Brando with his handsome, damaged face and his pained, fumbling inarticulateness. Brando, the critic Richard Schickel later writes, was "a star to lead a revolution—against the well-spoken, emotionally disconnected acting style that had long prevailed . . . His needs and rages somehow spoke for a silent generation, privately nursing our grievances at the bourgeois serenity of our elders."

It was James Dean who starred in *Rebel without a Cause*, but it was Brando who understood that the urge to rebel was a cause in itself. And all those kids like Levinson, sitting in the darkness of movie theaters across the country, understood this instinctively in the cautious, uptight 1950s.

In *On the Waterfront*, Brando's an ex-fighter and a punk for the mob, but he's also an open wound, and he's all alone as he moves from confusion to rage. He's up against John Friendly, played by Lee J. Cobb, the mob boss who's exploiting dock workers. Alfred Kazin will write, "Cobb no more resembled a tough dockside Irishman than Menachem Begin does, but he did carry the sense of a life that had begun with a tenement childhood, that ethnic memory of being put upon."

The key word here is *ethnic*. In the fifties, movies are still shying away from certain minorities. America likes to call itself a melting pot. We're not supposed to notice our differences; it's considered a little bit rude. Levinson notices. To notice isn't to denigrate, it's to open a door to telling new kinds of stories and celebrating them. The lesson stays with him: Look for the unnoticed people, the ones along the edges, the ones America hasn't exactly heard from yet.

In *Diner*, there are stretches of dialogue that might echo bull sessions from fifty years ago at his old hangout. It's funny stuff, but it's not one-liners for superficial chuckles. These sound like real postwar guys poised somewhere between adolescence and adulthood, hungry for a little sexual action and cracking wise to cover their envy and their disbelief that one of the guys might actually score.

"I'm taking out Carol Heathrow," says Boogie, played by Mickey Rourke.

"You're taking out Carol Heathrow?" says a stunned Fenwick (Kevin Bacon).

"No, *you're* taking her," says Boogie.

As if.

"She is death," says Shrevie (Daniel Stern).

"You want to bet she goes for my pecker on the first date?" says Boogie.

"The only hand on your pecker is gonna be your own," says Fenwick.

"You want to bet me twenty bucks?"

"I'm in . . . But we'll need validation for this."

"All right," says Boogie, "I'll arrange it."

"How?" says Shrevie. "You gonna get finger prints? I'm telling you, I'm not gonna do the dusting."

There's something else going on here besides the sexual give-and-take of horny midcentury young men. They're ethnics—they're Jewish. The scene takes place in 1959, when we're only a few heartbeats past World War II and the devastation of the Jews. If Hollywood paid any explicit attention to Jews of that era, they were still portrayed as victims: as the Holocaust survivors of *Exodus* and *The Pawnbroker*, as targets of American anti-Semitism in *Gentleman's Agreement*.

The guys in *Diner* are incidentally Jewish, but they're mainly American, and they're like any other Americans of their age and era: talking football, cracking wise, getting into misdemeanors, and holding high-level debates on the make-out virtues of Frank Sinatra versus Johnny Mathis. They're nobody's victims. They're openly expressing a rambunctious, wise-ass spirit previously kept under wraps—and announcing, maybe for the first time in an American movie, that they are full, un-self-conscious citizens of a nation where Jews had felt so marginalized, and so muted, for so long.

In *Diner*, Levinson offers a soundtrack that's equal parts rock and roll and standard midcentury pop. Jerry Lee Lewis and Dion are there, but so is Jane Morgan. Fats Domino and Elvis are there, but so is the spirit of Sinatra and Mathis.

It's a reflection of the cultural crossroads the country's reached, the choices that are about to be made. It's in the music, and it's on the television.

The sixties are beginning to come into view. Soon it will be time for parents to lock up their children, if they can find them.

The teenage kids—especially the ones out there in suburbia—are now driving around at all hours of the night. What are they supposed to do, walk? Everything's too spread out now. They're driving around, and they're playing rock and roll up loud on the car radio, and they're looking for parties to crash, like Kenny Waissman.

Unless they were like a new kid in the midcentury adolescent consciousness, named Holden Caulfield. In an era when young people still value the written word, they're discovering J. D. Salinger's *Catcher in the Rye*. Enough with *Ivanhoe*, enough with *Silas Marner*. The street-corner language, and Holden Caulfield's sullen sense of rebelliousness, will change young people's lives—and, when adults call the book obscene and try to stop them from reading it, they only succeed in making the book seem cooler.

As the country moves from the Eisenhower era to John Kennedy's, there are high school English teachers brave enough to assign *Catcher* to their students, who read the book and hear a language never previously heard in assigned school literature: their own. Holden could be a kid from homeroom. He's insecure, like them, and hiding it behind a mask. Also, like them. He's voicing familiar misgivings at a time when they're feeling alienated from their parents' materialism and conformity.

The first words out of Holden's mouth sound so familiar in tone and texture: "If you really want to hear about it, the first thing you'll probably want to know is where I was born and what my lousy childhood was like, and how my parents were occupied and all before they had me, and all that David Copperfield kind of crap, but I don't feel like going into it, if you want the truth."

For those stumbling onto the shores of adolescence when they read this, it sounds like the voice in their own heads. Maybe they don't understand exactly why they feel this way, but they do. And maybe this Caulfield kid will explain it to them. At the very least, he validates a generation's disaffection and its sense of alienation.

When *Catcher* first appears, in 1951, nobody in America's talking about adolescent alienation. We'd just emerged from the forties, when everybody was still busy trying to win a war. *Catcher* offers a permission slip to let loose with all these pent-up emotions, all that dread that previously seemed too self-indulgent for postwar adolescents.

Barry Levinson was among the millions mesmerized by *Catcher*. It's five decades later, but he still remembers that kid back at Baltimore's Forest Park High School, feeling slightly suffocated by the mainstream culture and finding himself with another English paper to write. And another failing grade, most likely. So he figures he'll take a chance. He'll write this book report as though he's Holden Caulfield. "If you really want to know the truth of it, I hate to write book reports," he writes.

"I was trying to mimic Holden's voice," he remembers now. This is completely revolutionary for a high school classroom and utterly unacceptable. At this time, all high school English compositions are expected to mirror the linguistic stylings of nineteenth-century English noblemen. It's such a brilliant notion by the great thinkers in education—pushing aside traces of all original voice—that it will turn off generations of would-be writers (and readers). But Levinson goes further.

"I wrote another paper," he remembers, "that was one sentence long and went three pages. It was about World War II. Just one long stream-of-consciousness sentence. And you know you're gonna fail when you write one sentence, but . . . I liked that it was unconventional. That was important."

You break convention or suffocate. You keep looking around the culture, at its movies and music and books, and choosing what feels right and what doesn't. When it doesn't feel right, you start to push at its margins.

Holden becomes the spokesman for a generation. As Kenneth Slawenski will write in *J. D. Salinger: A Life*:

> The call to rebellion that the public had come to associate with Salinger's work began to bleed into mainstream society. The theatre became infused with the ideas of playwrights . . . who depicted the alienation of individuals in conventional society in ways remarkably concurrent with the complaints of Holden. American book shelves began to collect works of writers such as John Updike and Kurt Vonnegut, authors who had been profoundly influenced by Salinger . . . Not even Hollywood was immune to Salinger's influence. James Dean was in many way Holden personified.

As was Brando, who would follow. And Presley, whether he understood it or not. And the young Bob Dylan.

Catcher gives young people license. It opens a door, gives the go-ahead to feel rebellious, to test dangerous waters where young people hadn't previously dipped more than a toe.

As the culture loosens up Americans begin to discover a new kind of humor, as well. We're finding laughs where we never laughed before. A new generation of stand-up comics gives up mother-in-law jokes for a new brand of cynicism.

There's Mort Sahl, whose material reads like outtakes from the daily newspapers. Like Bob Hope, he's got jokes about Eisenhower and golf—but with more slice. When Arkansas's Little Rock High School closes the door to black students, Sahl cracks that Ike was going to make the grand gesture "and walk a little Negro girl to school by the hand. But he couldn't decide whether to use an overlapping grip."

There's Lenny Bruce. On Bruce's album cover he's having a picnic—at a cemetery. The old folks call this "sick humor." Teenage girls are cautioned by their protective parents not to listen to this material, lest they hear curse words (as though such language is never uttered at home). Teenage boys, meanwhile, gather by the hour in club basements and memorize these new comic routines word for word and repeat punch lines to each other like a secret tribal language. The material's not only a hoot but slightly subversive, which naturally adds to the enjoyment.

Bruce is the one who gets to Barry Levinson. Now remembered as part comedian and part martyr, Bruce got busted for cursing in public. But he was also taking on issues that made some listeners squirm. He said people were "straying from the church and going back to God."

Levinson was knocked over by Bruce's material. "At that time," he says, "nobody thought a comic was cool. The comics we knew were Milton Berle, Myron Cohen, Buddy Hackett. Those kinds."

One night Levinson's hanging out with his usual crowd at the Hilltop Diner. Lenny Bruce is doing a one-nighter at the Lyric Theater. Levinson says, "Let's go down there." The other guys are lukewarm. The only comics they know are the old farts spouting Borscht Belt material that's flat as seltzer water opened long past its expiration date.

"But we went," Levinson remembers. "Five of us. And there weren't a lot of people there, and the first five minutes, there weren't many laughs. But then he started talking about gas money, about guys chipping in for gas when you're driving around town. It hit a nerve. It was finally something we could relate to. And then he's talking about dating and then about getting laid.

"And I remember distinctly, at the diner later that night, we're all saying how it felt like hanging out with one of the guys. Comedy was something we understood, as opposed to what came before us, which we didn't understand. It's what was relevant to our lives. And this was the first guy connecting to our lives. He wasn't just a comic, he was a commentator. That was the real connection. Lenny was the first to do that for us. Everything else was following in his footsteps."

Levinson makes a lot out of television in *Avalon*. It's his third Baltimore film, after *Diner* and *Tin Men*, but it's earlier chronologically. TV's just arriving in everybody's living room. The whole extended family gathers around the first set as the thing is pulled from its delivery box and turned on.

Everybody stares. Since it's still the early 1950s and it's afternoon, there's nothing on the screen but an unchanging test pattern. But, since it's television, everybody keeps staring anyway. They've never seen such a thing.

"So that's television," somebody finally says.

"Better hope they start getting some more interesting programs."

Then, maybe twenty minutes into the movie, the TV's a visible presence in nearly every nighttime interior shot. Who needs front stoops to chat with neighbors, who needs family around, when there's entertainment waiting right there in the living room?

But, in the fifties, all of this was still bubbling subconsciously in Levinson's head. He was living on Springdale Avenue, a short walk to both Garrison Junior High and Forest Park Senior High. These schools, and the neighborhood, were then overwhelmingly Jewish. Levinson never gave it a second thought.

"We didn't know we were a minority," he says, "until we began to get driver's licenses. Then somebody would have a car, and for the first time you'd leave your own neighborhood. You found out there was a place called Loch Raven and a place called Roland Park. And there were great looking girls out there. We began to realize the world wasn't Jewish. And then you realized almost no one in the world is Jewish. We'd been completely isolated. Who in the hell would know there were people out there who weren't Jewish?"

That was the nature of Baltimore neighborhoods in the postwar years: a series of ethnic isolations. The Jews here, the various white gentiles in their own ethnic pockets, the blacks restricted to theirs but beginning to break out.

Levinson's family moved to Springdale Avenue in northwest Baltimore, just as millions more postwar white families were headed to the suburbs all over America.

"Ever been in the suburbs?" the little boy Michael asks a cousin in *Avalon* as moving day arrives. They live across the street from each other.

"I never even heard of the suburbs until this thing happened," the cousin replies.

The exodus was fueled by many things. The cities were crowded, and the suburbs offered space for growing families. Children could stretch their limbs. The cities' old row houses were falling apart, and the suburbs had new homes being built by the hour. These new homes had picture windows. The pricier ones had air conditioning. The schools were newer out there. And, never to be minimized, those schools and the surrounding neighborhoods were still white.

For a while.

By the autumn of 1954, the first full year after the Supreme Court integrated the nation's public schools, no blacks had yet arrived at Garrison Junior High. It stayed that way through Levinson's years there. At Forest Park High, he remembers three blacks.

"But there was so little contact, it was almost like a curiosity," he recalled. "I think we didn't understand them. It was never, 'Why are you here?' Nobody was challenging their right to be there. But we didn't understand what was going on, we'd had so little contact."

When Levinson and his pals weren't hanging out at the Hilltop Diner, they'd cross busy Reisterstown Road and hang at Mandel's Deli. One night, Levinson recalls, maybe half a dozen black people came to the restaurant, which still refused to serve African Americans. It was the late 1950s.

"And I remember thinking," he says, " 'They live down in West Baltimore. Why would they come all the way up here just for a corned beef sandwich?' We were so naive. It didn't even occur to me that they were trying to integrate the place—and getting turned away."

Clarence Mitchell stares down the mob. White parents stand outside Baltimore's Gwynns Falls Park Junior High as Mitchell's son Keiffer attempts to enter after the U.S. Supreme Court ordered integration of the nation's public schools. The mob shouts, "Go back to Africa." The sign is Mitchell's response. (Courtesy Denton Watson)

"I Am An American, Too"
Clarence Mitchell Jr. and Thurgood Marshall

In 1933 Clarence Mitchell Jr. graduates from Lincoln University and lands work as a reporter for Baltimore's *Afro-American* newspaper. The salary is fifteen dollars a week, and he's lucky to get it in the endless Depression. At this time the *Afro-American* has thirteen editions around the country and reaches several hundred thousand readers. The big numbers come from a disgraceful fact of American journalism that lingers deep into the innocent 1950s and beyond: in the nation's daily newspapers, owned and operated entirely by white people, news coverage of the lives of black people is limited strictly to acts of crime or sport. There's news from London and Lower Slobovia, sure. But coverage of those persons living a mile away in black West Baltimore? This is considered a foreign land too distant to cover.

And so, having no other place to find news about their lives, black readers breathe vigorous economic life into black-owned newspapers.

The *Afro*'s editor is Carl Murphy, a diminutive black man with a master's degree from Harvard who holds the newspaper's top job for forty-five years. Within that lengthy era comes George Armwood, a twenty-three-year-old man who lives with his mother on Maryland's Eastern Shore. Armwood allegedly assaults a seventy-one-year-old woman named Mary Denston but runs off when she screams. Denston is white, Armwood black. The mob that gathers a day after Armwood's arrest is all white, and they pull the terrified Armwood from his jail cell, cut off his ears, and pull gold teeth from his mouth. His body is hanged from the branch of an oak tree on an old woman's front lawn near the jail.

Clarence Mitchell Jr. is sent to Princess Anne to cover the story.

"This," says Michael Mitchell, "was my father's real awakening about man's inhumanity to man. He had the tough years growing up, but he always said this was the turning point. You know, he came out of college wanting to be a doctor, but found work at the *Afro* to support himself. And then this moment that really makes him rededicate his life—to calling on the fundamental decency in people."

Editor Murphy sends forth the young Mitchell, along with a photographer named Henderson and a reporter named Jolley. On the Eastern Shore they find Armwood's brutalized corpse still on display, intended as a grotesque signal to other blacks: Go ahead, step out of line. This could happen to you.

On October 21, 1933, Mitchell puts these details into his front-page story for the paper:

> Silent groups of our people on their way to work . . . solemnly gazed at the horribly-mangled corpse which had been stripped of all clothing and was covered with two sacks. The skin of Armwood was scorched and blackened while his face had suffered many blows from sharp and heavy instruments.
>
> A cursory glance revealed that one ear was missing and his tongue between clenched teeth gave evidence of his great agony before death. There is no adequate description of the mute evidence of gloating on the part of whites who gathered to watch the effect upon our people.

"The turning point of my father's life," Michael Mitchell says again.

The newspaper work ties Clarence Mitchell to politics. The *Afro-American* becomes a major advocate for the National Association for the Advancement of Colored People (NAACP) and helps Lillie Carroll Jackson win election as its Baltimore president. Jackson's daughter Juanita, now a college graduate, creates a cauldron of social activism known as the City-Wide Young People's Forum, and here she and Clarence, the two former schoolmates, find each other.

Their wedding's the big social event of 1936 black Baltimore. About fifteen hundred people pack the Sharp Street church. Their old high school classmate, Anne Wiggins Brown of *Porgy and Bess*, serenades them as they set off for their honeymoon.

In 1942 they move into the Druid Hill Avenue row house where they'll raise four sons and live for the rest of their lives. That first year

Juanita leads two thousand people urging the hiring of black police. She leads a citywide registration campaign that adds eleven thousand names to the voter rolls. Clarence begins years of daily commuting to Washington, where he lands government work.

When the war ends he joins the NAACP national staff as labor secretary. In 1950 he becomes director of the Washington bureau. By this time, he's getting a name for himself, working the halls of Congress, trying to open the job market for black people in the federal work force.

Everywhere he goes Mitchell carries in his wallet a small copy of the U.S. Constitution. He's a gentle but insistent voice arguing against discrimination in federal agencies, against the denial of voting rights to blacks, against segregation in the nation's capital.

And he's joining hands at the NAACP with his old friend from Baltimore, Thurgood Marshall.

Marshall departs Lincoln University with a diploma in one hand and a new bride, Vivian "Buster" Burey, a University of Pennsylvania student, in the other. The new couple moves back to Baltimore so they can live with Marshall's parents and save money for law school tuition. From West Baltimore Marshall could walk to the University of Maryland's downtown law school. But the law school's policy says no: it has never opened its doors to blacks and will not change now.

History will prove they stood in the wrong man's way.

Now Marshall rises at five each morning, walks to Baltimore's Pennsylvania Railroad Station loaded down with books, and takes the train to Washington, D.C., where he walks to the Howard University School of Law.

Every penny counts. His mother pawns her wedding ring for cash. Then her engagement ring. Lillie Carroll Jackson hears about the tight money and sends a few bucks to help with tuition.

Howard's kind of a mess. It's known as a law school of last resort. But the new dean—tall, blunt Charles Hamilton Houston—declares a new day for the school. He's a Phi Beta Kappa graduate of Amherst who served in the U.S. Army and then went to Harvard, where he was the first black student to edit the *Harvard Law Review*.

Houston greets Marshall's incoming freshman class by telling them he'll flunk anybody who's not serious about the work. He means it. There are thirty-six students in the freshman class; by graduation day, only six remain.

At Howard, "for the first time," Marshall recalls years later, "I found out my rights." He also found his great mentor in Houston.

Marshall graduates as Howard's valedictorian. He rents a small office in Baltimore, hires a secretary at $7.50 a week, and starts taking clients. Most of them are broke. In his first year of practice he ends up solidly in debt.

He's losing money but winning a reputation. The local NAACP starts sending him cases. The organization's boycotting white-owned stores in ghetto neighborhoods where blacks are permitted to spend their money but are never hired for a job. When the store owners sue the NAACP for damaging their business, Marshall's brought in as defense counsel. He immediately enlists Charles Houston's help, and the two of them win the case. It's the beginning of NAACP ties that will last for the next quarter-century.

The two men begin a crusade. They tour public schools attended by black children in the South. Usually these are shacks with dirt floors and leaky roofs. Houston takes movies to document these conditions. Marshall sits in the back seat of a car with a typewriter on his lap, putting the shabbiness into words. Sometimes the two of them are threatened by whites.

Their convictions deepen: America is cheating its black children, often beyond redemption. Education will be the battleground for a defining national fight on race. This is the beginning of the road to the Supreme Court case on school integration, and the two men decide on a natural early foe: the University of Maryland Law School that turned Marshall away for his color.

They find Donald Gaines Murray, a newly minted graduate of Amherst College who suffered the same turndown as Marshall. Here's a chance for revenge as well as justice. Marshall and Houston sign on. The law school pleads tradition: Maryland's part of the segregated South.

Never mind your traditions, says Marshall. "What's at stake here is more than the rights of my client. It's the moral commitment stated in our country's creed." Sitting in the courtroom, taking notes, is the young *Afro-American* reporter Clarence Mitchell Jr.

Marshall assumes he will lose. He assumes here is one more racist judge siding with "tradition," siding with money interests, siding with white people. Instead the judge says: Open the law school doors. In the midst of a courtroom eruption, the young reporter Clarence Mitchell leaps to his feet and bolts from the building. He runs all the way from the courthouse to the *Afro-American* offices nearly a dozen blocks away and immediately begins to type. He knows history when he sees it unfolding.

With the Maryland law school doors opened, who follows Donald Murray there but Juanita Jackson Mitchell. She graduates in 1950 and becomes the first African American woman to practice law in Maryland.

For Thurgood Marshall and America's schools, the Murray case is the merest starting point. In the coming years Marshall will take thirty-two cases to the U.S. Supreme Court and win twenty-nine of them. As the NAACP's chief counsel, he runs all over the country. He wins primary election voting rights for black people in Texas—a case that reverberates across the South. He wins entrance for blacks to the University of Texas and then the University of Oklahoma—cases that open state universities in eleven more states across the South. He wins cases allowing blacks to serve on juries, and he wins cases ending housing discrimination.

The job takes him wherever the angriest civil rights cases are fought.

"Thurgood had a vision," Mitchell will say years later. "His overcoat was thin, and he drove a car that you were never sure would take him to the end of the block. But local lawyers couldn't do it. There was too much local pressure. When it came to civil rights, the nicest people would go into cahoots with the worst rednecks."

In Tennessee there was a shootout. When Marshall accused the police of improper use of force, the cops arrested him and threatened imprisonment. Only national outrage saved him. His life was threatened repeatedly when he took South Carolina to court over voting rights. There were riots in Florida when Marshall investigated racially motivated murders, and then a bomb exploded outside his hotel on a Christmas night. In Tennessee he was forced into the back of a police cruiser and taken to a river where angry white men waited for him. He narrowly escaped with his life.

And all of this was mere prologue to Marshall taking his biggest case to court: finally, the racial integration of America's so-called public schools.

In 1950 the U.S. census takers count 949,708 persons living in the city of Baltimore. Three-quarters are white, one-quarter black. In the next ten years more than one hundred thousand of these whites will leave the city, and more than one hundred thousand blacks will arrive. The coming and the going are not unrelated.

All of that anxiety and exiting that started in the postwar years along Fulton Avenue now touches scores of neighborhoods in every section of the city. Lots of white people are telling each other: "How do you like the colored these days? They want to sit next to us at our lunch counters and movie theaters." Some whites can't get over this. It feels like black people are moving into their living rooms.

Or their schools. In 1953, the last year before the beginning of integration, the public schools of Baltimore are precisely 60 percent white. Ten years later, when the innocent fifties are ending and integration has kicked in, the schools are 43 percent white.

And many of these public schools are shaky even before the onset of racial integration. The postwar baby boom means that classrooms designed for maybe thirty kids are now bursting with forty. Some kids are sitting in classroom doorways, halfway into the hall. Overmatched teachers struggle to cope with too many kids each day and too many papers to grade long into each evening.

In 1950 the Baltimore newspapers carry stories of this great overcrowding, in which nearly ten thousand city children go to school only half a day because there isn't enough room to keep them for a full day. But the school system's statistics carry a more textured story. It's about race. In these final years before court-ordered integration, roughly 85 percent of the overcrowding's in schools strictly for African American children. The white kids are moving into modern new schools, while the black kids, cheated on class time by their abbreviated days, are still sitting in outdated, overcrowded, third-rate buildings. Across white America, this kind of racial disparity is known as "separate but equal."

And so, in places like Baltimore, there are tiny little offerings of racial accommodation. Toss these Negroes a little bone, maybe that'll soothe 'em for a few years while we figure out a new dodge on integration. In 1952 the prestigious high school A Course at Polytechnic Institute reluctantly opens its doors to a couple of "qualified Negro boys" seeking accelerated college prep engineering courses. It's the first time in Maryland public education that blacks and whites will attend the same school.

A year later two African American students, Carl E. Smith and James A. Grove, are admitted to another city high school, the Mergenthaler School of Printing. This happens under duress. Lawsuits are filed. The kids' attorneys? Juanita Jackson Mitchell and Donald Gaines Murray.

A little step here, a little step there. And each step so small that it sends signals to segregationists, who dig in their heels and imagine they can hold back the future.

When a young black man named George Washington Jr. helps integrate the University of Texas law school, the Ku Klux Klan burns a cross in front of the main building. When an ex-schoolteacher, George McLaurin, integrates the University of Oklahoma law school, he has to sit at a separate library table and a separate cafeteria table, and he's assigned a separate toilet.

These are the real-life reactions to Thurgood Marshall's courtroom triumphs at those schools. And all of this is innocent America's system of schooling when Thurgood Marshall turns to the U.S. Supreme Court on public schools—and Clarence Mitchell Jr. turns to his young son Keiffer.

The two of them, up from segregated West Baltimore, up from segregated Douglass High and Lincoln University, now must work two distinct sides of the same fight against American apartheid. Marshall has to confront the law of the land; Mitchell, the law of the jungle.

Marshall confronts the esteemed justices of the U.S. Supreme Court, these great men who sit there through the years with their insights into every layer of jurisprudence and human history but somehow fail to notice generations of white children getting a decent public school education while black children get the national brush-off.

Mitchell confronts the mob. He carries no law books in his hand. He stands outside a Baltimore junior high school on an autumn afternoon, alone and vulnerable, listening to this mob scream obscenities at him.

They're screaming about Mitchell's twelve-year-old son Keiffer. They don't want him in their school. The boy's not thinking about making history, he just wants to go to the seventh grade. The mob wants him to do it at his old school, one of those dumps where black kids are warehoused until they're old enough to leave with outdated skills. All right, let the mob scream, let 'em threaten. Clarence Mitchell stands right there on the sidewalk and says: This is my country, same as yours. And it's my child's country. Same as your child's.

But we come to that day in fits and starts.

The argument over public school integration first reaches the U.S. Supreme Court in December 1952, a month before Dwight Eisenhower's inauguration. At this time in America, school segregation's the law in seventeen states, including Maryland, and it's an unofficial fact of life in most other states. At this time, also, we have the most strident voices of segregation attempting to keep it that way as the justices prepare to hear arguments.

There's Georgia Gov. Herman Talmadge, who announces, "As long as I am governor, Negroes will not be admitted to white schools." There's South Carolina Gov. Jimmy Byrnes, who says, "If the court changes what is now the law of the land, so that we cannot maintain segregation, we will abandon the public school system." There's Bill Hendrix, grand dragon of the Ku Klux Klan, who says, "If segregation is abolished, the American Confederate Army" will march in armed rebellion. Wonderful, let's choose up sides for another Civil War.

So there's poison in the air on that December morning as hundreds line up outside the Supreme Court building. Some have shivered in the cold all night long. They stand there in their overcoats and their dress-up outfits, and never mind the weather and never mind the wait. They've waited all their lives for this moment, and it feels like history's about to change, right in front of their eyes. They fill up every seat in the courtroom: whites and blacks, scattered randomly, and nobody trying to separate them. This alone is pretty good for 1952 America.

They watch Marshall match up with John W. Davis, who represents segregation's side. Davis arrives here from a long career linked with Wall Street and the big banks and the entrenched Washington political establishment. Marshall arrives from the slums of West Baltimore.

Davis, with his white hair and craggy face, looks like a walking coin.

He was a U.S. congressman, he was U.S. Solicitor General, he was Ambassador to the Court of St. James. He ran for president in 1924 but lost to Coolidge. He's argued 140 cases before the Supreme Court. This is more than any other attorney, living or dead.

Marshall represents those whose entire lives are determined by their skin color.

He already knows Davis beyond any resume. When he was a law student at Howard twenty years earlier, Marshall cut classes whenever the brilliant Davis came to Washington to argue a case. "Every time John Davis argued," Marshall recalled, "I'd ask myself, 'Will I ever, ever . . .' and every time I had to answer, 'No, never.'"

Now, in the final weeks of 1952, Davis rises before this packed courtroom and says, "There is no reason why this court or any other" should change any laws separating children by race. Let the states run their own schools, he says. Let the federal government mind its own business. He's taken this case pro bono because he believes in it, believes the law is on his side, as is grand American tradition.

"Is it not a fact," he asks, "that the very strength and fiber of our federal system is *local* self-government in those matters for which *local* action is competent? Is it not of all the activities of government the one which most nearly approaches the hearts and minds of people: the question of education of their young?"

The old man talks law, he talks money, he talks nostalgia for the good old days. To those who say the schools aren't equal, why, look at South Carolina, he says. Only last year the state built these colored children some brand new schools and raised the salaries of Negro teachers to the level of white teachers. And never mind that it took a court order to do it. And never mind that it took years of foot-dragging and open contempt before the state finally made these grand, belated gestures.

None of this matters, Thurgood Marshall responds. "Racial discriminations in and of themselves are invidious," he says. His big voice booms around the courtroom. He's wrapping himself in constitutional essentials, in the "equal protection" clause of the Fourteenth Amendment.

So Davis gets folksy. He recalls the distant days of his boyhood, when children walked along dusty roads to school—separate dusty roads, presumably—swinging their books as they went merrily along.

Never mind all this talk of constitutional rights, he says. This is about custom, and it's about state's rights: the right to segregate people by age, by sex, by mental capacity. Or, if they wish, by race.

But all words vanish into the air.

The justices call time-out. In a few weeks the nation will get its new president, and they're concerned Eisenhower will need time to deal with such an emotional case. The justices make no decision. Instead they issue new questions for both sides to answer, and schedule arguments for a year later—five separate state cases to be gathered under the name of one: *Oliver Brown v. the Board of Education of Topeka, Kansas*.

So now it's December 1953. A new round of arguments and a new chief justice listening to them: Earl Warren, who got the job two months ago. Warren's presence causes mixed concern. During the war he headed California's program to put Japanese Americans into internment camps. But it was also Warren, as governor of California in 1943, who said, "I don't want to hear of any of my department heads refusing to hire anyone for reasons of race, color or creed." And he added, "We must insist upon one law for all men . . . Anything that divides us or limits the opportunities for full American citizenship is injurious to the welfare of all."

In midcentury America, this is rare and powerful language. It doesn't mean Warren's a lock on school integration. Maybe he wants to leave it up to the states. Maybe he believes this baloney about "separate but equal." But at least his history indicates a desire for fairness.

Once again people stand all night in the December cold waiting to pack the courtroom. Once again, blacks and whites are sitting together inside, watching as Marshall tells the court that the Fourteenth Amendment's "equal protection" clause deprives individual states of the power to impose segregation.

The justices can barely conceal their boredom. They've heard this argument before; what else have you got for us?

It's coming, it's coming.

For more than a year the NAACP legal team looked at psychological tests conducted by Dr. Kenneth Clark, a black psychologist from City College of New York. Clark showed four plastic, diaper-clad dolls to children between the ages of three and seven. The dolls were black and white. The children were black. They were asked which dolls were good and which dolls were bad; which ones were prettier, smarter, better; which ones they liked and which they did not.

Almost every time, these black children preferred the white dolls.

"Prejudice, discrimination and segregation" created a sense of inferiority and self-hatred in these children, says Clark.

Marshall understands this in his bones. He remembers all those neighborhood kids growing up in segregated West Baltimore, each one considered a city's excess baggage. And they know it. All they have to do is look at their surroundings. Marshall thinks about all the kids he's met here in midcentury America, all over the damned country, who understand that their future extends no further than segregation's limits. They must have done something bad—isn't that why they're being punished? The white kids must have done something really good—isn't that why their lives seem so blessed?

Hell, Marshall knows adults still fighting this kind of self-hatred. He can look at any black-owned newspaper or any national magazine—*Ebony* or *Jet*—and see pages of advertisements for skin lighteners and hair straighteners, all designed to make black people look more like white people, to obscure their true selves.

What about his own colleague, the NAACP executive director Walter White? He wrote a piece for *Look* magazine urging blacks to try a new chemical compound that would lighten their skin. He said there were new methods to make their hair "permanently straight." He said there was surgery to make their noses and lips look more like white people's.

Self-hatred, from cradle to grave.

"The average Negro," says Marshall, "has this complex that was built in as a result solely of segregation." He's caught the justices' attention with the Clark study. He tells them that black children's self-respect has been harmed, and here's a telling piece of evidence. He tells them that segregation and second-rate schools inflicted "not theoretical injury" but "actual injury."

And he waits for Davis to dispute any of this, and Davis's answer is hollow: America's history is too long, says Davis, and its race relations too complex and too volatile, to allow black and white children to sit together in the same classrooms.

Marshall hears this malarkey and knows he's been waiting all his life to respond. He says,

I got the feeling on hearing [Davis] that when you put a white child in a school with a whole lot of colored children, the child would fall apart or something. Everybody knows that is not true. Those same kids in Virginia and South Carolina—and I have seen them do it—they play in the streets together, they play on their farms together, they go down the road together, they separate to go to school, they come out of school and play ball together. They have to be separated in school . . . Why, of all the multitudinous groups of people in this country [do] you have to single out the Negroes and give them this separate treatment?

Now comes Justice Felix Frankfurter. "Mr. Marshall," he asks, "can you explain what you mean by 'equality?'"

"Equality," Marshall says, "means getting the same thing at the same time and in the same place."

So Davis replies with more history. He doesn't understand what's happening right in front of his eyes: his kind of history is running out. He says, "It is a little late—after this question has been presumed to be settled for ninety years—it is a little late to argue that the question is still at large."

But it is, and this is the very moment when it's finally being answered. Marshall's backed up by NAACP attorney James M. Nabrit, who tells the court that the fundamental basis of any segregation is an assumption of racial inferiority: that black children aren't as good as whites, aren't as smart, aren't as talented.

And here sits Marshall, who knows all about "inferior" black kids. He knew them back in Baltimore, back at Douglass High, back when every one of them was regarded as naturally "inferior" simply by reason of color.

Like the inferior Clarence Mitchell who now strides the halls of Congress and helps change the laws of the land.

And the inferior Anne Wiggins Brown and Avon Long who brought *Porgy and Bess* to life and changed the face of the American musical theater.

And the inferior Cab Calloway who lights up the jazz world for half a century.

And the inferior Juanita Jackson Mitchell, now a great civil rights attorney.

And the inferior Marshall himself, the former class cut-up banished to the school basement to memorize the constitution by a principal who saw the face of untapped potential instead of the stamp of inferiority.

All of these kids from just one isolated school in one city in one tiny moment in time. Each considered inferior because of race and national dictate. And each one an American legend.

Now they join the others gliding through Marshall's memory: the young people he helped enter previously segregated colleges, and the working people whose voting rights he won, and those now able to buy decent housing because of legal arguments he laid out.

They're all there in spirit, listening somewhere out there in America, as Marshall reaches his finish. He tells the court: "You can have them voting together, you can have them not restricted because of law in the houses they live in. You can have them going to the same state university and the same college. But if they go to elementary and high school, the world will fall apart?"

He's bringing two decades of his courtroom history—and his own history in the segregated public schools of Baltimore—into play here.

"We submit," he says, "the only way to arrive at that decision is to find that for some reason Negroes are inferior to all other human beings. The only thing it can be is an inherent determination that the people who were formerly in slavery, regardless of anything else, shall be kept as near that stage as is possible. And now is the time, we submit, that this Court should make it clear that that is not what our Constitution stands for."

It takes six months for the justices to make up their minds.

On May 17, 1954, the clock says eight minutes before one o'clock when Earl Warren starts to speak and everybody else in his courtroom goes silent. He speaks for the next twenty-eight minutes, and the words will change the face of America as nothing has since Lincoln's emancipation decree.

"I have for announcement," he says, "the judgment and opinion of the Court in *Oliver Brown v. Board of Education of Topeka*."

Finally, a day of reckoning. Reporters in the big courtroom, including some from the nation's African American newspapers, lean forward and listen with extra care. Departing from custom, the justices handed them no advance copies of the opinion.

Warren's only a few paragraphs into his reading when the Associated Press (AP) sends out its first bulletin to newsroom editors around the country: "Chief Justice Warren today began reading the Supreme Court's decision in the public school segregation cases. The court's ruling could not be determined immediately."

He's twenty minutes into his reading when a second AP bulletin goes out. It says Warren's attacking segregation in schools but adds ominously, "The Chief Justice has not read far enough in the court's opinion for newsmen to say that segregation was being struck down as unconstitutional."

Education, says Warren, "is the very foundation of good citizenship. Today it is a principal instrument in awakening the child to cultural values, in preparing him for later professional training, and in helping him to adjust normally to his environment."

Marshall likes what he's hearing so far. Warren's not saying *white children* need an education, or *black children* need it; he's saying *children* need it.

"In these days," says the chief justice, "it is doubtful that any child may reasonably be expected to succeed in life if he is denied the opportunity of an education. Such an opportunity, where the state has undertaken to provide it, is a right which must be made available to all on equal terms."

Marshall looks around and sees some reporters from the Negro press. They're scribbling notes with tears coming out of their eyes.

"To separate Negro children from others of similar age and qualifications solely because of their race," says Warren, "generates a feeling of inferiority as to their status in the community that may affect their hearts and minds in a way unlikely ever to be undone."

It's the Clark study—the justices understood. All those little black children, instinctively reaching for those little white dolls because this is how America has conditioned them from birth.

"We conclude," Warren finally says, "that in the field of public education the doctrine of 'separate but equal' has no place. Separate educational facilities are inherently unequal."

The words will reverberate across the coming generations. The court's decision is unanimous: The same American classrooms, the same teachers, the same textbooks, now belong to all children, and their color doesn't matter. Legalized school segregation is finally done.

The AP bulletins start clacking away in newsrooms around the country. An exultant Marshall, standing with reporters outside the big courtroom, calls it "the greatest victory we ever had."

He spots a little white boy and lifts him into the air, thinking "Don't be afraid, son, I'm not here to hurt you." The big man doesn't know what to do with all his happiness. So he starts to run. There he is, bursting all over, running up and down the stately corridors of the U.S. Supreme Court with this little white kid on his shoulders. The boy begins to smile. One white smile, a hundred fifty million to go.

Across the country, newspaper front pages are dominated by the decision. In Baltimore the final edition of the day's *Evening Sun* carries a page 1 banner: "RACE SEGREGATION BANNED." The front page of the next morning's *Sun* says, "Supreme Court Bans Segregated Schools." "MIX SCHOOLS," trumpets the *Afro-American*. "THURGOOD WINS." The paper runs three full pages on it.

In London the *Daily Mail* says the ruling "has helped to spike the Communist propaganda that Americans treat their colored people like dogs." In Paris *Le Monde* calls it "the victory of justice over race prejudice." In India, the powerful *Indian Express* chain calls it "a healthy change in enlightened American opinion."

America's daily papers, all owned and staffed by whites, all wary of anxious white readers, are not so exultant—especially newspapers in the South. In Chattanooga, the *Tennessee Times* editorializes, "Any man who thinks that a social custom of a century can be immediately overthrown without dangerous repercussions is stupid . . . [But] this is a country of law and however unpalatable to individual minds a law may be, it is eventually accepted." In Richmond, Virginia, the *Times-Dispatch* says, "We had hoped that the Court would uphold the 'separate but equal doctrine,' but since it did not do so, this is a time for calm and unhysterical appraisal." In Columbia, South Carolina, the *State* newspaper asks the high court not to rush integration but to "allow years to elapse before invoking its decree."

Yes, yes, by all means, more years, to pile upon all the others.

At the *Baltimore Sun*, even those editors who applaud the court know that most of their readers are white and many of them are already rattled by midcentury changes. Now their children will be touched. Many have never known a Negro child, much less sat in a classroom with one. The culture didn't permit it. Parents now whisper with their neighbors. All this summer of 1954 they're out there on street corners, they're taking laundry off their adjoining backyard clothes lines, they're sitting on front stoops, and this is all they talk about. The colored, the colored. They're comparing notes about how worried they should be or how angry. Maybe there's one guy who tries to calm things by talking about a colored guy down at the plant, and he's not such a bad guy, and maybe we should give this thing a chance. Some of the others will then attach a familiar pejorative to this guy: nigger lover.

All their lives, they've learned to ascribe certain qualities to black people. They were passed down by word of mouth and were reinforced by newspaper headlines that landed on their front steps every day:

"Negro, 49, Held in Burglary."

"65 Negroes Arrested in Gambling Raid."

"Rape Charge against Negro."

Such people will invade their children's schools next fall. And so, never mind all this business about the American melting pot, and never mind those words in the daily classroom pledge about "liberty and justice for all." A lifetime of casual slander has to be reevaluated or tossed aside. Or left behind, by packing the family off to some safe, distant place out there in the promising new suburbs. Thousands of angry white readers send letters to newspaper editors capturing the national anxiety.

Here's one from the *Sun*: "I am writing this because I feel that my thoughts are also the thoughts of the average white person living in a community where we are surrounded on all sides by Negro people. I hope that the people who have ended segregation are aware of the monstrous thing they have done to society."

And this: "A Negro who wants to worship the Lord may do so very well without sitting next to a white person, just as a colored child may also learn in school without sitting next to a white child. The way the authorities go on you would think a colored person could hardly breathe unless they were in a group of white people."

And this: "What about the social aspects? Will my child have to go to a school prom and dance with colored children? Where will these things lead? Suppose we do tell our children that everyone is alike, that these people who have only three hundred years of civilization behind them are the same, then a son or daughter brought home a Negro boy or girl friend. Would you be happy?"

And this: "If God had wanted us to be alike He would have created us so. He made some black and some white, and I am all for keeping things that way. The birds, animals and fish all instinctively practice segregation. Aren't we as smart as they are? The end of segregation is strictly to please the colored people. Aren't we white people supposed to be happy, too?"

Politicians around the country see such reactions and pounce on the opportunities presented. In Georgia, Gov. Herman Talmadge says he will never allow integration of the schools. South Carolina Gov. James Byrnes says the same.

Here in the innocent fifties their defiance will set the tone for a generation of southern politicians standing in schoolhouse doors to protest integration. Talmadge and Byrnes will give courage to Faubus in Arkansas, who will give us George Wallace in Alabama, which will encourage Richard Nixon's Southern Strategy and generations of politicians speaking in racial code.

On this May afternoon in 1954, nine justices in Washington, D.C., have spoken unanimously. But beyond their courtroom not a single black child has yet moved into an all-white classroom.

In Maryland, Gov. Theodore McKeldin, a liberal Republican before such a phrase disappears from American politics, reacts to the court's decision with careful parsing of the language: "Maryland prides itself upon being a law-abiding state." That's the tone of the day for even the bravest liberal: like it or not, folks, this is the new law. It's not my decision, and maybe it's not your choice, but let's all try to make the best of it.

That spring in Baltimore, it falls upon Walter Sondheim, president of the school board and a supporter of the Supreme Court decision, to seek out Mayor D'Alesandro. It's one thing for the high court to issue pronouncements; it's another for local leaders to carry them out.

D'Alesandro's a man who understands the American melting pot in all its complexities. An Italian American who faced early ethnic rejection, he knows what it means to be an outsider. But he also knows his city and knows many whites feel threatened by any talk of integration.

Now the future seems to be arriving for the entire city, and Sondheim doesn't know what to expect when he reaches D'Alesandro. He finds relief.

D'Alesandro knows Sondheim had rounded up school board support for the high court's ruling. So the mayor, in his confusion, turned instinctively to those he trusts most.

"I don't know whether what you did was right," he tells Sondheim, "but the priests tell me you were right." That's good enough for D'Alesandro.

And, in the city of Baltimore, that sets the stage for the opening of schools in the autumn of 1954.

≋

"What I remember about that time," says Dr. Keiffer Mitchell, nearly sixty years after the attack outside his new junior high school, "is the punch in the jaw. Pow! My jaw, and a minor concussion. And then somebody getting me inside to the principal's office."

"What I remember," says Michael Mitchell, "is my brother Keiffer going into this howling mob. And my father telling him, 'My second son is my tallest son. And I was never more proud of him.'"

What everyone should remember is the father, Clarence Mitchell Jr., with a sign in his hand. He stands all alone on the sidewalk outside Gwynns Falls Park Junior High School on this autumn day in 1954, and he demands an equal chance for his son. Nothing more, but nothing less. He's been making the case every damned day for years now, cornering the most powerful people in the nation's political corridors, hiding all his anger and all his grief and frustration with them, laying out arguments for racial equality in the most reasonable way, and these powerful men smile politely and they dig in their heels with every legal and political tool in their arsenals.

And now they're leaving it to the mob in the street.

"My father," says Michael Mitchell, "always felt he needed to deal with reason and logic and use the law. If you appeal to people's emotions, those change from time to time. So he kept his emotions in check. But now you had this mob outside Gwynns Falls Park Junior High, and they're saying the most horrible things. And my father's courage in the face of it—oh, my. He never had a fear in him."

Except he'd feared all along that it might come to this, and he'd watched it coming over the past decade, starting back there on Fulton Avenue in the closing days of the war, back when black people first started slipping deeper into West Baltimore and whites started pushing back or moving away.

Was this a new day in America, or wasn't it? The high court said so last May, just before the schools closed for summer vacation. And then, when classes went back into session just a few weeks ago, things in Baltimore looked pretty good.

For a while.

"City Schools Open, Some with Mixed Enrollment," the *Sun*'s headline declared on the morning of September 7, 1954. "Public education in Baltimore entered a new era today as some 143,000 children began classes in schools from which the labels 'White' and 'Negroes' have been removed," the *News-Post* said.

The newspaper arrived on doorsteps late that afternoon, after its reporters had had a chance to watch the first day of classes play out for a few hours.

Typical of the activity in schools through the city this morning was that at the Sidney Lanier Elementary School at Linden Avenue and Wilson Street [in West Baltimore]. The school has about a dozen colored pupils assigned to various grades. Their appearances caused no reaction whatsoever.

The Negro children seemed not disturbed to find themselves in classrooms with white youngsters and the latter seemed unworried by their occasional neighbor of a darker hue. Among the late registrants, white and colored mothers sat side by side in the waiting line, chatting now and then.

But elsewhere in the city the transition was not being made entirely without difficulty.

And not without reason. At Holabird Avenue and Broening Highway on the east side of town, at school no. 200, a few hundred white children were getting their first look at a school previously reserved for black children. The white parents were appalled. "A firetrap," they said. Its lavatories were antiquated. There was no medical office, no cafeteria, no recreational equipment. A "dangerous cesspool" lay adjacent to the school. The white parents said this place wasn't nearly as nice as their children's previous school.

"We want it abolished," a white mother told school officials. "You thought you could cram it down our throats and we would sit and take it." In this moment these white parents were discovering the true meaning of the phrase that had seemed to satisfy them just fine across so many segregated generations: "separate but equal."

For a few weeks, the general city response was pretty calm. And then it wasn't.

> From September 7 to the present time [said a *Sun* editorial], Baltimore has been an object lesson to all Americans in how a city with many deep Southern convictions can adjust itself in a quiet, orderly manner to the Supreme Court's announcement that school segregation is unconstitutional. There was some grumbling, to be sure . . . But, at the schools themselves, harmony has prevailed to a stimulating degree.

Then comes the change.

In mid-September, white housewives picket Charles Carroll Barrister Elementary School no. 34, in southwest Baltimore's Pigtown neighborhood. These women are angry, and they've reinforced each other's anger over the long summer months. They're the ones whose husbands work the factory assembly lines, who drive transit buses and haul cargo on the city's shipping piers. Nobody's getting rich. What are the colored complaining about? We're the ones, these white people tell each other, whose lives are about half a step better than those of some of the blacks.

Now there are dozens of these white women picketing outside Charles Carroll Barrister Elementary and carrying signs. "Segregation—It's Our Heritage." They vow to keep marching "until we can't walk anymore." They're stopping little white children, telling them not to go into the school, telling them to go back home, telling them they won't be safe inside Charles Carroll Elementary.

There are 546 white children at the school. There are 11 black children, all in kindergarten.

Go home, white children. It's not safe for you here.

White people down in South Baltimore are watching this and taking courage from it. They see that they're not alone. Some make telephone calls. Many are made anonymously. They're spreading stories about violence at Southern High School, about dangerous conditions for white kids there, about the colored carrying knives and guns. They're telling stories about some black kid stabbing a white girl to death, about schools around town being set afire, about blacks gathering to attack whites. These stories are lies, every one of them.

On the first day of October, about five hundred white students gather outside Southern High, at Warren Avenue and William Street. There are roughly eighteen hundred students at Southern. Thirty-nine are black.

Some of the protesters carry signs: "We Want Southern Back." "Negroes Not Allowed."

Black students are roughed up outside the building, and riot police are brought in. Several whites are arrested. Then the organized protests spread here and there.

More than a thousand students gather outside Mergenthaler High School, at Hillen Road and Thirty-Sixth Street. They march all the way to City Hall. Six hundred police are called out as the kids spread across War Memorial Plaza and chant for Mayor D'Alesandro to come out. The mayor's not there. Some of the kids sing "God Bless America," failing to notice that it's not just their America. Police, unimpressed by the singing, announce that arrests will commence if they don't "break it up."

"Come and get us," the kids chant. But it's only the fifties, when these teenagers haven't yet figured out their own strength. They still yield to authority figures. When police move toward them, the crowd breaks up. Some head down to Southern High, about two miles away. Four of them hoist a big sign saying, "Southern Don't Want Negroes."

Clarence Mitchell watches all of this, and finds it troubling, and also knows it doesn't matter. His son's education will be different from his. His oldest boy, Clarence III, takes the train to Washington every morning, where he's the only black student at the Catholic Gonzaga High. Young Michael Mitchell's still in elementary school, and in three years he will be among the first to integrate Pimlico Junior High. George is still a toddler.

When he looks at his twelve-year-old son Keiffer, Clarence Mitchell sees a sensitive boy whose strength is being denied him. The kid's an artist. He won a citywide contest. But he goes to historically segregated Booker T. Washington Junior High School, where there's no art instruction. The classes are overcrowded, the textbooks outdated.

"One time," Keiffer Mitchell remembers many years later, "I painted a picture of people waiting at a train station. My mother pointed something out to me. Everybody in the station had white faces."

It isn't lost on him, all these years later, that it's Kenneth Clark's psychological study put to canvas, Thurgood Marshall's argument in the *Brown* case. It's all those black children instinctively reaching for the white dolls, the ones that are nicer, smarter, more lovable.

White people at a train station, running away. To the suburbs, probably.

The Mitchells transfer Keiffer to Gwynns Falls Park Junior High, near Edmondson Village on the western edge of the city. There are two thousand white students there. There are seven blacks besides Keiffer. Nearby residents, all white, find this upsetting. So many of them are out there in the street that snack vendors are making the rounds, selling sodas and candy and sticky apples. Some protesters—quite a few arriving in cars with out-of-state license plates—carry signs: National Association for the Advancement of White People.

Michael Mitchell remembers his father looking Keiffer in the eye that first school day and asking, "Son, do you want to go to that school?"

"Yes, Daddy, I want to go."

"My son will never be taller than he is today."

"And then," says Michael Mitchell, "my brother went into that howling sea of a mob."

Now it's September 30, the midday lunch hour, when Keiffer's outside in the schoolyard. Two big guys—it's still unclear if they're teenage students or young men from the neighborhood—approach him.

"You know what time it is?" one of them asks.

"I don't have a watch," Keiffer says.

Boom, he's blind-sided. The two guys run off as Mitchell staggers and falls.

"In the jaw," Keiffer remembers now, and the next thing he knows, he's in the principal's office with a concussion. The cops are called in, but an investigation goes nowhere.

And the mob's still outside the school, and they're telling white children they should go back home and screaming for these black kids to go somewhere, too.

Go back to Africa.

Clarence Mitchell sees this, and he's had enough. You punch my child in the jaw, we'll both turn the other cheek. You stall me across years and years, I'll maintain my civility, I'll play it out in the courts and the Congress. You stand outside my child's school screaming obscenities at him after you've attacked him, and now you're issuing more threats his way, and that's enough.

The accumulation has gotten to him.

He heads downtown, to school headquarters on Twenty-fifth Street, and finds Dr. John Fischer, the school superintendent, and Sondheim, the school board president. Sondheim's not surprised by any of this trouble. He's the guy who solidified the school board vote last spring, backing integration. He paid for it. All summer long he's had anti-Semitic telephone calls to his house. Once he found a cross burning on his front lawn. He knows the anger out there.

But he's never seen Clarence Mitchell like this. Mitchell tells them about the mob outside Gwynns Falls Park Junior High. He tells them about his boy getting attacked. He tells them he's going back to the school, and he's going to challenge the mob. They tell him not to do it, that the mob will come after him. Mitchell doesn't hear them. He's already out the door, heading west to Druid Hill Avenue, to his row house. Those white people outside Keiffer's school had signs saying, "Go Back to Africa." Mitchell makes his own sign.

Look at him out there now. He's all alone, holding up his sign, as the mob loses its collective mind.

"Go home, nigger."

"Go back to Africa."

Mitchell's answer is five words on this sign he carries in his hands, and it becomes a banner to carry into a crusade.

"I AM AN AMERICAN, TOO!" it says.

While many of Maryland's counties continued to stall public school integration after the Supreme Court's decision, the city of Baltimore proceeded. Here, an elementary schoolteacher oversees her newly integrated class. But suburbia, fueled by the growing white exodus from the city, remained heavily white for years. (Hearst Newspapers LLC / Baltimore News-American)

Hello Towson, Hello Pikesville
The Suburban Exodus

Maybe this is where the fifties really begins: on a West Baltimore sidewalk outside Gwynns Falls Park Junior High, on this autumn afternoon in 1954, with Clarence Mitchell Jr. staring down the howling mob. Let 'em scream, let 'em holler. Mitchell's not going anywhere.

And maybe the fifties begins with these black children heading toward Charles Carroll Barrister Elementary School. They're slipping through these angry white housewives telling them to go away, they don't belong here. But the children want to go to kindergarten.

And maybe it begins with all those angry white people filling the streets outside Southern High with their signs and their screams and their final attempts to hold back the future, while a few real good bigots start the newest lie about some colored kid stabbing some innocent white girl to death.

It's enough to make anybody move away.

But it's white people who moved away first, because they could. They had a few bucks, and they had the right skin color. They moved by the millions from Baltimore and countless other big, crowded cities across America. Some of them moved because they wanted more room to spread out. They said they always wanted a yard. They learned how to barbeque, and they gathered the whole family on their new backyard patios. They bought little plastic wading pools for the children. This became the Good Life. It wasn't just the intrusion of black people in the city schools and the old neighborhoods that made so many whites move away. They had other reasons. But race was a real big part of it for a lot of panicky families.

And so, across the country, white people went to places called Elm-wood and Lakewood and Kirkwood and Forest Hills and Forest Grove and Forest Park. From the row-house streets of Baltimore they went to leafy Towson, where the 1940s population barely tops twenty thousand, by 1955 the population reaches fifty-five thousand, and by 1963 it reaches eighty-six thousand.

And Essex–Middle River, whose population in 1950 is still so sparse that the addition of a traffic light merits headline coverage atop the front page of the News-Post's Metro section ("New Traffic Light Allotted to Essex")—and the population grows by sixteen thousand in the next five years.

And Arbutus and Lansdowne, where it jumps by the thousands, and Randallstown, where it jumps by so many thousands more that they can't build schools fast enough for all the new children.

And when the newly minted middle-class blacks start following them to those suburbs a decade or so later, many of these whites will move even further out, to places like Columbia and Bel Air and Owings Mills and Westminster. Suburb after suburb after suburb.

By now all those formerly stay-at-home mothers needed cars whenever they went somewhere. No more of this sitting on the front stoops waiting for a little summer breeze while you watched the kids play hopscotch and curb ball and stickball. Hell, the kids weren't out there playing ball; now they were down in the new paneled basement watching TV in the air conditioning. Which is why everybody's windows were shut, to keep the cool air from escaping. And so you no longer heard music wafting out onto the sidewalk from somebody's open window. And you didn't hear snatches of ballgames where you learned that Brooks Robinson just hit one out or Hoyt Wilhelm had a no-hitter going, and you couldn't wait to pass these little bulletins to the guys down on the corner, when all of this made it feel like an actual shared community.

In suburbia there was no grocery store on the corner, where you sent the kids to grab a couple of snowballs to chill a sweaty summer evening. Now everybody shopped at the Food Fair at the new mall that was six miles away. There they also found the department stores that used to draw the big crowds downtown. Those downtown stores closed, one by one, and followed the money to the suburban malls. They left the heart of downtown deserted and eerie. And the drugstore and shoe store and movie theater were found at the new mall, as were the delicatessen and coffee shop and shoe repair that used to be down the block.

And because everything was now miles away, the kids, those turning sixteen, needed cars of their own. At war's end there were forty-three million cars on America's roads; only a decade later, sixty-nine million. Plus all those yellow school buses picking up children every morning, since the nearest school was too far away to walk.

For three years in the fifties, the city of Baltimore doesn't bother to build a single new school. What's the point, when so many families are moving away? Meanwhile, the counties are building their new schools as fast as they can. Baltimore County averages a new school every two and a half months over a three-year period—and yet, even that ferocious pace is too slow. From 1945 to 1955 Baltimore County's school population doubles, and it doubles again in the next five years, and nobody knows where to put all these kids.

There's Milford Mill High School, in Baltimore County west of the city, built to hold about seven hundred students. Suddenly they've got eleven hundred. Stemmers Run Junior High, built for fourteen hundred students, now has more than twenty-two hundred. Arbutus Elementary's averaging forty-seven children per class. Sparrows Point High's so crowded, they're putting kids in the basement of a nearby elementary school built at the turn of the century.

Thousands of county children go to class on half-day shifts. Or they sit in portable classrooms. Or they use gymnasiums and auditoriums and cafeterias as classrooms, and when school administrators run out of those, they use community halls and libraries and lease rooms in churches, and this is where the kids learn their multiplication tables.

In the aftermath of the Supreme Court ruling on integration, there's one other fascinating thing about suburban schools. In the Baltimore metro area, all of the county kids are white. Never mind what the Court said, and never mind what the city of Baltimore's doing—these counties claim they need time to think things through. A few days after the Court's ruling the state Board of Education votes unanimously that racial segregation in public schools and teachers colleges will remain in force. Edward Rollins, Maryland's attorney general, declares the Supreme Court "so far handed down only an opinion . . . not a decree." So, never mind that the city of Baltimore's letting black kids into its schools. The counties will get around to it when they can, maybe.

A year after the *Brown* decision, Baltimore County's schools are still segregated. In Carroll County 250 parents gather at a Union Bridge elementary school to protest the admission of six black children, and a county school spokesman declares, "There is nothing improper in circumventing the law."

Across Maryland only eight counties out of twenty-two were integrated a year after the Court's decision. Even the city of Baltimore's sending out mixed signals. It's two years after the *Brown* decision—late February, 1956—before the city's three all-black high schools—Douglass, Carver, and Dunbar—finally get permission to play sports against the other high schools.

It's three years after the high court's ruling, and Harford County's still fighting integration. In Baltimore County it's 1957 before seventy-eight schools finally integrate, and it's 1962—eight years after *Brown*—before the last five Maryland counties—Carroll, Calvert, Wicomico, Kent, and Dorchester—open their doors to black students.

In the summer of 1955, when it's clear that many Maryland school districts are dragging their feet, Democrat H. C. "Curly" Byrd runs for governor against Republican Theodore McKeldin. Byrd was director of the University of Maryland's (all-white) athletic program and then became president of the (practically all-white) school. Now he's running for governor, and he's asked as he leaves a political rally, "What are you going to do about the shines?"

"Keep 'em out," says Byrd.

McKeldin, meanwhile, urges the schools to be "prompt and reasonable" on integration. He's elected governor, in a race considered closer than it should have been. And he becomes a national voice urging racial healing.

For this, McKeldin looks out the front window of the governor's residence in Annapolis one night in 1957 and finds Confederate flags, a burning cross, and a sign quoting lines from "Maryland, My Maryland."

> Better the fire upon thee roll
> Better the shot, the blade, the bowl
> Than the crucifixion of the soul.

Beneath the quotation is written: "Down with Traitor McKeldin."

Awful, of course. Everyone with the slightest sense of civility agrees to this. But all these protests and all this foot-dragging send a signal to whites: maybe the Court's ruling was meaningless. Let 'em integrate the city schools—we can move to the counties, where our kids can go to school with white children the way it used to be.

By 1960 one-third of the country was living in suburbia. Robert C. Wood, in his book *Suburbia: Its People and Their Politics*, called Americans' midcentury exodus "the greatest migration in the shortest time of the nation's history."

The most famous suburban developer of the era is William Levitt. On Long Island he builds Levittown. It's practically Henry Ford's mass production assembly line transferred to housing. He's building three dozen houses a day and hundreds of thousands across the decade. All are strictly for white people.

From 1951 to 1957 America's suburbs grew six times faster than did its cities. Nearly all new homes were being built in the suburbs. In 1950 Baltimore's the sixth largest city in America. Its population's almost a million. Then comes the great leaving.

From 1954, when the public schools are first integrated, until 1963, the population of the city of Baltimore drops by an average of eight thousand people a year. Almost all those leaving are white. Over the coming decades, this pace does not diminish. By century's turn, barely six hundred thousand people still live in the city. About one-third are white.

Here's where the suburban migration really kicks into gear, in this autumn of 1954, with white people running amok through the streets in South Baltimore because thirty-nine black children want to go to public high school there.

Here's where it begins, with eleven kindergarten children causing panic as they weave through a picket line outside their public elementary school.

And here's where it begins, with Clarence Mitchell out on a sidewalk declaring, "I am an American, too."

The mobs disappear after that. But people go home and start getting friendly with realtors and moving companies. They take Sunday afternoon drives to shiny new developments where the builders are still hauling in bricks and concrete for all the new bungalows and semi-detached and split-levels and ranchers that are still going up, and they're hauling in young saplings to line the streets and fresh sod to put on the ground so all the new culs-de-sac will look green and inviting.

A day after Mitchell's protest, the city police commissioner announces that any pickets standing directly outside a school are breaking the law and will be arrested. That sends the mob home. When hundreds of Southern High parents keep their kids home from school, the principal declares that anyone absent the next day will be suspended. That gets everybody back in class. At Gwynns Falls Park Junior High, Keiffer Mitchell never sees another picket after his father defies the mob.

Nor does he make a friend at school in the coming years.

"No, no friends," he says nearly six decades later.

He says this without emotion. What's done is done. He sits in his Druid Hill Avenue medical office, a block from the row house where his parents lived most of their lives. The walls here are covered with photos of so many of the public moments, his mom and dad with John Kennedy and Eleanor Roosevelt and Lyndon Johnson. Look how happy everyone looks. And Mitchell remembers the struggles behind the smiles.

"There was so much hostility then," he says. He was alone at school most of the time. He found refuge in his art. Classmates mostly avoided him, but some taunted him. They found it amusing. Once, riding the bus, a couple of kids put lighted cigarettes in the hood of Keiffer's coat. He was beaten up on the playground.

"It was such a traumatic time," he says now, "the kids were afraid to extend themselves. Most of the teachers, too. I was isolated, day after day. I made no friends there. But the art department had materials I'd never had before. That was my safe haven. And that's why my parents sent me there. I was a day-dreamer as a kid, but I was interested in art. And that school had what I needed, and my old school didn't. It wasn't about making friends, it was about getting an education, it was about the revolution. From the time we were kids we were recruited for mass meetings, for handing out fliers. In 1956 my parents were hosting Hungarian freedom fighters. We made them tuna sandwiches."

He laughs at the memory and then at another, from the years when John Kennedy sat in the White House and a generation of young people found inspiration there. "In the early sixties," says Mitchell, "our house was filled with these gorgeous co-eds from out-of-state colleges. They camped out with us on the nights before sit-ins. We were all part of a revolution, and you could feel the world about to change."

In a lot of ways, it did. Keiffer Mitchell made it through Gwynns Falls Park Junior High, and then he went to high school at Baltimore City College, where he played football and threw the shot put and the discus for the track team. He went to Morgan State College, and Lincoln University, and the University of Pennsylvania's medical school. He found doors opening for him that had previously been shut to black people. And now he sits here on Druid Hill Avenue with years of medical practice piled up behind him, and he's never left this neighborhood that holds so much history dating back to Thurgood Marshall and Clarence Mitchell Jr.

In the aftermath of public school integration, Marshall spent another seven years as the NAACP's chief counsel. Then he was the first African American named U.S. solicitor general and the first African American named to the U.S. Supreme Court. He spent the next quarter-century there.

Clarence Mitchell Jr. spent thirty years as the NAACP's chief lobbyist. He became the driving force, and the conscience, behind a whole series of civil rights acts, the first to be passed by the U.S. Congress in nearly a century.

They were laws that finally prohibited racial discrimination at the voting booth.

That prohibited job discrimination based on color.

That prohibited a hotel or restaurant, or a store or a theater, from turning anyone away because of skin color.

"My parents," Keiffer Mitchell says, not for the first time, "were revolutionaries. And this is where it all leads."

He points across the room to a large political poster. It's a campaign sign for his son, Keiffer Mitchell Jr., who's a state delegate now. In his first political position he was a Baltimore City Councilman on the city's west side.

"Oh, if I could have seen the future," says his father. "My son representing the very neighborhood where I went to Gwynns Falls Park Junior High, and all those people stood there on the street and tried to keep me out."

≈

It's a great American story, except for this: You walk back outside Mitchell's medical office, onto Druid Hill Avenue, and the world is falling down in darkness. Block after block of cancerous row houses, their insides coming undone, plaster falling, linoleum floors crumbling, electrical fixtures coming apart, the plumbing rusty and rotting.

And some of these places are still occupied by human beings.

It's the barely living and the long-since dead, side by side. One block after another, occupied homes next to rows of vacated units that sit there like a mouth with rotted teeth, on crowded Druid Hill Avenue and all of its side streets. Boards over windows and doors, roofs caving in, signs on doors warning No Trespassing. As if something worth stealing had been left behind in the dark.

And so much of this decay comes out of the innocent fifties, in struggling neighborhoods like this one and in neighborhoods that were still thriving in the postwar years. This is when thousands of white people can't wait to head for the suburbs. They make the best deals they can for their old homes. They do it in haste and often in panic. They look frantically for a buyer. Race no longer matters, even when their remaining white neighbors eyeball them and declare: "You're selling to the colored? You're doing this to the neighborhood?" And then those families, too, desperate to get away, sell to black families, who are thrilled that they can finally escape the confines of the old ghettos.

When these white people can't find a buyer, they find a professional landlord. Let *him* take the heat. Let *him* worry about finding a tenant and collecting the rent. And here the problem deepens.

Never mind the crumbling of a neighborhood—these absentee landlords are looking to cash in. The math is simple: the more people they can squeeze into a house, the more money they get out of it.

From such arithmetic comes the brilliant idea of breaking the house into units. So now you've got two families living in these little row houses where there used to be one. If the house is a little bigger, maybe there are three families squeezed in. All sharing bathrooms. Or, if the place is even bigger, you go to four families, or five, or six. In a single house. This goes on in neighborhoods all over the city of Baltimore—and in cities across America.

In West Baltimore, for example, just below beautiful Druid Hill Park, you have the graceful Reservoir Hill neighborhood of fine old Victorian homes. Here you find the 1400 block of Linden Avenue. Once the Baltimore Blue Book listed more than fifty families of social prominence living on this block and the next. But now, as the midcentury flight to suburbia commences, absentee landlords are grabbing with both hands. Why should one family pay rent here when several could?

First, with the official blessing of the Board of Zoning Appeals, comes 1413 Linden Avenue, previously home to one family. The absentee landlord divides this into units. For seven different families. And it sets a zoning precedent for the entire block.

In quick succession, six families will share the house at 1404 Linden where there used to be one. Then five families at 1406 Linden. Then eight families at 1409 Linden. Five families at 1410 Linden. Eight families at 1411 Linden. Sixteen families at 1415 Linden. Each, where there used to be one family.

And on and on, until the zoning board approves fifty-two families living in seven houses that formerly held seven families.

On this one block. In this one neighborhood, reflective of scores more.

The houses suffer from the overload, and soon enough entire neighborhoods and schools show the strain. The working-class black families who first moved in save a few bucks and move to areas where the housing's a little better. The new renters, taking a look at the deterioration, stick around for a few months. Some of them, when the rent's due, slip off in the middle of the night. Most are poor; a growing number turn in despair to drugs.

Now there are new signs on such blocks: "Furnished Apartments." "Furnished Rooms." "Sleeping Rooms." "Rooms for Rent and Light Housekeeping." Each sign becomes a dagger to the heart of a neighborhood.

By 1954 a federal study cites two thousand blocks as "blighted." This covers one-third of the city of Baltimore. It covers 175,000 people. They live in 50,000 substandard homes. Many are half a century old. Some were built before the Civil War.

Such places were a mess when Clarence Mitchell Jr. and Thurgood Marshall were living in them as they grew up, and such homes were still here in the fifties, slowly coming apart when they should have been condemned, and thousands of them remain in the brand-new twenty-first century.

In the innocent fifties the most depressing units are two-room dwellings. One room's downstairs, one room's upstairs. There's a place called Ten Pin Alley, behind the 1400 block of East Baltimore Street, that's about as bad as it gets. Most of the block is made up of two-room hovels, though a few have rickety lean-to kitchens in the rear. If there's running hot water, this is considered a luxury. Most have no indoor toilets or tubs. Some lack windows. The floors sag. Rats are all over the place.

Slum housing is advertised in the city's newspapers: page after page of apartments for rent. Most of these places go for twenty-eight bucks a month, payable by the week. This averages out to a dollar a day. At least the gas and electric bills run pretty low, since most of these apartments have no central heating.

The bulk of these places are home to black families. Poverty put them there, and so did legalized racism. And so does migration, which is happening in unprecedented numbers in the 1950s. Mostly, this involves black people moving from the South, where they're still facing segregated drinking fountains and movie theaters and schools, to the North, where some of this is beginning to change and there's a little better promise of a decent job, as well.

Across 1950s America, black families earn barely half the income of whites. But there's disparity among blacks, as well. Those in the South earn only two-thirds of what blacks in the North make. In the North they're starting to find work as sales clerks and firefighters, as police officers and bus drivers. Even the women are doing better. In the war years two-thirds of all African American women with jobs in northern cities are employed as housekeepers. A decade later, that figure's cut by half.

And so they come north.

In 1900 only 10 percent of black people lived outside the South; by 1957, the figure's 40 percent. In the war years, roughly half a million black people lived in the city of New York; by 1957, it's more than a million. In Chicago, the figure goes from a quarter million to more than six hundred thousand. In Los Angeles, the number of blacks grows from about sixty thousand to more than a quarter million. In Detroit, there were 150,000 during the war and nearly half a million by 1957. In Baltimore, swelled by all those seeking wartime factory jobs, the black population goes from 160,000 to 280,000 by 1957.

Thousands of white people can't wait to move away from this. It's not that they're all bigots; far from it. Many are simply feeding off each other's fears. There's a tide that's washing them out to suburbia, based on history, based on money, based on the things they see with their eyes, like all those For Sale signs in front of their neighbors' houses. They don't want to be the last whites on the block. They don't want to lose whatever value remains on their property. The integration of schools unnerved them, and what follows rattles them more.

Black people want to go places they've never been allowed to enter. They want to enter restaurants that still won't serve them and movie theaters that won't sell them tickets. They want to walk into a Read's drugstore and sit down at the lunch counter the same as any white person. There are thirty-seven Read's outlets all around the Baltimore metropolitan area, and a black person can walk in and buy a nickel bag of potato chips but can't sit at a lunch counter and wash them down with a ten-cent Pepsi.

It stays this way until 1955, a year after the public schools integrate. The change comes suddenly. Half a dozen Morgan State College students stand in the January cold at the downtown intersection of Howard and Lexington Streets. They're waiting for a bus to school. This Read's has a first-floor lunch counter. The kids could get coffee or hot chocolate inside and warm up before their bus arrives, instead of standing in the miserable cold. Except Read's won't let them.

What the hell, somebody says, let's give it a try. These kids are well dressed, well spoken, and polite. But their gesture is brazen beyond precedent. One day the whole country will watch young people in Greensboro, North Carolina, protest segregation at an F. W. Woolworth lunch counter, and reporters will call it a sit-in and make it a stirring, iconic moment in civil rights history.

But the Read's sit-in in Baltimore happens five years before Greensboro. It's history without anybody particularly noticing. Nobody alerts the newspapers ahead of time. That kind of media savvy doesn't exist yet. The local TV stations couldn't run a camera crew downtown even if they wanted to.

This is a time when such things aren't done in America, when black people are still supposed to know their place—and their place is out there in the cold until the damned bus arrives. But they walk in and sit themselves down at the Read's lunch counter.

"You'll have to leave," a man tells them. It's the store manager, all fluttery.

"We just want something warm to drink," one of the kids says.

"Store policy," the manager says. "You'll have to leave."

"Just want some coffee."

"Or I call the police."

The police station's only a few blocks away. This mild confrontation lasts a few minutes, and then the kids get up and go back into the cold. They would rather go to school than to jail.

But the moment matters. Word of the protest spreads, and soon there are similar protests at other Read's around town. The chain's management sees the handwriting on the wall. Within days comes an announcement: the lunch counters at all Read's drugstores are now open to all citizens, just like that.

The change in policy gets a one-paragraph mention in the *Sun* on January 18, 1955.

But this is just the beginning. When some of these Morgan State students wander off their North Baltimore campus, they pass the Northwood Shopping Center, sitting in the very shadows of the school. And yet black people aren't allowed into the movie theater there.

A natural audience, a natural flow of money—and still the theater's owners say: No Colored.

Students begin demonstrating outside the theater in 1955. They're still out there in 1963. At first it's just a couple of kids—one from Morgan, one from Johns Hopkins—who want tickets to see a movie called *Untamed*. They're turned away. Within a week there are more than two hundred pickets outside.

White patrons holler at them, "Go to your own theaters."

Now it begins to dawn on protesters: Why are we focusing strictly on the theater? There's a whole row of lunch counters and stores here that won't serve us. This eight-year struggle becomes a crusade. Before it's over, hundreds of students—from Morgan, from Hopkins, from Goucher—are arrested for trespassing. Some spend weeks at the Baltimore City Jail next to killers and thieves. They're packed in six and seven to a cell, and some spill into the prison corridors. They sing spirituals every night. Other inmates tell them to shut up. It doesn't matter. The singing continues, and so does the picketing. By the time the protests are over, integration comes to all of the Northwood Shopping Center, including the movie theater.

But there's a price to pay.

White people grow weary of the confrontations. Yes, yes, these Negroes deserve to go to the movies and sit in restaurants. But why can't they wait a little longer? Why does everything have to happen now? These protests are going on all over town: at Woolworth's, at McCrory's, at Grant's. In one weekend, at a hundred different restaurants.

Better to leave such problems behind, thousands of whites tell themselves. And so the hunger for escape to suburbia deepens.

⇒

"Well, it felt pretty promising there for a while," Richard Holley says.

On a summer morning in 2009 he sits in his living room on Crawford Avenue, in northwest Baltimore, in the house where he's lived for about forty-five years. His teaching years at Hampstead Hill and Garrison Junior High are long behind him, as are all traces of the white students who went to those schools. There were white families in this neighborhood when he moved in, but they, too, started going away when the first black families arrived, and within five years virtually all whites were forever gone. The courts could change all the laws they wanted, but outside the courtrooms millions still lived by their own creeds.

"When we moved in back in the mid-sixties," says Holley, "we were all the first generation of black professionals. We were schoolteachers and post office workers and Social Security people." They were the first generation of blacks getting a shot at the American middle class. They arrived in this neighborhood during John Kennedy's and Lyndon Johnson's presidencies.

Kennedy sounded the first calls for racial fairness but couldn't move his civil rights bills through an intransigent Congress. In the emotional aftermath of Kennedy's assassination, Johnson gathered up a nation's grief, and its perception that Kennedy had been some latter-day Lincoln, to steer through the landmark legislation. For all those voicing the great hope for racial conciliation, the future seemed quite bright. For black families such as Holley's, Crawford Avenue with its grassy yards and its neighborhood school with black and white children was a world away from Fulton Avenue, where even the ministers had dug in their heels against integration.

Generations later some of those original black families remain, as do the neighborhood's charms: well-kept homes, clean streets, children playing outside the Grove Park Elementary School. But none of the children are white. The school opened in 1959 and was home a few years later to a handful of black students and about three hundred whites. By the end of the 1960s all whites were gone.

"A lot of us," says Holley, "it was the first time we ever lived in a neighborhood with trees and grass. Beautiful neighborhood, beautiful. Still is. I'm sorry all those white people felt they had to leave. Nobody got mad or raised any fuss with us the way they did on Fulton Avenue. They just kept moving out. Seemed like every day, somebody was moving. It was quiet and civilized, but it came down to the same thing. Black folks moving in, white folks moving out."

In Holley's living room are photos of Louise, his wife of fifty years, and their three sons, all dressed formally. Golf clubs rest on a nearby stand, like a testament to the good life. This is a long way from dreary Fulton Avenue.

In northwest Baltimore in the fifties there were no overt protests over school integration. Out here, many of the white students were Jewish. Their parents knew the sting of bigotry and knew that, even in postwar America, there were neighborhoods with restrictive religious covenants. When they moved into previously gentile neighborhoods, these Jews heard themselves called pushy and unrefined. They understood the mindlessness of prejudice. Many of them became great voices for tolerance, declaring that there was no room in America for racism. They stressed this to their children as they sent them off to school each new integrated morning.

And yet, when the dust clears in the great civil rights movement of the fifties, the Jews are as quick as anyone to bolt for the new, white suburban neighborhoods.

"For a while," Holley says now, "it looked like America tells itself it's supposed to look." He means this neighborhood before all the whites cleared out, and he means Garrison Junior High. The era of serious integration in the public schools of Baltimore lasted for about a decade.

"At Garrison," he says in soft, measured tones, "we had something that looked real promising for a while. Like that moment in the cafeteria."

He means that moment when all racial distinctions seemed to be pushed aside—when the black kid Claude Young climbed atop a table and began singing Ray Charles's "What'd I Say," and scores of kids, black and white, chanted back and forth with him.

"You can't plan a moment like that, like some school assembly, or some lecture on brotherhood," Holley says. "It has to be spontaneous. And then, when it is, there's no telling where it can take you. Listen, most of the time the kids were fine. But the parents were different. Even the ones talking all that talk about tolerance and brotherhood. The schools had a shot at working things out with the kids, but the parents were already scouting out new houses out in the counties."

In the early years at Garrison, the student body was a legitimate mix of black and white, and so was the staff. All these years later, Holley can still rattle off the names of the first generation of African American colleagues who were there with him—the science teachers Marcia Mills and Sarah Grey, the English teachers Carole Lomax and that sweet lady, Miss Millburn, the gym teacher Clarence Craig, and the assistant principal, Dr. Elaine Davis, all of them young, all of them standing there every day in front of these crowded classrooms of baby-boom kids of all backgrounds. Finally, it looks the way America's supposed to look.

He thought about that professor back at Morgan State College the day after the Supreme Court ordered school integration—the one who told the classroom full of young black men, "You better understand something. They are never going to let you people in a classroom with any of those young white girls."

But they did, didn't they? It was white girls and boys, and black girls and boys, and for a little while there it seemed like the old divisions might slip into the American past.

"And these kids were so bright," he says, "and you felt like you were bringing something into their lives they'd never had before."

Not just the foreign language that Holley taught, but the lesson every white kid absorbed: here was a black man, and he was just like any white man. And that was a lesson as big as any language skill.

But the lesson began slipping away as the kids did.

In the first autumn after 1954's high court ruling on school integration, Garrison Junior High opened its doors to 2,516 students. Twelve were African American. By the time Holley arrived five years later, the school was one-third black. Five years later, there were more than two thousand blacks and less than three hundred whites. A few years later, virtually all whites were gone.

Mostly, they went to suburbia. Nobody was singing any Ray Charles songs across the racial divide down in the cafeteria.

Holley lived on Crawford Avenue for nearly half a century. He organized a Cub Scout pack in the neighborhood. He coached amateur baseball and lacrosse teams. He was chairman of the governance board of the Frederick Douglass High School Alumni Association.

He moved in the 1960s from Garrison Junior High to Lake Clifton Senior High, where he continued teaching foreign languages. When he left Garrison, the last of the white students were leaving. When he arrived at Lake Clifton, there were no white students at all. Then he was named assistant principal at Lemmel Middle School. Lemmel's white students were all gone. In 1980 he became principal at Calverton Middle School, and he stayed there until he retired in 1990. Calverton had no white students.

Holley died of cancer in the spring of 2010. He was seventy-four.

Meaningful racial integration in the public schools of Baltimore City had died much earlier.

When President John F. Kennedy named former Baltimore Mayor Thomas D'Alesandro Jr. to the Federal Renegotiation Board, they were joined by Nancy D'Alesandro and by young Nancy, the future Speaker of the House. (Courtesy D'Alesandro family)

The *Sun* Sheds Its Light
John F. Kennedy

$\mathcal{A}t\ the\ dawning$ of the 1950s more than two-thirds of all Americans say they read a daily newspaper. We've got printer's ink all over our smudgy fingers. We read a paper over breakfast and another around the dinner hour while the kids have temporary custody of the only TV set in the house. Well, let 'em watch for a while. No adult with a three-digit IQ in the fifties would bother turning on a television to find serious news coverage.

The five to seven o'clock hours are strictly kids' stuff from the dawn of the fifties until the era's curtain time in 1963. Take Baltimore. The dinnertime TV offerings across the 1950s include *Paul's Puppets*, *Howdy Doody*, *Bozo the Clown*, the *Mickey Mouse Club*, *Popeye*, the *Cisco Kid*, *Amos 'n' Andy*, *Our Miss Brooks*, *Woody Woodpecker*, *Ramar of the Jungle*, *Kit Carson*, and actor Richard Dix starring as Officer Happy and hosting old *Little Rascals* and *Laurel and Hardy* movies.

At the tail end of such programs comes fifteen minutes of local news. This consists of an anchorman reading copy lifted from the local newspapers and wire services, a weather man delivering forecasts while wearing an Atlantic Oil cap in case somebody doesn't know who's sponsoring him, and a sportscaster whose visual effects consist of a photo or two from one of that day's newspapers. There are no street reporters yet; local TV hasn't discerned that in order to uncover news they first have to hire an actual reporter.

The networks aren't much better. The most popular TV news program in the early fifties is John Cameron Swayze's fifteen-minute *Camel News Caravan*, and the only thing anybody remembers about Swayze's coverage is his nightly lead-in, "Let's go hop-scotching the world for headlines." Hop-scotching the world in fifteen minutes, good luck with that. You want some semblance of real news in the 1950s, you read a newspaper.

In 1950 an American Newspaper Publishers Association survey says 78 percent of us read editorials. (This is no doubt a lie on a grand scale, since almost nobody really reads editorials, but at least it shows we're lying in the right direction, pretending to be a *serious* people.) Eighty percent read the sports pages. And 84 percent of us can't get through the day without Blondie and Dick Tracy. (This is a figure clearly closer to the truth, especially with the appearance of a new strip, called *Li'l Folks*, which changes its name to *Peanuts* and does pretty well.) Even more important to the great men who publish newspapers, 82 percent of their readers say they pay close attention to the advertisements, which are abundant.

In the 1950s newspapers are so healthy that they take out national magazine ads boasting of circulation and advertising gains. We've got roughly four hundred morning papers around the country and another fifteen hundred evening papers. Most are fat and rich and cocky, and their publishers cannot imagine that most of the evening papers will not survive the twentieth century, nor many of the morning papers, either.

In 1950, in a nation of 150 million people, the combined daily newspaper circulation is more than 100 million.

Sixty years later, in a nation that has more than doubled its size since the postwar years, 379 daily newspapers reporting to the Audit Bureau of Circulations declare a combined circulation of just over thirty million.

In 1950, the newspaper sits there at the heart of all public life. In Baltimore, if you want to know about Captain Emerson's latest vice squad raid to break up a pinochle game in Highlandtown, you check the paper. You want to know which ships docked at the city's bustling harbor last night with bananas from Central America, it's in the paper. You want to know which inmates were paroled from state prisons, there's a regular listing. ("Edward Harris, 49, Negro, sentenced to seven years, served five.")

You walk into any newspaper city room in Baltimore and hear the clackety-clack of Underwood typewriters and wire service machines and some editor yelling, "Boy! Copy!" as you inhale air thick with stale, lingering aromas: cigars, cigarettes, paste pots, carbon paper, raw ambition.

Take a deep whiff, boys, because all of it's on the way out, including the clackety-clack of all those Underwoods.

At the *Sun* editors await the latest dispatches from their overseas bureaus. The paper gives readers all the latest news from South Africa while overlooking every nuance of South Baltimore. At the *Evening Sun* the doyennes of the Women's Section will put something nice together on the city's upcoming Flower Mart. At Hearst's *News-Post* they're sending a small battalion of reporters over to The Block to uncover the highly important news of last night's felonious disrobing by Irma the Body.

You go to City Hall and there are newspaper guys covering the mayor, the city council, the Housing Department, the Department of Public Works. You go to the municipal courthouse and there's a busy press room with desks and typewriters and dial telephones set aside for the newspaper guys who camp out there daily, and there's another one right across Calvert Street at the federal courthouse. It's the closing era of "Hello, Sweetheart, get me rewrite." School board meetings are covered, and the liquor board, too. Hordes of newspaper guys cover the cops, cozying up to every desk sergeant they can find. There are newspaper reporters going through land records, court files, rap sheets, housing records. They're watching the governor, the legislature, the county executives. They do this every day.

How else do you find out what's going on if you don't have somebody watching on a daily basis? This is a question that will never occur to TV news executives, who will hire handsome and well-groomed poseurs and make lucrative careers swiping stories out of the daily papers and declaring, "Eyewitness News has learned . . . " while stealing away generations of readers.

In the 1950s newspapers are justifiably proud of their great names. This is still a time of Walter Lippmann and Murray Kempton, of Arthur Krock and James Reston, of Red Smith and Jimmy Cannon. Sure, it's also a time of the gossips like Walter Winchell and Louella Parsons but, what the hell, in these big, fat newspapers there's room for all kinds of voices.

The people who run Baltimore's *Sun* believe their paper is one of the country's most serious. The *Sun* has a bureau in Washington with eleven reporters. It has bureaus in London and Paris, in Moscow and Tokyo and other major capitals around the world. But, by the twenty-first century, the paper can't even afford a bureau in Baltimore County.

It's this way for newspapers all over America, and the great change-over starts now. In the 1950s most big cities boast more than one daily newspaper. New York has seven, whose combined 1953 Sunday circulation is just under eight million. Only three of Manhattan's big dailies will survive the century. Of Baltimore's three dailies, only the *Sun* will survive.

In December 1950, the deep thinkers at the *Sunpapers*—morning, evening, and Sunday editions—make their first major concession to change. They move the entire operation. The paper's been a fixture at downtown's Baltimore and Charles Streets, the very heart of the city, at so-called Sun Square. But now, like so many in postwar America, they feel the need to change homes. It's a pretty emotional moment.

"This newspaper's departure from its birthplace," says an *Evening Sun* editorial,

> from the scenes of its childhood, the place where it came of age, arouses a sentimental pang in the hearts of all who work [here].
>
> Farewell to the Sun Square traffic cop, to the Savings Bank of Baltimore, to the Hansa Haus, to the B&O, to the place where all the parades passed, where The Evening Sun Newsboys Band played Sousa marches, where the first election returns used to be flashed upon a white sheet by a magic lantern, where World Series were played upon a mechanical scoreboard . . . where the ends of two world wars and the doom of national prohibition were celebrated. To all this and the perfume of printer's ink in Sun Square, good-by!

Behind the sentiment is anxiety. The *Sun* can't get its delivery trucks through all that new postwar traffic. Worse, their readers have begun moving to the suburbs, meaning the trucks have to travel farther than ever before. They've got a nineteenth-century delivery system in a time when television's gearing up to deliver instant news from anywhere on the planet, if TV ever decides to get serious about it.

This is an era when the *Sun* has a highly respected national reputation. In a 1960 feature on the paper, *Time* reports, "The Sun abides like the oysters in Chesapeake Bay. Residents set such store by the *Sun-*

papers that they accept the *Sun*'s word as though coming from above, follow its paternal advice in running the city, and generally vote just the way the *Sun* tells them to . . . Everything in Baltimore revolves around the *Sun*."

In another flattering piece, three years later, *Newsweek* notes, "Coverage of foreign news by *Sun* correspondents in bureaus scattered from Moscow to Rio is thorough, thoughtful, and professional. Its Washington bureau is one of the finest. Its editorial cartoonist, R.Q. (Moco) Yardley, belongs in the same league with Herblock and Mauldin. Its history, dominated by the late H. L. Mencken, abounds with wit and influence. The *Sun* is a distinguished newspaper . . . President Kennedy includes it among his daily morning papers . . . Yet, in Baltimore nearly everyone avoids the *Sun*."

"The *Sun*," says its editor-in-chief, Price Day, "is the best unread newspaper in the world."

In a metropolitan area of 1.5 million people, the *Sun*'s circulation in 1963 is only 188,000. It's dropped by ten thousand in the last three years. Its sister newspaper, the *Evening Sun*, has dropped another eight thousand. Its afternoon competition, the *News-Post*, has slightly higher circulation but only a fraction of the ads.

The ground is shifting beneath their feet, and the *Sun*'s deep thinkers can't figure out how to stop it. Some of the trouble's staring them in the face: the paper's awful looking. There are many days when they don't bother running a single photo on the front page. Television's bringing us an age of visuals, and the *Sun*'s offering us eight front-page columns of nothing but words. Haven't these people heard about the invention of the camera?

But the biggest problem is that history has finally begun to catch up with them, and with all newspapers, and in November 1963, no one will capture that history the way television will.

≈

John F. Kennedy comes to Baltimore in 1957, when the mayor is Tommy D'Alesandro Jr., whose daughter Nancy is finishing her high school years at the Institute of Notre Dame. The mayor's got a seat at Kennedy's table at a big political dinner at the Emerson Hotel. Tommy's wife is supposed to sit next to JFK. But the wife is Big Nancy, deeply Democratic, passionately Catholic, veteran leader of armies of political women. This is a mother whose daughter is going places no American woman has ever gone.

"Tonight you go to the dinner," she tells the daughter.

The future Nancy Pelosi, the first woman Speaker of the House, sits next to the young Senator John F. Kennedy, the first Catholic who will be president of the United States.

They talk about his book, *Profiles in Courage*. They talk about politics. They find they can talk like a couple of grownups since teenage Nancy's already been at the political game about as long as Kennedy has.

She brings photographs of Kennedy to school and shows them to her girlfriends. Nobody looks at these pictures and talks about politics or profiles in courage. The girls (including the nuns, who know a good Catholic when they see one with political promise) all swoon as though it's Tab Hunter.

Such reaction is not exactly news to the Kennedy people. By the time he campaigns for the White House, his aides know they have more than a candidate on their hands. He's a sex symbol such as America has never seen in national politics.

Three years later, when his presidential campaign kicks into action, Kennedy returns to Maryland and speaks to the Montgomery County United Women's Democratic Club. These women in their flowery spring hats are all over him. They beg for his autograph. Hats are falling from heads. They do everything but run their fingers through his marvelous hair.

When Kennedy comes to Baltimore a few days later, the *Sun*'s editors are savvy enough to work the sex angle harder. Normally the paper wouldn't dream of such coverage—the *Sun* likes to think of itself as the poor man's *New York Times*, serious as hell and unconcerned with matters of the flesh—but this is too good to pass up. They assign a feature writer, Dinah Brown, to cover him. The story reads like fan magazine fluff.

Kennedy's "wooing the women of Maryland," Brown writes. And the women, "forgetting to be flirtatious and coy . . . followed the national vogue, mobbing the blond candidate at shopping centers, rallies and tea parties.

"One woman pried herself loose from the crush, subsided against a stone pillar and announced, 'It just about killed me, but I shook his hand.' A teenager ran shrieking from the crowd, saying, 'I got it, I got it.' An almost illegible 'J. Kennedy' was scrawled.

"A housewife who missed the Massachusetts Casanova's appearance by two minutes gazed wistfully after the car and murmured, 'Was he really good looking?' At an evening rally, women ranging from 8 to 80 waited more than an hour for the senator to make his appearance. Dowagers in furs, dowdy matrons in sweaters and skirts, and young women in cocktail gowns tagged by reluctant escorts lined the walls of the Emerson ballroom."

Nobody ever covered Eisenhower this way, or Truman, or Roosevelt.

Nobody even imagines covering Richard Nixon this way.

What we're witnessing here is not only the dawning of the Kennedy years, but the seismic shift of politics into pop culture theatrics. Eisenhower thought television cheapened the political process and made it seem juvenile. Kennedy understands the future has arrived. Get used to it, or get out of the way. Eisenhower detested TV news conferences and avoided them whenever he could; Kennedy will use them to charm viewers with his grasp of issues and, never to be minimized, his wit and his good looks. He and television have come of age simultaneously, to each one's good fortune.

When Kennedy debates Nixon, the postgame analysis is startling. Those who hear them on the radio believe Nixon the winner; those who watch it on TV believe Kennedy wins. Nixon needs a shave, and the poor guy can't stop sweating. If he's nervous against young Kennedy, how's he going to stand up to Khrushchev?

This isn't just the argument at office water coolers. The professional analysts are jabbering the same way. Never mind what the candidates might have mentioned about nuclear war. It's as if these political reporters are reviewing a TV show instead of a presidential debate about the future of a nervous world.

"Reactions to the debate," *Newsweek* writes, "were largely based on the physical appearances and manner of the candidates. Women in particular tended to dwell on Kennedy's personal appeal and on the fact—which almost everyone noted—that Nixon looked 'haggard,' 'tired,' or 'sick.'"

The star system is being introduced to American politics. From now on, we will judge our prime-time political figures the same way we judge our movie and TV heroes: not only by what they stand for but by how they look and how they touch us in ways we can't quite put into words. The days of seasoned old men working everything out in the smoke-filled rooms of political clubs are ending. Television is the new political boss, starting here and now.

America's about to fall in love with the Kennedys. They're giving us back our youth. *Time* and *Newsweek* run pieces on the romance between reporters and the new president. On Inauguration Day, millions watching from the warmth of their living rooms see Kennedy bare-headed in the frigid January sunlight, Prince Valiant standing tall while the old men like Eisenhower huddle in the cold, and Kennedy calls upon everyone to "ask not what your country can do for you, but what you can do for your country."

He's attached conscience to charisma.

Kennedy stares down the bully Khrushchev and gets us through a crisis in Cuba that threatens all life on the planet. He's cheered madly on all overseas journeys, thus reassuring us that a world choosing up sides between the commies and the good guys still loves America. He gives us the beautiful wife Jacqueline, who leads us on a TV tour of the White House. The two of them bring art and music and high fashion there. FDR gave us Kate Smith. Harry Truman played "The Missouri Waltz" on his piano. Ike read his Zane Grey westerns. The Kennedys bring Pablo Casals and Stravinsky to the White House and make it seem pretty cool. The country's finally coughing up the cultural cobwebs left over from the Ike and Mamie years. Kennedy reads James Bond spy novels. Now it feels cool to read. It feels cool to be young and educated, to sneer a little at those uptight years we're so happy to be leaving behind, and to vent endlessly about it.

The imagination of a generation of artists and writers, comedians and film makers, has been unleashed. As has a new generation of television news.

In the last two months of John F. Kennedy's life, network TV decides to grow up a little. Early in September 1963, *CBS News with Walter Cronkite* increases the length of its evening newscast from fifteen minutes to thirty. (Twelve minutes of that first half-hour newscast is Cronkite interviewing Kennedy one-on-one; the CBS boys know what sells.) A week later NBC goes to half an hour with Chet Huntley and David Brinkley. The noise heard in newspaper city rooms everywhere is the beginning of a death rattle.

For television the chill of the Eisenhower years has finally thawed. Across the 1950s Eisenhower sneered at TV and kept it at arm's length. Ike considered TV child's play; politics and government was the work of serious men. Let television give us *Romper Room* and *Roy Rogers*. Leave the work of adults to the grown-ups.

Then John F. Kennedy arrives. The young man smiles into a camera and a nation clutches its collective heart. "So smart, so handsome! Let's all watch!" The TV networks are not so stupid that they do not notice a few things: politics can be theater; politics can draw viewers.

Eisenhower was two years into his first administration before he reluctantly allowed TV cameras into his press conferences. Until then it's mainly Ike and some newspaper guys having an occasional chat, minus any theatrics. When Eisenhower finally relents, early in 1955, and allows TV cameras into his press conferences, he grumbles, "I hope it doesn't prove to be a disturbing influence."

Good luck with that.

Newspaper editors start imagining the future. In the *Sun* the editorial cartoonist Moco Yardley draws Lincoln and Patrick Henry and a whole ghostly political gang gathered around a TV set, where they're told, "You boys would have to learn a new technique today."

Kennedy understands this, and he also knows how to add. Consider Baltimore, at this time the sixth biggest city in the country. In 1948, the Baltimore Television Circulation Committee reports just eighteen thousand homes here with TV sets. A year later, the number doubles. A year later, the number quadruples, and thereafter there are TVs everywhere you look, familiar as indoor plumbing.

It's this way across the country. In 1950 the Television Broadcasters Association reports 3,700,000 American homes with TV sets. By 1955, ten times that many.

By Kennedy's era the whole country's plugged in. When he and Richard Nixon hold their televised presidential debates in the fall of 1960, sixty million people tune in. That's more than the number of people who voted for president four years earlier.

And reaction to the debates is like nothing previously heard. It's no longer analyzed as mere politics, but as theater, as cosmetics. *News-*

week does an "on-camera" rundown on each man. Nixon's "handicapped by heavy beard, reduced but still noticeable jowls." Kennedy's "highly dependent on studio lighting to give him a needed mature look. Shock of hair, though recently trimmed a bit, often looks as if it needs a thorough combing."

Nobody ever talked about Eisenhower in such terms, or Roosevelt.

Campaign financing is revolutionized. In 1952 the two political parties spend an estimated three million dollars for TV. The figure doubles in 1956. By 1960 the parties are spending more for TV spots than they do for newspaper ads. (In the 2012 presidential race the two parties spent an estimated six billion dollars for TV advertising and almost nothing on newspaper ads.)

By the late fifties both parties are experimenting with new TV gimmicks: animated cartoons, canned interviews, biographies modeled after the popular *This Is Your Life* TV show. America's never seen the likes of this.

By September of 1963 the networks are ready to hold up their end of the new marriage of politics and TV. Two months before the shots in Dallas, CBS and NBC have doubled the length of their evening news broadcasts. No longer will these programs be limited to a piddling fifteen minutes (minus commercials) each evening. No, sir. Now the great accumulation of news gathered by seasoned reporters and photographers from every corner of the world, every major capital and tiny hamlet, every government office and police station, every catastrophe large and small—all of this will be covered each evening in a piddling thirty minutes (minus commercials).

Never mind that eight minutes of commercials leaves viewers with a paltry twenty-two minutes of news from around the planet—somehow, it still has the sound of legitimacy when Walter Cronkite declares, at the end of each show, "And that's the way it is . . . "

And that's the way it is?!

Cronkite makes it work because he has the look of legitimacy. He's an old print guy who covered Europe and World War II for United Press before joining CBS in 1950. He looks trustworthy. Trust is important in television, where you're asking millions of viewers if you can enter their homes each evening while they're sprawled in their underwear. Personality is about to play an outsized role in who delivers the news.

But how do the networks shoehorn in as many stories as they do in twenty-two minutes? Easy. Some stories get fifteen seconds. Some get thirty seconds, or sixty. It's the rare story that exceeds ninety seconds, since the network execs make a startling discovery: viewers get accustomed to quick, punchy stories. A kind of Pavlovian effect takes over: at a certain point, we salivate for something new. Tell us another story, and then another, and make it quick, pal.

This is the beginning of the narrowing of the American attention span. A nation will discover its inner laziness. Who needs detail, who needs texture, when you've got those nice people on the air telling you some reasonable facsimile of the news? Just give us the headlines, and we'll convince ourselves we know more than we actually do. We'll watch TV news the way we watch all other TV shows: as an audience, not an electorate. We know these telecasters aren't giving us details, but so what? TV is new. We're charmed that they're here at all. And they're taking us off the hook, telling us we don't have to wade through all those words in those smudgy newspapers. They'll do the reading for us.

Huntley and Brinkley are NBC's front men. Their huge popularity stems less from any news-gathering than it does from chemistry, from the give-and-take between the two men. Huntley's the somber, philosophical older brother with the kind of rugged face that belongs on Mount Rushmore; Brinkley's the puckish, glib, witty younger sibling. He's got some *rascal* in him. The two of them are paired in 1956, and they're an immediate hit.

"An accident of casting," says their NBC producer, the legendary Reuven Frank. *Casting*: now there's a word never previously tossed around in journalism circles. "A phenomenon of show business, rather than of the news business."

When the two newscasters bid farewell each evening, signaling everyone's heavy thinking for the day is over, the sign-off becomes a national catch-phrase.

"Good night, Chet."

"Good night, David. And good night for NBC News."

The chemistry of Huntley-Brinkley versus Cronkite becomes a national debate. It's no longer the news, it's the personalities behind the news that juice the ratings. And, as ratings go up, evening newspaper circulation continues downward.

Two months after the networks expand from fifteen to thirty minutes, the shots are fired in Dallas. The networks have geared up just in time. For this is the weekend when America moves irrevocably from a nation of newspaper readers to a nation of television watchers.

We will watch like junkies getting their first real fix. And we'll find it so compelling that we'll return, night after night, looking for that same kind of high, until we find ourselves addicted.

This is the moment when the daily news changes dramatically—and so does America's way of absorbing that news.

The Day the Sixties Started

On $November$ $22,$ $1963,$ the day America drapes in mourning cloth for the martyred John F. Kennedy, the great fire at Saint Jerome's Parochial School, on West Hamburg Street in southwest Baltimore's Pigtown neighborhood, gets four paragraphs in the afternoon newspaper. Three hundred eighty children who might have been incinerated at their little desks instead huddle safely on the school playground and gaze upon the destruction. Of the day the fifties ended, this is the memory they will carry in their heads forever. The fire goes to four alarms. It demolishes the brand new auditorium dedicated only a week ago to celebrate the school's seventy-fifth anniversary. Thirty firemen clamber onto the roof to keep the blaze from spreading to the church and rectory next door. An inferno, they call it.

Four paragraphs in the afternoon newspaper, and that's it.

There is no room for any more coverage, nor heart for it.

"KENNEDY ASSASSINATED," says the late-edition *Evening Sun* page 1 banner.

This removes all other stories from the English language.

By the time the evening paper reaches people's homes Frank Luber, racing back from covering the Saint Jerome's fire, has been broadcasting the story for a couple of hours. The Kennedy story, that is; Saint Jerome's is strictly in God's hands now. Luber sits in this tiny studio at WCAO radio, and each new wire service bulletin out of Dallas carries fresh details for him to read aloud to all those who haven't got a TV set to turn on.

"The most important story of my lifetime," says Luber, who's still doing radio fifty years later. "And yet it was surreal. I couldn't believe it was happening, even as I'm telling everybody it's happening. I'm just reading wire copy, which was our source of news. We didn't verify anything. I was twenty-five. I wasn't a hard news person, I only had a couple of years under my belt, really. And we're a Top Forty station. You weren't doing investigative work at City Hall, you were just doing five minutes of spot news at the top of the hour. Fires, murders. So many murders, you feel jaded, day after day.

"And now this. People are walking around like they're in a daze. Nobody could have dreamed it was possible. You heard about these things in third world countries, but not in America. Afterwards I thought, Gee whiz, I just announced the president is dead. I wonder how many people heard it and said, 'What did he just say?' People thought they were hearing things. It really was the end of the fifties. Which we thought would never end."

Luber's voice—and all those radio voices just like his—carry everywhere.

On Baltimore's Calvert Street, outside the federal courthouse, sweaty workmen are digging into concrete with air hammers that rattle away like old-fashioned dental drills inside everybody's heads. Then silence replaces the noise. All work ceases as the usual afternoon courthouse crowd, workmen and passers-by, attorneys and uniformed cops, witnesses and defendants, all gather around one guy's transistor radio to hear the news.

Inside the courthouse a few floors above them, a grinning Joseph Tydings prepares for his farewell party. He's the outgoing U.S. attorney, and a future U.S. senator. He's got ties to the Kennedy family. When the news comes over the radio, Tydings goes completely to pieces. Sobs uncontrollably. Locks himself in his office with orders not to be disturbed. There will be no farewell party, not on this day.

In north Baltimore a woman sitting on her front porch with a transistor radio bringing the bad news finds herself surrounded by giggly junior high school girls who want to know what's going on. One of them, hearing the story for the first time, claps her hands over her ears, not to hear any more, and runs inconsolably into the distance.

The little chapel at Mercy Hospital, empty much of the day, fills to capacity as the news breaks. Patients in hospital gowns arrive, and nuns, and surgeons standing alongside janitors, all gathering in their grief and confusion. They're lighting candles and praying, and wondering how heaven could let such a thing happen. Down a nearby hallway a man named George Schoor, just out of surgery, lies in bed gripping his wife's hand when a patient from the room next door appears in the doorway like some angel of death.

"They said it on the radio," he says. "They said it twice."

"What's that?"

"The president of the United States is dead."

Jack Bowden's a young reporter for WBAL radio on this day. He'll go on to a half-century career as a TV newsman in Baltimore and Washington. But as news spreads of Kennedy's shooting, Bowden's driving up Baltimore's Charles Street, heading for the radio station after an interview.

"Ironically," Bowden recalls, "it was an interview with a guy from Dallas. And I see all these people on Charles Street, and they're crying. They're standing on the sidewalk and crying, and I'm thinking, What is this? And then I'm looking into people's cars and they're crying, too. What in the world?! But I didn't have the radio on, so I didn't know what they were crying about. People crying all along Charles Street. That's what I've never forgotten."

Nancy Pelosi was another who hadn't heard the news. She's a young housewife living in New York when her husband arrives home unexpectedly early.

"I was excited to see him," she says fifty years later. "He thought I had heard the news. He came home early to console me. He knew I was such a devoted supporter of President Kennedy's. But I had not heard the news . . . that devastated our entire nation."

That's as far as she'll go. An aide to the House Democratic leader, Drew Hammill, says that, fifty years later, "This is still a very emotional topic for her."

In 1963 Ann Werner's a student at Baltimore's Seton High School. At the end of the day she'll put her thoughts to paper: "Dismissal from school," she writes, "which is usually filled with noise and laughter, today took on a silent solemnity. Sobs, not laughter, filled the halls of my school. It was the death . . . most of all, of a friend . . . the most complete sorrow I have ever witnessed."

Barry Levinson's a student at American University in Washington,

D.C. He's running late for class. He's racing across the campus quadrangle to a classroom located on the basement level of a big academic building. There's a classmate, a young lady, sitting on a step next to a railing with a transistor radio in her hand.

"I remember the moment," Levinson says, traces of awe still in his voice. "I grabbed onto the railing, swung over the top of this girl, and ran down the steps into class. A minute later the girl walks through the door, holding her radio up, and she's in shock. Everybody looks up at her, like, What are you doing playing a radio in class?"

"The president's been shot," she said.

"And we all sat there," says Levinson, "and listened to this little portable radio, trying to make sense of what just happened. I remember that little transistor, and she's holding it up, and we're all sitting there in silence, just listening."

At the University of Maryland's Cole Field House, in College Park, boys gather for a required freshman phys ed lecture on hygiene. The instructor's a crew-cut gym teacher named Fluke. Early radio reports out of Dallas have begun drifting through the field house, but nobody knows the extent of the awfulness.

These are eighteen-year-old kids here, who came of age inspired by Kennedy. *Ask not what your country can do for you, ask . . .* Now their instinct is to rush from the classroom to find out what's happening to America.

"Everybody just sit there," Fluke orders. His tone is a sneer. He sees the anxiety on these kids' faces and seems halfway to mocking it. "I've got a lecture to deliver," he says. "When I'm done, *then* you can find out whether or not the president's dead."

Nobody moves. Something awful is happening outside this classroom, and these young men, immobilized by a sneer, are frozen in place, sitting here while this moron delivers a freaking *hygiene lecture*. They should toss Fluke through a window. They should beat him to a pulp for his attitude. Come on, guys, at least march out en masse. But they sit there and let Fluke drone on. Of course they do. This is their generation's last moment of innocence. They've been raised to respect authority figures. Now the sixties will arrive and they'll all make up for lost time.

At twenty minutes before two on the East Coast, those watching the soap opera *As the World Turns* find themselves staring at a grey screen. There's nothing there but the CBS eye and a graphic slide reading "CBS News Bulletin." Then comes Walter Cronkite's voice—no video, just the voice—announcing, "We interrupt this program."

Housewives pause over the laundry they're folding, or the family dinner they're preparing, or the carpet sweeper they're pushing. *What's this? They're interrupting my soap opera? Why are they interrupting my soap opera?*

"Here is a bulletin from CBS News. In Dallas, Texas, three shots were fired at President Kennedy's motorcade in downtown Dallas. The first reports say that President Kennedy has been seriously wounded by this shooting."

And then the picture comes back on, and it's *As the World Turns* again.

There's nothing else to report. Dallas has erupted in chaos, but reporters don't know the extent of it yet. NBC won't get on the air for about another minute. That's an eternity in a moment when people across the entire country are already reaching for their phones to tell each other, "Turn on your TV. Did you hear Walter Cronkite? Yes, it's on CBS! Yes, he said the president's been shot!"

A few more moments of *As the World Turns*, and then a commercial break for Nescafe coffee. In that moment, millions hovering over their TV sets—no remote controls yet—bend over to change channels. If Cronkite's got it, maybe NBC's got something! Maybe ABC! Or maybe we didn't hear what we thought we heard, maybe it's some terrible misunderstanding.

When they flip back to CBS, Cronkite's on the air again.

"More details just arrived," he announces. He's at a little desk now, glasses on, in his shirtsleeves, no jacket, pretty disheveled for a TV anchorman, which adds to the moment's unsettled feel. He's reading from a piece of wire service copy. He's as lost as everybody else but for this little piece of paper in his hand, this piece of paper that connects him to Dallas and makes him the nation's authority figure.

"These details just arrived," he says. "These details, about the same as previously: President Kennedy shot today just as his motorcade left downtown Dallas. Mrs. Kennedy jumped up and grabbed Mr. Kennedy. She called, 'Oh, no.' The motorcade sped on."

Something has happened out there in the shadows of sunny post-war America, something we've never imagined while so many of us were having such a good time for so long. We're out there in our shiny new suburban neighborhoods. We ran there in search of the American dream. We sit in the air conditioning of our new homes so we can block out the heat of the day, and the troubles. We watch our glamorous president on our brand new television sets. The television brings us America as we wish to see it, with people like that nice Anderson family on *Father Knows Best*, living in a comfortable suburban neighborhood that's only slightly better than our own. There are no drugs in that neighborhood, no crime, no surly teenage drapes, and no people of color marching into classrooms to sit next to white children. The television only breaks from its happy little comedies to bring us helpful commercials telling us about the latest space-age products to help make our happy lives even happier. The television networks allow twenty-two minutes of news each night to cover the entire planet. The stories run thirty seconds, maybe sixty seconds; any longer, and we might get bored and turn the channel. In thirty-second installments we learn that in India people starve and in Africa they put each other's tribal leaders to death. In America we only amuse ourselves to death. David Brinkley wraps up the news each evening with a charming, upbeat anecdote leading into the closing commercials and then says, "Good night, Chet." "Good night, David," Chet Huntley replies. That's our signal to relax, the heavy lifting's over. Sleep gently, America. Walter Cronkite assures us, "That's the way it is." Beautiful. Twenty-two minutes, and that's the way it is, the problems of the day are now behind us. Somebody turn on *Ozzie and Harriet* and we'll all put our brains on automatic pilot.

Whoever imagined the news could be this bad? Apparently we'd left a few disaffected people behind in sunny America, and one of them emerged from the shadows this very day and took aim at the whole damned complacent country.

Twenty minutes after the first stunning reports, the news gets worse. UPI quotes a Secret Service agent saying the president has died. CBS radio says a priest and a doctor confirm the death. They must be kidding; this must be some kind of cosmic joke. But then Cronkite comes back. In half an hour he's become America's grisly go-to guy.

"We just have a report from our correspondent Dan Rather in Dallas," says Cronkite, voice holding firm for the moment, "that he has confirmed that President Kennedy is dead. We still have no official confirmation of this, however. It's a report from our correspondent Dan Rather in Dallas, Texas."

Now he's stalling for time waiting for confirmation. Everybody's hoping there's been some mistake. Maybe Rather got it wrong, maybe UPI got it wrong, maybe the priest and the doctor got it wrong. Cronkite starts talking about the atmosphere in Dallas in the weeks leading up to Kennedy's trip, the political antagonism there. Then somebody off-camera hands him a note.

The look on his face says the news could not be worse. For years, when people talk about the things they saw on television this day, they'll recall Cronkite taking a beat to compose himself. He removes his glasses, puts them back on, glances at a clock on the wall, tries to get words out. He's everyman now, he's the mirror image of millions of us, trying somehow to get through this dreadful moment and make sense out of the senseless.

Finally, he says, stumbling slightly: "From Dallas, Texas, the flash apparently official. President Kennedy died at one o'clock p.m. Central Standard Time, two o'clock Eastern Standard Time, some thirty-eight minutes ago."

It was John Kennedy dying, and the fifties dying alongside him. The sixties are now upon us. They're a little late by the calendar, and they blindside us since the day starts like any other from the dying era. In Baltimore on this day a special legislative committee urges censorship of all movie nudity, which is "seriously detrimental to the mental and physical development" of all those under eighteen.

Of course, of course. Movies, *they're* the great threat to our postwar innocence.

In U.S. District Court Louis "Boom Boom" Comi is fined eight thousand dollars and ordered to spend eighteen months in prison for taking off-track horse racing bets.

Of course, of course. It's still the closing moments of the innocent fifties, when gambling's considered serious crime and a threat to our way of life.

Meanwhile a stranger with a gun shoves us from our sleepy mid-century America into something much darker, faster, out of control, deranged. We're ushered into the sixties against our will, still looking over our shoulders at the slain Kennedy. We watch the same newsreels over and over across an endless, haunted weekend. The networks will all stay with the Kennedy coverage, non-stop, until the president lies in the ground. For the first time ever, the whole country's watching the end of a life from our living rooms. It's our new form of mourning. We will learn it across the coming years like a macabre dance step.

On television the visuals of Kennedy's motorcade yield to scenes of horrified people on the streets of Dallas. These yield to Lyndon Johnson on Air Force One with his right hand raised in oath. These yield to Lee Harvey Oswald in handcuffs and Jack Ruby with a gun, and these in turn yield to the bright streets of Washington and a funeral procession watched by the whole world. And all will be shown over and over.

This is the beginning of a new kind of ritual. It is televised grief therapy. It will be repeated at all times of great tragedy in the coming years: the killing of Martin Luther King and of Bobby Kennedy, the *Challenger* explosion, the shooting of Ronald Reagan, the bombing in Oklahoma City, the terrorist attacks of September 11, 2001. And the death of John F. Kennedy Jr.

As the president is laid to rest, the newspaper columnist Mary McGrory tells the congressman Daniel Patrick Moynihan, "We'll never laugh again."

"Heavens, Mary," says Moynihan. "We'll laugh again. It's just that we'll never be young again."

Goodbye, willful innocence.

Hello, cynicism as national defense mechanism.

It's the death of the old Norman Rockwell America, the one where we saw ourselves as the good guys, handing out chocolate bars to orphans after winning a world war, and the birth of an America whose sons will machine-gun babies in Asian villages.

It's the death of an America whose bustling cities are emptying out, and those who remain behind are increasingly the old, the infirm, the impoverished, and the addicted. And one day soon many, in the wake of another assassination, will take out their frustration, and the rage of generations, by setting fire to those cities.

It's the death of an America whose college kids jammed themselves into telephone booths, staged panty raids, had a last fling at foolishness before settling into adulthood. In the sixties they're out there dodging tear gas and chanting, "Hey, hey, LBJ, how many kids did you kill today?"

It's the death of an America that had a brief flirtation with public school integration. By the end of the next decade the new suburban schools are virtually all white and city schools are almost all black.

It's the death of an America where children in public schools held organized prayer each morning. The schools are only a small piece of the change. In the sixties *Time* magazine's cover will famously ask, "Is God Dead?"

It's the death of an America that saw Perry Como and Patti Page yield to Elvis and Little Richard—all of them singing light-hearted and often silly love songs—and the birth of an America where Bob Dylan cries, "Something is happening here, and you don't know what it is, do you, Mr. Jones?"

No, we didn't know. It was all happening too fast now.

John Kennedy's death seemed to set off so much of it. His charmed life and awful death will leave us spiritually bereft for a long time. He becomes not just a martyr but a point of reference: here is where so much hope died.

But the man we thought we knew back then turned out to be somebody more complicated than we imagined.

The cold warrior stared down Khrushchev over missiles in Cuba, but he also helped set into motion a monstrous arms race that would last decades and eventually drain billions that might have salvaged neglected American cities.

He talked of civil rights, but it was late in the game by then. He feared the political fallout on race and had to be coaxed into the fight by those moved by simple fairness instead of political concerns.

He had wit and style and grace, yes. And women who dropped in when no one was supposed to be looking. In hindsight he sometimes seems an impossible gambler, a man outrunning his own sense of boredom.

But something beyond Kennedy himself stays with us. We remember how our hearts broke when we heard the news of his dying. This is the thing that stirs us across the years. He was the last fling an entire generation had with grand ideals.

November 22, 1963, took not only Kennedy's life but our own illusions. Dallas is where they were buried.

To watch Kennedy now in the old footage, even on that final day in Dallas, is to receive a perverse kind of gift: the knowledge that we could be so touched so many years later. Half a century after his death, the old images can still tear us up. Out of the ordinary numbness of daily life, it's nice to have this reminder that our hearts are still capable of such emotion.

But the pictures that touch us most deeply aren't specifically Kennedy, not any more. They're the surrounding players, who happen to have faces like our own. Some stand there on the streets of Dallas when they hear the news. They're crying their eyes out. They cover their faces in despair and in abject shame for their city.

And you see the crowd scenes from around the country as people hear what has happened, and all who were alive then remember how it was in their own lives that day: all those children hearing the news over school intercoms, who arrive home to find a mother weeping over the kitchen sink; and strangers gathering on street corners to hear reports coming out of car radios and transistors; and that lost weekend when millions stared at their television sets, transfixed, watching the previously unimaginable.

So November 22, 1963, the day the fifties died, becomes a sentimental journey. Look, there's John Kennedy in his youth! But it's more than that. There's the rest of America, in our own youth, still nurturing our ideals, still clothed in our innocence, not yet knowing how our hearts will ache for such a long time to come.

Notes on Sources

The Day the Fifties Ended

Much of the flavor of this chapter comes from being alive in America on the day John F. Kennedy was murdered. I was a college freshman at the University of Maryland and hitchhiked from College Park to Baltimore in the immediate aftermath of the Kennedy assassination. I watched two communities reeling in grief and disbelief.

The accounts of Frank Luber's reporting that day come from interviewing Luber. The accounts of the fire at Saint Jerome's Parochial School come from the *Sun's* story of November 23, 1963, "School Damaged by 4-Alarm Fire," and from Luber's memory. The accounts of WCAO radio that day come from Luber and disc jockey Johnny Dark.

The KBOX radio account is drawn from the Columbia Records album, *I Can Hear It Now: The Sixties*, written and edited by Fred W. Friendly and Walter Cronkite. The Robert McNeil and Edwin Newman radio accounts are drawn from the RCA Victor recording, *A Time to Keep: 1963, Voices and Events of the Year*, written and edited by William Alan Bales.

The account of the courtroom trauma is drawn from the *Sun's* story of November 23, 1963, "Naturalization Ceremony Becomes Mourning Scene," by Theodore W. Hendricks, and the account of the Lord Baltimore Hotel gathering comes from "Death Shocks Rights Group," by Frank Somerville, *Baltimore Sun*, Nov. 23, 1963.

White Boy at Doo-Wop's Dawning

In the beginning of this chapter, much of the flavor comes from living in Baltimore during the 1950s and '60s.

Much of the Jerry Leiber portion is drawn from interviewing Leiber a year before his death and visiting his old West Baltimore neighborhood. The Leiber interview was supplemented by *Hound Dog*, by Leiber and Stoller (Simon & Schuster, 2009), and *Rhythm and the Blues: A Life in American Music*, by Jerry Wexler and David Ritz (Knopf, 1993).

Accounts of Bethlehem Steel come from Mark Reutter's *Making Steel: Sparrows*

Point and the Rise and Ruin of American Industrial Might (University of Illinois Press, 1988); "Plant Soot Called 'Gold Dust,' It Means People Are Working," by John Ahlers, *Evening Sun*, Nov. 12, 1951; and *Roots of Steel: Boom and Bust in an American Mill Town*, by Deborah Rudacille (Pantheon Books, 2010).

Accounts of Baltimore's public baths come from *Sun* stories—"25 Spend 20 Minutes for Public Bath Scrub," by David Cullhane; "Our Man Finds Best Nickel Buy in Town"; and "Walters No. 1 Torn Down after 8,670,380 Baths," by William Manchester. All were written in the early 1950s. The parking meter information came from "Parking Meters Coming to City," a 1955 *Sun* story.

"Swallows and Orioles Make Saga of Success," in the September 15, 1951, *Baltimore Afro-American* newspaper, was helpful in writing about Sonny Til and the Orioles.

Magazine circulation figures of the era come from Publisher's ABC Statements, July–December 1953.

Pete Hamill's remarks about American music come from a 1970s Hamill column in the *New York Daily News*, "Music History Lives on WNEW-AM."

Passport across the American Racial Divide

Much of the material on Clarence Mitchell Jr. comes from interviewing his sons, Dr. Keiffer Mitchell, Michael Mitchell, and Clarence Mitchell III. They were interviewed specifically for this book. I also draw from numerous interviews across the years with all of the Mitchells, including Parren Mitchell and Juanita Jackson Mitchell.

Also helpful was Denton L. Watson's monumental biography, *Lion in the Lobby: Clarence Mitchell, Jr.'s Struggle for the Passage of Civil Rights Laws* (William Morrow & Co., 1990), and *A Defiant Life: Thurgood Marshall and the Persistence of Racism in America*, by Howard Ball (Crown Publishers, 1998).

Antero Pietila's book, *Not in My Neighborhood: How Bigotry Shaped a Great American City* (John R. Dee Publishers, 2010), was helpful on Fulton Avenue material, as were numerous articles in Baltimore's *Afro-American* newspaper, including R. B. Rea's "Pennsylvania Avenue" column of April 8, 1950; "Churches Lead Hate Crusade," March 10, 1945; "Fulton Avenue Home Stoned," March 10, 1945; "Frontiers Ask Member on Housing Planning Bodies," April 7, 1945; "Of Men and Jobs," by Alexander J. Allen, May 17, 1945, and such *Sun* articles as "Real Estate Men Scored: McKeldin Committee Blames Them for Race Strife," May 17, 1945, and "Real Estate Board Warns on Ill Feelings," May 28, 1945.

Clarence Mitchell Jr.'s arrest for entering the White Waiting Room was reported in "Retreat from Reason," *Time*, April 2, 1956. William F. Buckley's editorial, "Why the South Must Prevail," arguing against voting rights for African Americans, was written for the *National Review* in 1957.

A 1960 report from the Sidney Hollander Foundation, Inc., "Toward Equality: Baltimore's Progress Report," delineated the painfully slow year-by-year integration of the city's workplaces and recreational institutions, and Kenneth D. Durr's

Behind the Backlash: White Working-Class Politics in Baltimore, 1940–1980 (University of North Carolina Press, 2003) was helpful in understanding neighborhood and school race relations.

Juan Williams's biography, *Thurgood Marshall: American Revolutionary* (Times / Henry Holt, 2000), was helpful, as was *Up Close: Thurgood Marshall*, by Chris Crowe (Viking, 2008).

Clarence Mitchell III, Dr. Keiffer Mitchell, and Michael Mitchell offered additional material on Marshall, who was a frequent visitor to their home and was their father's close confidant.

Also helpful was "High Court's Tenth Member," by John Dorsey, *Baltimore Sun*, Feb. 20, 1966; "Marshall Quiet, Scholarly in 'Mr. Civil Rights' Role," *Baltimore Sun*, Sept. 24, 1961; and "Integration Gains Hailed: Marshall Notes 'Startling Change' in 10 Years," *Baltimore Sun*, Jan. 7, 1954.

Thrown Together on Both Sides

Richard Holley was the author's ninth-grade Spanish teacher at Garrison Junior High School during the 1959–60 school year. Much of the information here came from interviewing Holley on several occasions over the ensuing years, including a June 22, 2009, interview for this book.

Information about Garrison Junior High also came from the author's experiences at that time, including the cafeteria incident with Claude Young and the singing of Ray Charles's "What'd I Say."

Material about Morris Goldseker came from Holley's recollections. Also from Antero Pietila's "Not in My Neighborhood: How Bigotry Shaped a Great American City," and from "The Riddle of Morris Goldseker's Legacy," by Eric Siegel, *Baltimore Sun*, Feb. 5, 1978.

Material on Johnny Dark and Jack Edwards and reaction to rock and roll in the 1950s came from interviews with the two disc jockeys.

Material on Jerry Leiber came from an interview with Leiber and from *Hound Dog*.

Time and Opportunity

Rep. Nancy Pelosi was interviewed for this book on October 7, 2011, in her Capitol Hill office. Her memories formed the spine of this chapter, along with numerous other interviews: with her brother, the former mayor of Baltimore, Tommy D'Alesandro III; and, through the years, interviews with her parents, Annunciata and former Baltimore Mayor Tommy D'Alesandro Jr.; with former Gov. William Donald Schaefer; with Pelosi's brother Nick D'Alesandro; and with Ann Seely, former Pelosi classmate at Notre Dame who was the school principal when Pelosi became Speaker of the House.

These interviews were supplemented by Vincent Bzdek's *Woman of the House: The Rise of Nancy Pelosi* (Palgrave/Macmillan, 2008); "Case of the Bouncing Mayor,"

Saturday Evening Post, Sept. 11, 1954; and "Most. Effective. Speaker. Ever," *Ms. Magazine*, Winter 2011. Also, "The Little World of Tommy," *Time*, April 26, 1954, and "Big Leaguer," *Time*, May 16, 1955.

There were scores of newspaper and magazine articles attesting to female second-class citizenship of the era, including the following: "Marry 'Em Dumb, Boys; They're Less Inhibited," *Evening Sun*, May 5, 1953; "U.S. Lacks Equal Rights, Woman Lawyer Says," *Baltimore Sun*, Feb. 25, 1951; "Charm Class Offered Woman Teachers Only," *Baltimore Sun*, April 1, 1950; "Women Cabbies Undaunted: Kidding and Uneven Tan Worst Perils," *Baltimore Sun*, Sept. 1, 1950; "For 1st Time County Has Woman Prosecutor," *Baltimore Sun*, April 29, 1963; "A Woman Judge," *Baltimore Sun*, Aug. 3, 1961; "It Won't Hurt Because Dentist Is a Lady," by Robert Blake, *Baltimore Evening Sun*, June 2, 1959.

Also, "Hates Housework, So She Drives a Truck," by Donald Klein, *Baltimore Sun*, Sept. 1, 1958; "Women's Emotions Called Handicap in Politics," *Baltimore Evening Sun*, Dec. 1, 1950; "Now It's a Woman Traffic Cop—Maybe," *Baltimore Evening Sun*, Oct. 14, 1950; "Girl Is Sent Home from School, Skirt Is Called Too Risque," by Donald Bremner, *Baltimore Sun*, June 9, 1962; "Hair Tinted, Girl Kept from Class," *Baltimore Sun*, March 3, 1958; "Girls Squealing Too Much—'Rek' Dances Called Off," *Baltimore Sun*, May 10, 1956; "Ann Landers Says: Sex Is Like Football, Girls Should Hold the Line," by Louis Rukeyser, *Baltimore Evening Sun*, March 3, 1959; "Girls Reveal Strategy on Dating and Kissing," by Eleanor Johnson, *Baltimore Evening Sun*, Feb. 25, 1951.

Also, "U.M. Cracks Down on Girl Overnight Absences," *Baltimore Sun*, Oct. 31, 1963; "If You Can't 'Keep It Short,' Longer Kisses Aren't Really Dangerous," *Baltimore Evening Sun*, Nov. 25, 1952; "Cars and Good Grades Don't Mix, Students Say," by Francis Rackemann, *Baltimore Evening Sun*, April 28, 1959; "Eastern Girls Like Neat, Humble Boys," by Francis Rackemann, *Baltimore Evening Sun*, Oct. 1, 1958; "Recreation Center Molds Hamilton Teen-agers' Life," by Burke Davis, *Baltimore Evening Sun*, July 10, 1950; and "Teen-Age Financing: Girls Keep the Boys Poor," by Robert Blake, *Baltimore Evening Sun*, March 14, 1958.

Other helpful material included: "The Elvis Presley Fan Club Meets Once a Month to Talk about Their Hero," by Ralph Reppert, *Sun Magazine*, May 5, 1957; "Teddy Square on Rock, Roll," *Baltimore Sun*, May 5, 1956; "Vassar and Virginity," *Newsweek*, May 21, 1962; "The 'Confused' Young," *Newsweek*, July 1, 1957; "Teen 'Monkey Suits,'" *Newsweek*, March 11, 1957; "Books as Bombs: Why the Women's Movement Needed 'The Feminine Mystique,'" by Louis Menand, *New Yorker*, Jan. 24, 2008; and "Our Good Teen-agers," *Newsweek*, Nov. 23, 1959.

The Original Cast of *Grease*

Kenny Waissman was interviewed on August 13, 2010, at Joe Allen's Restaurant in New York City's theater district. His recollections formed much of the chapter's content, as did the author's own recollections of Baltimore's drapes, northwest Baltimore, and the Forest movie theater of that time.

These memories were supplemented by newspaper and magazine articles of the era, including "Drapes Branded as Wild, Detrimental to Youth," *Baltimore Evening Sun*, Jan. 30, 1950; "Zoot Suiters Unwelcome at Many Rek Centers," *Baltimore News-Post*, Jan. 26, 1950; "Drapes Extend Influence but Turn Conservative," by Frank Porter, *Baltimore Evening Sun*, Dec. 5, 1950; "Fourth of Juvenile Crime Linked to Gangs," by Burke Davis, *Baltimore Evening Sun*, Dec. 11, 1950; and "'Blackboard Jungle' Removal in Venice Laid to Mrs. Luce," *Baltimore Evening Sun*, Aug. 28, 1955.

Also helpful was Deborah Rudacille's "Roots of Steel: Boom and Bust in an American Mill Town."

The Vice Man Cometh

The author spent several decades writing occasional newspaper columns about Baltimore's gambling figures, all of whom had vivid memories of Capt. Alexander Emerson. Among them are vice squad Lt. George Andrew and such "sporting figures" as Albert Isella, George "Puddin'" Barry, Philip "Pacey" Silbert, Michael "Bo" Sudano, Jesse Bondroff, Daniel "Nookie the Bookie Brown" Brozowsky, William "Little Willie" Adams, and former *News-American* assistant Sunday city editor Jack Ryan, creator of the "Boom-Boom" in Louis Comi's name.

Their memories were supplemented by numerous newspaper articles of the era, including "Emerson Raid Seizes 54; 2 on Bail," *Baltimore News-Post*, Jan. 4, 1950; "Emerson Sued for $25,000 for Hamburger Error," *Baltimore News-Post*, May 4, 1951; "Pennsylvania Avenue," by R. B. Rea, *Baltimore Afro-American*, May 17, 1951; "Sodaro Warns Gamblers Due Stiff Terms," *Baltimore Sun*, Jan. 3, 1958; "17 Card Players Fined $25 Each, Put $340 in Poor Box," *Baltimore Sun*, Jan. 24, 1960; "Gamblers Are Losing to Rackets Division," by James White, *Baltimore Sun*, Sept. 30, 1957; "Urges Dope Fight under Capt. Emerson: Griebel, Mayoral Candidate, Cites Success against Bookmakers," *Baltimore Sun*, March 20, 1951; "63 Negroes Arrested in Pearl Street Raid," *Baltimore Sun*, Jan. 1951; "5 Held in $1,000 Bail Each in Numbers Case," *Baltimore News-Post*, Dec. 5, 1950; "Numbers Day in Court," by Burke Davis, Aug. 12, 1950; "State Asks Right to Try 'Little Willie' Over Again," *Baltimore Sun*, Oct. 14, 1950.

Also, "6 Men Seized in Crap Game," *Baltimore Sun*, Sept. 12, 1954; "Anti-Numbers Drive Staged by Police," *Baltimore Sun*, May 3, 1957; "Players in $1,950 Dice Game Fined," *Baltimore Sun*, July 7, 1951; "Poet Freed in One Grand Bail after Ode on Numbers Tale," *Baltimore Sun*, Feb. 14, 1951; "Some Numbers Dream Books Not Illegal," *Baltimore Sun*, Feb. 25, 1951; "Police Close Bingo Place; 'Benefit,' Sponsor Says," *Baltimore Sun*, March 3, 1950; "Bookie Office's Daily Take Put at More than $14,000," *Baltimore Sun*, April 17, 1962; "Man Is Held on Numbers Ring Charge: Police Seize 14 Others Following Reports of Crap Game," *Baltimore News-Post*, Jan. 10, 1952; "Emerson Nets 50 in Poolroom Raid: Captain Confiscates Dice, Money," *Baltimore News-Post*, March 1953.

Also, "That Man Emerson," by Donald Kirkley, *Sun Magazine*, Jan. 6, 1946; "Emerson: That Man with the Maul," by Donald Kirkley, *Sun Magazine*, Jan. 13, 1946; "Lieut. Emerson Makes 250th 'Bookie' Raid: Squad Smashes into House on Ashburton Street, 3 Men Arrested," *Baltimore Sun*, April 11, 1946; "Haircutting Goes

On during Raid," *Baltimore News-Post*, Dec. 6, 1946; "Mob Stymies Emerson Tactics, Leaves Vice Squad Flat-Tired," *Baltimore Sun*, Oct. 12, 1945; "Emerson Sets the Table—with Garbage Pail," *Baltimore Sun*, Oct. 14, 1950; "Judge Criticizes Emerson Tactics," *Baltimore News-Post*, Feb. 7, 1950; "Emerson Raid on Pool Hall Nets 76 Men: Three Face Bookmaking Charges after Frederick Avenue Arrests," *Baltimore Sun*, n.d.; and "Vice Squad Retiree Won't Quit," by Roger Twigg, *Baltimore Sun*, Jan. 15, 1977.

For information on the growing narcotics traffic of the era, the newspaper and magazine selections included "Text of Senate Crime Findings," *Baltimore Evening Sun*, Sept. 30, 1951; "Narcotics Move in Sellers' Market Where Customer Is Always Wrong and Broke," *Baltimore Evening Sun*, Oct. 1, 1951; "Dope Here 'Well Under Control,' Police Report," *Baltimore Evening Sun*, May 15, 1952; "Residents Hit Sherbow's Statements on Dope," *Baltimore Evening Sun*, Nov. 14, 1951; "Marihuana Use Leads to Heroin Addiction," by William Manchester, *Baltimore Sun*, March 23, 1951; "Marihuana Is Easy to Get, Cabbie Says," by Burke Davis, *Baltimore Sun*, March 22, 1951; "3 Jockeys Facing Dope Indictments," *Baltimore Sun*, Aug. 10, 1951; "Schoolgirls Tell Court of Dope Parties Here," *Baltimore Evening Sun*, Sept. 9, 1951; "Prison Inmates in Dope Cases on Increase," *Baltimore Evening Sun*, Dec. 11, 1951.

Also, "New York Wakes up to Find 15,000 Teen-Age Dope Addicts," *Newsweek*, Jan. 29, 1951; "Narcotics: An Ever-Growing Problem," *Newsweek*, June 11, 1951; "The Junkies," *Time*, June 25, 1951; "Heroin and Adolescents," *Newsweek*, Aug. 13, 1951; "Narcotics: Degradation in New York," *Newsweek*, June 25, 1951.

The author and his contemporaries' coming-of-age experiences filter through the section of this chapter on sex in the fifties, as does the analysis of JoAnn Rodgers and newspaper articles of the era on Captain Emerson and his new censorship assignments.

Also helpful: "Museum to Show Italian Film, Cut or Uncut," *Baltimore Evening Sun*, April 5, 1950; "Dispute in Dubuque," *Time*, April 2, 1951; "All About Eve: Kinsey Reports on American Women," *Newsweek*, Aug. 24, 1953; "The Censors," *Time*, Jan. 11, 1954; "Movie Morality," *Time*, June 11, 1956; "Sex & Censors," *Time*, Oct. 22, 1956; "What the Public Wants?," *Time*, Aug. 18, 1958; "Tabooed in Taunton," *Newsweek*, April 4, 1960; "Sex—Here and There: Co-Eds Fast, Not Loose," *Newsweek*, Sept. 12, 1953; "Sex vs. America," *Newsweek*, Aug. 31, 1953; "K-Day," *Time*, Aug. 31, 1953; "5,940 Women," *Time*, Aug. 24, 1953; "'Taboo' on Television," *Newsweek*, Dec. 9, 1957; "The Hidden Problem," *Time*, Dec. 28, 1955; "What Is a Homosexual?" *Time*, June 16, 1958; "One Man's Obscenity," *Time*, Nov. 25, 1957; "Playboy: Sassy Newcomer," *Time*, Sept. 24, 1956; "Movies Are Too Dirty," by John Crosby, *Saturday Evening Post*, Nov. 10, 1962; "Sinful & Suggestive?" *Time*, Dec. 29, 1952; "Tin from Sin," *Time*, March 25, 1957.

Also, "Legislative Unit Seeks Movie Curbs," *Baltimore Sun*, Nov. 25, 1963; "Club Seeks Rehoboth Beach Curfew on Bathing Suits," *Baltimore Sun*, May 23, 1961; "Sex and Celluloid," *Newsweek*, Dec. 11, 1961; "Feminine Neckline Plunge Creates Problem for TV," *Baltimore Evening Sun*, March 14, 1950; "Film Censors' Ban on 'Hell' Opposed," *Baltimore Sun*, Sept. 11, 1954; "Indecent Photo Sale Case Defense Cites Pratt Book," *Baltimore Sun*, Sept. 14, 1954; "Striptease Bill Is Called Unfair to Working Girl," *Baltimore Sun*, Jan. 23, 1957; "Tea and Sympathy," *Time*, Oct. 8, 1956; "Graham Calls Art Exhibit 'Trashy, Disgraceful,' Wants It 'Closed Up,'" by Peter Young, *Baltimore Sun*, July 17, 1962; "Library's Classics Seized in 'Lewd-Book' Raid," *Baltimore Sun*, March 10, 1951; "Obscene-Book Bill Planned by Goodman," *Baltimore Evening Sun*, July 17, 1957; "Trashy Books, Crime Linked," by Lawrence C. McDaniel, *Baltimore Sun*, Sept. 5, 1957.

Also, "Lewd-Picture Terms Go Up to 7 Years," by T. Denton Miller," *Baltimore Evening Sun*, June 27, 1958; "'Girly' Books Thrive, Md. Seeks New Law," by Bruce Winters and Philip Evans, *Baltimore Evening Sun*, Dec. 7, 1960; "Decency Group to Sift Books for Obscenity," *Baltimore Sun*, Oct. 17, 1961; "Could Clean Up Clubs in Week, Emerson Says," *Baltimore Evening Sun*, June 25, 1962; "Censors Plan Deletions in Jayne Mansfield Film," by Bruce Winters, *Baltimore Sun*, Oct. 24, 1963; "Prelate Forbids Catholic Seeing Of 'Baby Doll,'" *Baltimore Sun*, Dec. 12, 1956; "The Nation's Last State-Wide Movie Censors," by James Dilts, *Sun Magazine*, June 25, 1967; "Three Movie Censors at Work," by John Dempsey, *Sun Magazine*, Oct. 6, 1968; "When Hollywood Dared," by Geoffrey O'Brien, *New York Review of Books*, July 2, 2009.

The Most Hated Woman in America

The reminiscences of Madalyn Murray's attorney, Leonard Kerpelman, were very helpful for this chapter, as were the author's recollections of that era's classroom prayer rituals and of Baltimore's reaction to Murray's courtroom battles.

Also helpful were *The Atheist Madalyn Murray O'Hair*, by Bryan F. LeBeau (New York University Press, 2003), and *America's Most Hated Woman: The Life and Gruesome Death of Madalyn Murray O'Hair*, by Ann Rowe Seam (Continuum International Publishing Group, 2005). Also "From Sunday's Sermons: Heard in Baltimore's Churches," the publishing of church sermons each week in the *Baltimore Evening Sun* in the 1950s, and "From the Choir Loft," the lengthy schedule of choir performances published each week in that newspaper.

Also: "Boy, 14, Balks at Bible Reading," by Stephen Nordlinger, *Baltimore Sun*, Oct. 27, 1960; "Book Objections Listed by Schoolboy's Mother," by Michael Naver, *Baltimore Evening Sun*, Oct. 29, 1960; "No Suspension Slated in Bible-Reading Case," by Michael Naver, *Baltimore Evening Sun*, Oct. 31, 1960; "Lord's Prayer Reciting also under Fire," *Baltimore Sun*, Nov. 1, 1960; "Pupil in Bible Row Kept Out of Class," by Michael Naver, *Baltimore Evening Sun*, Nov. 28, 1960; "Atheist Mother to File Suit," *Baltimore Sun*, Dec. 2, 1960; "Atheist Suit to Bar School Religion Is Dismissed," by T. Denton Miller, *Baltimore Sun*, April 28, 1961; "Beall Plans Prayer Action; Decision Splits Clerics," *Baltimore Sun*, June 26, 1962; "Teachers Call School Prayer Helpful to Some, Just Rote to Others," by Edwin Hirschmann, *Baltimore Evening Sun*, July 7, 1962.

Also, "The Court Decision—and the School Prayer Furor," *Newsweek*, July 9, 1962; "Prayer Ruling Asked by Md.," by Edwin Hirschmann, *Baltimore Sun*, July 28, 1962; "School Prayer Rules Here Hit in Supreme Court," *Baltimore Sun*, Dec. 10, 1962; "Mrs. Murray, Judge Wrangle in Court," *Baltimore Sun*, Sept. 27, 1962; "Mrs.

Murray, Son, Atheists Protesting," *Baltimore Evening Sun*, Feb. 27, 1963; "Supreme Court Justices Debate Prayer in Schools," by Anthony Lewis, *New York Times*, Feb. 27, 1963; *Life*'s editorial of March 15, 1963, and Madalyn Murray's response of April 12, 1963; "2 Cases Decided: Government Must Be Neutral in Religion, Majority Asserts," by Anthony Lewis, *New York Times*, June 17, 1963; "Supreme Court Bans Required Bible Reading, Prayer in Schools," *Baltimore Evening Sun*, June 17, 1963; "Organized Prayers Said Last Time in City Schools," *Baltimore Evening Sun*, June 18, 1963; "The Supreme Court: A Loss to Make Up For," *Time*, June 28, 1963; "Mrs. Murray Fighting Tax Exempting Churches," *Baltimore Sun*, Oct. 7, 1963; "3 Housewives Campaign for School Prayers," *Baltimore Sun*, Oct. 23, 1963; "Atheist's Son Moves Away from Home," *Baltimore Sun*, Nov. 12, 1963.

Also, "The Most Hated Woman in America," by Jane Howard, *Life*, June 19, 1964; "Mrs. Murray's War on God," by Robert Liston, *Saturday Evening Post*, July 11, 1964; Bynum Shaw's Oct., 1964, piece in *Esquire*; and the *Playboy* Interview of October 1965.

For general material about religion in America in the 1950s, the following were helpful: "Insecurity Brings Religious Upsurge," by George Cornell, *Baltimore Evening Sun*, Feb. 2, 1951; "Bishop Fulton J. Sheen Preaches Absorbing Sermons in 'Life is Worth Living' Series," by Jack Gould, *New York Times*, Feb. 22, 1952; "Bishop Sheen, Microphone Missionary," *Time*, April 14, 1952; "The Bishop Looks at Television," by Val Adams, *New York Times*, April 16, 1952; "Do Americans Believe in God?—99 to 1," *Time*, Oct. 20, 1952; "Video Departure: Bishop Sheen's Program to Be Sponsored," by Jack Gould, *New York Times*, Oct. 28, 1952; "A Clergyman Discusses Sponsors and Video," by the Rev. Clyde D. Williams, *New York Times*, Nov. 2, 1952; "Plaque for Bishop Sheen: Advertising Club Names Him Our Television Man of the Year," *New York Times*, April 30, 1953.

Also, "More Church Members," *Newsweek*, March 24, 1953; "The Bible in Modern Undress," *New Yorker*, Nov. 14, 1953; "Oral Roberts' Deadline from God," *Time*, July 11, 1955; "Is Communism Christian?" *Time*, July 11, 1955; "The American Religion," *Time*, Sept. 26, 1955; "Americans and Religion: State of the New Revival," by Reinhold Niebuhr, Billy Graham, and John LaFarge, *Newsweek*, Dec. 26, 1955; "Clergy Sees Rapid Increase in U.S. Desire for Religion," by William Blair, *Baltimore Evening Sun*, Jan. 2, 1957; "Billy and Benny," by E. J. Kahn Jr., *New Yorker*, June 8, 1957; "The Christ Doll & All," *Time*, Dec. 29, 1958; "Parish Politics: After World War II, Roman Catholicism and the American Image Converged," *New York Times Book Review*, Aug. 17, 1997; "Oral Roberts: The Man Who Made God His ATM," by Michelle Goldberg, *Daily Beast*, Dec. 19, 2009.

The Diner Guy

Much of this chapter comes from interviewing Barry Levinson over the past few decades, including two interviews in 2012 specifically for this book. Other interviews conducted by the author through the years also added to this chapter's flavor: with Paul Reiser, Leonard "Boogie" Weinglass, Donald Saiontz, Richard Sher, Gary

Huddles, Gene Modell, Clarinda Harriss Lott, and Paul Stamas, owner of the Hilltop Diner in the post–World War II years.

Also helpful: "Same Time, Same Station: Creating American Television, 1948–61," by James L. Baughman (Johns Hopkins University Press, 2007); "Right Here on Our Stage Tonight: Ed Sullivan's America," by Gerald Nachman (University of California Press, 2009).

Also, "Sonny: An Introduction," *Time*, Sept. 15, 1961; "Holden at Fifty: 'The Catcher in the Rye' and What It Spawned," by Louis Menand, *New Yorker*, Oct. 1, 2001; "Marlon Brando: Hostage of His Own Genius," by Richard Schickel, *Time*, July 12, 2004; "J. D. Salinger, Literary Recluse, Dies at 91," by Charles McGrath, *New York Times*, Jan. 28, 2010; "Of Teen Angst and an Author's Alienation: An Appraisal of J. D. Salinger," by Michiko Kakutani, *New York Times*, Jan. 29, 2010; "Special Order: 'Diner' may be 30, but its cast and influence are timeless," by Michael Sragow, *Baltimore Sun*, Dec. 4, 2011; "How Barry Levinson's 'Diner' Changed Cinema, 30 Years Later," by S. L. Price, *Vanity Fair*, Feb. 2012.

"I Am an American, Too"

The author spent much of a year reviewing microfilm of Baltimore's daily newspapers from the dawn of 1950 through the close of 1963. Coverage of public school integration provided a treasure trove of information to supplement interviews with Dr. Keiffer Mitchell and Michael Mitchell and above-noted biographies of Thurgood Marshall and Clarence Mitchell Jr.

Particularly helpful on insights into Marshall and Mitchell: "Negro Files Suit for Admittance," *Baltimore Sun*, April 21, 1935; "Negroes Organize Here for Own Advancement," *Baltimore Sun*, Oct. 10, 1935; "Status of Negro Student the Same," *Baltimore Sun*, Jan. 17, 1936; "Negro High School in County Sought," *Baltimore Sun*, May 15, 1936; "Segregation Issue Debated," *Baltimore Sun*, Jan. 9, 1948; "Negro Asks U.M. Admission," *Baltimore Sun*, Aug. 16, 1950; "Association Will Probe Negroes' Army Trials," *Baltimore Sun*, Jan. 11, 1951.

Also: "Lawyer Raps Segregation: Marshall Says Discrimination is 'Unlawful and Immoral," *Baltimore Sun*, Oct. 19, 1951; "This is the NAACP: The Leaders—the Target," *Newsweek*, Oct. 14, 1957; "Marshall Quiet, Scholarly in 'Mr. Civil Rights' Role," *Baltimore Sun*, Sept. 24, 1961; "High Court's Tenth Member," by John Dorsey, *Baltimore Sun*, Feb. 20, 1966.

Particularly helpful on Supreme Court coverage of the Brown case: "The Segregation Issue," *Time*, Dec. 22, 1952; "When the Barriers Fall," *Time*, Aug. 31, 1953; "Attack on Segregation Opened in High Court," by Gerald Griffin, *Baltimore Sun*, Dec. 8, 1953; "May It Please the Court.," *Time*, Dec. 21, 1953; "The Fading Line," *Time*, Dec. 21, 1953; "High Tribunal Bans Race Segregation in Schools," *Baltimore Evening Sun*, May 17, 1954; "Supreme Court Bans Segregated Schools," by Gerald Griffin, *Baltimore Sun*, May 18, 1954; "The School Segregation Cases," *Baltimore Sun*, May 18, 1954; "Court Ruling 'Disappointing' to Southern Congressmen," by Dewey Fleming, *Baltimore Sun*, May 18, 1954.

Also "Western Press Hails Ban of Segregation," *Baltimore Evening Sun*, May 19, 1954; "Southern Call for Calmness," editorials from the *Times* of Chattanooga, Tenn., the *Times-Dispatch* of Richmond, Va., and the *State*, Columbia, S.C.; "To All on Equal Terms," *Time*, May 24, 1954; "Historic Decision," *Newsweek*, May 24, 1954; "Talmadge and Segregation: He Makes His Stand," *Newsweek*, May 31, 1954; "Integration Gains Hailed: Marshall Notes 'Startling Change' in 10 Years," *Baltimore Sun*, June 7, 1954; "Report Card: Progress of the States toward School Desegregation," *Time*, Sept. 19, 1955.

Particularly helpful on Baltimore's school integration: "Public School Crowding Affects 11 P.C. of Children, Study Shows," *Baltimore Sun*, March 1, 1950; "Poly 'A' Course to be Opened to Negroes," *Baltimore Sun*, Sept. 3, 1952; "Printing School Entry Sought for Negroes," *Baltimore Sun*, June 5, 1953; "Mix Schools: Court Rules Segregation Illegal," *Baltimore Afro-American*, May 18, 1954; "Races to Join in Teaching," *Baltimore Sun*, May 31, 1954; "Segregation's End Here," *Baltimore Evening Sun*, June 5, 1954; "U.M. Regents Vote to Drop Segregation," *Baltimore Evening Sun*, June 25, 1954; "City's Preparation for End of Segregation Is Praised," by Odell M. Smith, *Baltimore Sun*, Sept. 6, 1954.

Also "Segregation Concluded as Schools Open: First Day Passes with Few Complaints, No Serious Clashes," *Baltimore Sun*, Sept. 8, 1954; "Groups to Fight Desegregation," *Baltimore Sun*, Sept. 13, 1954; "State P-TA Gives View on Integration," *Baltimore Evening Sun*, Sept. 14, 1954; "Integration Notice Filed with Court; State Wants Method and Pace Left to School Boards," *Baltimore Sun*, Sept. 15, 1954; City Schools Open, Some with Mixed Enrollment," by Gwinn Owens, *Baltimore Evening Sun*, Sept. 17, 1954; "Women Picket School No. 34; Classes Small," *Baltimore Evening Sun*, Sept. 30, 1954.

Also "School Boycott Spreading in City," *Baltimore Evening Sun*, Oct. 2, 1954; "Police Battle Milling Crowd; Traffic Blocked on Light Street as Integration Fighting Flares Up," *Baltimore News-Post*, Oct. 2, 1954; "'Crackdown' Order Issued," *Baltimore News-Post*, Oct. 3, 1954; "Integration at Southern Stirs Unrest," *Baltimore Sun*, Oct. 3, 1954; "Students March in Integration Protest," *Baltimore Evening Sun*, Oct. 4, 1954; "Parents Defy Police; 600 Extra Cops on Duty," *Baltimore News-Post*, Oct. 4, 1954; "Students March on City Hall, Southern High School," *Baltimore News-Post*, Oct. 4, 1954; "The Ugly Episode at Southern High School," *Baltimore Sun*, Oct. 5, 1954; "Dr. Byrd Hints Attitude on Segregation," by William Jabine, *Baltimore Sun*, Oct. 5, 1954; "Coolness Needed," *Baltimore Evening Sun*, Oct. 6, 1954; "Notes on the Mess," by Louis Azrael, *Baltimore News-Post*, Oct. 7, 1954; "What the Reds Might Say," by Louis Azrael, *Baltimore News-Post*, Oct. 8, 1954; "Segregation," *Baltimore News-Post*, Oct. 10, 1954; "Friends School Will Admit Negroes," by Gwinn Owens, Nov. 21, 1954.

Hello Towson, Hello Pikesville

I was part of the suburban exodus, as were many of my family and friends, and our experiences contribute to this chapter's flavor, along with interviews of Keiffer and

Michael Mitchell, Regina Wright Bruce, and Richard Holley, and extensive newspaper and magazine coverage of the era.

Among the most helpful stories: "New Traffic Light Allotted to Essex," *Baltimore News-Post*, Feb. 1, 1950; "School Building Score: County, 14; City, 0," by Odell M. Smith and Lawrence Efford, *Baltimore Evening Sun*, April 1, 1950; "Population Up 48% in Harford Co.," *Baltimore Evening Sun*, June 25, 1950; "County Schools Enroll Record 40,046," *Baltimore Evening Sun*, Oct. 4, 1950; "Dundalk Population Up 160 Per Cent in 10 Years," by John Goodspeed, *Baltimore Evening Sun*, Dec. 11, 1950; "Baltimore County's Headache: School Enrollment Rising Rapidly, Pupils May Double in Five Years," by Robert Moyer, *Baltimore Evening Sun*, Feb. 14, 1951.

Also "State School Segregation End Delayed," *Baltimore Sun*, May 27, 1954; "State to Map Plans to End Race Bias," *Baltimore Evening Sun*, May 27, 1954; "Negro Teachers," *Newsweek*, July 19, 1954; "Back Streets of Baltimore: 2,000 Blighted Blocks Housing 365,000 Cover Nearly Third of City," *Baltimore Evening Sun*, Sept. 12, 1954; "Absentee Landlords Find Slum Realty Pays," *Baltimore Evening Sun*, Sept. 13, 1954; "Slums Cost City's Taxpayers Cold Cash," *Baltimore Evening Sun*, Sept. 14, 1954; "School Segregation Comes to Quiet End in Washington," by Peter Kumpa, *Baltimore Sun*, Sept. 14, 1954; "Negroes Enroll at First Dixie White School," *Baltimore Evening Sun*, Sept. 15, 1954; "Zoning Breakdown Leads to Blight," *Baltimore Evening Sun*, Sept. 15, 1954.

Also "First Family to Move into New Apartment," *Baltimore Evening Sun*, May 20, 1955; "McKeldin Asks State to Avoid School Integration Delays," *Baltimore Evening Sun*, June 1, 1955; "The Plight of Suburbia," *Time*, July 25, 1955; "4,000 Students Facing Half-Day Schedules," by Gwinn Owens, *Evening Sun*, Aug. 29, 1955; "8 Counties End Tradition with Integration," *Baltimore Evening Sun*, Sept. 2, 1955; "1,000,000 Population Still Eludes City as Suburbs Mark Up Gains," by Martin Millspaugh, *Baltimore Evening Sun*, Oct. 1, 1955; "City Population Gains 32% in 37 Years, That in 2 Abutting Counties 320%," by Martin Millspaugh, *Baltimore Evening Sun*, Oct. 4, 1955; "Two Booming Urban Centers Make State Population Jump," by Martin Millspaugh, *Baltimore Evening Sun*, Oct. 5, 1955; "6 High Schools Are Integrated," *Baltimore Evening Sun*, Sept. 7, 1955; "Cars, Trucks Jam Former Carriage Road," by Richard K. Tucker, *Baltimore Evening Sun*, Oct. 10, 1955; "Industry Draws Baltimore's Suburban Exodus," by Richard K. Tucker, *Baltimore Evening Sun*, Oct. 13, 1955; "Arbutus-Lansdowne Growth Tops 4,000 since 1950," by Richard K. Tucker, *Baltimore Evening Sun*, Oct. 14, 1955; "Growing Northwest Baltimore: The City Takes the Liberty, Reisterstown Roads," by Richard K. Tucker, *Baltimore Evening Sun*, Oct. 17, 1955.

Also "Integration Resistance," *Baltimore Evening Sun*, Oct. 15, 1955; "Substandard Schools," *Baltimore Evening Sun*, May 7, 1957; "Park Pool Shut, Too Few Swim," *Baltimore Sun*, July 20, 1956; "Attendance at Public, Private Pool Drops," *Baltimore Evening Sun*, Aug. 1, 1956; "Mondawmin to Open as Shopping Center," *Baltimore Evening Sun*, Sept. 18, 1956; "Eastpoint, City's Newest Shopping Center," *Baltimore Evening Sun*, Oct. 9, 1956; "Desegregation Policy Upheld for Harford," by Gwinn Owens, *Baltimore Evening Sun*, March 3, 1957; "Living Atop a Civic Mushroom,"

Newsweek, April 1, 1957; "County Schools Face Worst Housing Crisis," by Lawrence Efford, *Baltimore Evening Sun*, May 13, 1957; "25 Schools End Segregation," *Baltimore Evening Sun*, Aug. 30, 1957; "FBI Probe of McKeldin Cross Burning Asked," *Baltimore Evening Sun*, Sept. 7, 1957.

Also "The Critical Spots: The Real Victim of School Crowding—The Child," by Gwinn Owens, *Baltimore Evening Sun*, Sept. 25, 1957; "Mobile Classrooms Used in Baltimore County," by George Eagle, *Baltimore Evening Sun*, March 7, 1958; "268.8 Acres of Blighted Land Erased—5,600 Acres to Go," by Colin MacLachlan, *Baltimore Evening Sun*, March 11, 1958; "Rented Classrooms to Be Used This Year, Superintendent Reports," by Bruce Winters, *Baltimore Evening Sun*, Aug. 8, 1958; "Latest Problem for Cities in North: 'Blockbusting,'" *U.S. News & World Report*, Dec. 5, 1958; "Cozy Catastrophe: Suburbia: Its People and Their Politics," *Newsweek*, Jan. 19, 1959; "Metropolis in a Mess," *Newsweek*, July 27, 1959; "Americana: The Roots of Home," *Time*, June 20, 1960.

Also "Record 86,145 Pupils at Baltimore County Schools," by Lawrence Efford, *Baltimore Evening Sun*, Aug. 15, 1960; "170,440 Pupils Will Troop into City Schools," by Robert Highton, *Baltimore Evening Sun*, Aug. 19, 1960; "Rise Reported in Non-White Population," by Bruce Winters, *Baltimore Evening Sun*, May 13, 1961; "2 Negro Youths Seized at Restaurant Sit-In," *Baltimore Evening Sun*, Aug. 12, 1961; "Baltimore County Record Enrollment Near 6,000 More Than Last Year," by Lawrence Efford, *Baltimore Evening Sun*, Aug. 9, 1961; "Decline in Detroit," *Time*, Oct. 27, 1961; "Md. Considers Integration in Hospitals," Nov. 8, 1961; "The City: Deplanning the Planners," *Time*, Nov. 10, 1961; "Student Pickets Sing Hymns at 100 Restaurants Here," *Baltimore Sun*, Nov. 18, 1961.

Also "Population Growth Continues throughout Baltimore County," *Baltimore Evening Sun*, Dec. 14, 1961; "Won't Drop Color Bar, Ocean City Mayor Says," by Richard Pollak, *Baltimore Evening Sun*, May 17, 1962; "Integration Seen Hurting Ocean City," *Baltimore Evening Sun*, May 20, 1962; "5 More Counties Integrate Schools; Only Three in State Aren't Biracial," *Baltimore Evening Sun*, Sept. 5, 1962; "Morgan Bail up to $600," *Baltimore Evening Sun*, Feb. 19, 1963; "Baltimore Movie Ends Segregation," *Washington Post*, Feb. 22, 1963; "Races: The Price of a Ticket," *Newsweek*, Feb. 26, 1963; "Owners Agree to Integrate Theater," by Jerome Kelly, *Baltimore Evening Sun*, Feb. 21, 1963.

Also "Industry Threatens Harford's Rural Character," *Baltimore Evening Sun*, April 17, 1963; "100 Parents Protest School Integration in Hamilton," *Baltimore Sun*, Sept. 5, 1963; "Parents Map Fight against Negro Shifts," *Baltimore Evening Sun*, Sept. 7, 1963; "The Changing Face of Towson: When They're Through You'll Hardly Recognize the Place," by Alan Lupo, *Baltimore Evening Sun*, Oct. 23, 1963; "City Population Drops 2%," by Richard Frank, *Baltimore Evening Sun*, Nov. 21, 1963; "Richard Holley: Calverton Middle School principal spent 32 years in education and was a Grove Park neighborhood official," by Jacques Kelly, *Baltimore Sun*, April 24, 2010; "Freedom Trains," by David Oshinsky, *New York Times*, Sept. 2, 2010; "The Uprooted," by Jill Lepore, *New Yorker*, Sept. 6, 2010.

The *Sun* Sheds Its Light

Accounts of newspaper conditions in the 1950s come from the author's lengthy career in the newspaper business, plus these articles: "Newspapers Hit All-Time High in Readers," *Baltimore Evening Sun*, Feb. 17, 1950; "What You Read: Death and Weather," *Newsweek*, Jan. 29, 1951; "The Century's Daybook," *Newsweek*, Sept. 24, 1951; "The Anatomy of a Real Foreign Correspondent," *Newsweek*, March 5, 1958; "New York without Papers," *Time*, Dec. 22, 1958; "Do You Belong in Journalism?" by A. J. Liebling, *New Yorker*, May 1, 1960; "Punditry & Partisanship," *Time*, Nov. 7, 1960; "Ever on Sunday," *Time*, Dec. 1, 1961; "Shattered Mirror," *Time*, Oct. 28, 1961; "Death in the Family, *Newsweek*, Oct. 28, 1963; "Newspapers across the Country Show Steep Declines in Circulation," by Jennifer Saba, *Ad Week*, Oct. 26, 2009.

Material on the *Sun* came from: "Sunpapers Moving Plant to New Calvert St. Site," *Baltimore Sun*, Dec. 22, 1950; "Good-by, Sun Square, *Baltimore Sun*, Dec. 23, 1950; "We're Moved," *Baltimore Evening Sun*, Dec. 26, 1950; "This Is First *Evening Sun* Printed in New Building," *Baltimore Evening Sun*, Dec. 26, 1950; "The Sun's Orbit," *Time*, April 11, 1960; "Sun Shine," *Newsweek*, May 6, 1963.

Material on Kennedy and Richard Nixon came from "Grady, Tommy Huddle with Kennedy," by Louis Rukeyser, *Baltimore Evening Sun*, July 14, 1959; "Kennedy Campaigns in Md. Supports Education Aid," by David Culhane, *Baltimore Evening Sun*, May 12, 1960; "Ladies Look and Listen to Kennedy," by Dinah Brown, *Baltimore Sun*, May 16, 1960; "The Romance," *Time*, July 18, 1960; "Kennedy & the Press," *Time*, July 25, 1960; "Nixon & the Press," *Time*, Aug. 8, 1960; "Kennedy's State Visit Successful," by David Culhane, *Baltimore Evening Sun*, Sept. 25, 1960; "TV Debate Backstage: Did the Cameras Lie?" *Newsweek*, Oct. 10, 1960; "The Campaign: Debate No. 2," *Time*, Oct. 17, 1960; "Climate: Chilly," *Time*, Oct. 24, 1960; "The Vigil on the Screen," *Time*, Nov. 16, 1960.

Material on TV news came from "TV Keeps More People Home, Survey Says," *Baltimore Sun*, May 25, 1950; "You Boys Would Have to Learn a New Technique Today," by Yardley, *Baltimore Sun*, Nov. 10, 1950; "123,767 TV Sets Here, Survey Shows," *Baltimore Sun*, Jan. 30, 1950; "29 Million Seen at TV Sets by Next Year," *Baltimore Sun*, Jan. 18, 1951; "First for Ike," *Newsweek*, Jan. 31, 1955; "37 Million People Can't Be Wrong," *Time*, July 8, 1957; "Television and Politics: Who Projects the Image of A Winner?" *Newsweek*, Sept. 5, 1960; "CBS and NBC: Walter vs. Chet and Dave," *Newsweek*, Sept. 23, 1963; "Political Ads Boost Broadcasters," by Miriam Gottfried, *Wall Street Journal*, July 12, 2012.

The Day the Sixties Started

Much of this chapter's flavor comes from the author's memories, as well as those of Barry Levinson, Jack Bowden, Nancy Pelosi, Frank Luber, Ken Waissman, Leonard Kerpelman, and Richard Holley.

These were supplemented by "Kennedy Assassinated," *Baltimore Evening Sun*, Nov. 22, 1963; "Shock Gives Way to Empty Feeling as Baltimore Mourns a Martyr," by Alan Lupo, *Baltimore Evening Sun*, Nov. 23, 1963; "Shock Voiced at Kennedy Death; Silence Replaces Friday's Bustle," *Baltimore Sun*, Nov. 23, 1963; "Legislative Unit Seeks Movie Curbs," by Stephen Nordlinger, *Baltimore Sun*, Nov. 23, 1963; "Business of Shopping Forgotten as People Cluster at Radios," *Baltimore Sun*, Nov. 23, 1963; "Telephone Bells Toll Grief," *Baltimore Sun*, Nov. 24, 1963; "The Mourners," *Baltimore Sun*, Nov. 25, 1963; "Marylanders Mourn at Special Services," *Baltimore Sun*, Nov. 25, 1963; "In Memoriam," by Ann Werner, *Baltimore Sun*, Nov. 25, 1963; "Kennedy's Death Topic of Sermons," *Baltimore Sun*, Nov. 25, 1963; "City Streets Still, Quiet," *Baltimore Sun*, Nov. 26, 1963; "All Faiths Here Mourn at Services," *Baltimore Sun*, Nov. 26, 1963; "Mrs. Kennedy Tearful as She Leaves Grave," by Muriel Dobbin, *Baltimore Sun*, Nov. 26, 1963.

About the Author

Michael Olesker started writing in high school for the Baltimore City College newspaper, where he first realized that nothing in the world could be more enriching than meeting interesting people and writing about them. He was sports editor of the University of Maryland's *Diamondback* and then spent ten years writing for the *News American* and twenty-five years writing columns for the *Sun* while simultaneously delivering nightly commentaries for WJZ-TV's *Eyewitness News*.

He is the author of five previous books, including *Michael Olesker's Baltimore: If You Live Here, You're Home, Journeys to the Heart of Baltimore,* and *The Colts' Baltimore: A City and Its Love Affair in the 1950s,* all published by the Johns Hopkins University Press, as well as *Leap into Darkness: Seven Years on the Run in Wartime Europe* and *Tonight at Six: A Daily Show Masquerading as a TV News Program.*